# CREDIT MANAGEMENT REVIEW

## A GUIDE TO PROFESSIONAL ACCREDITATION

*By Maurice H. Margotta, Jr.*

*Second Edition*

*National Association of Credit Management*
*8815 Centre Park Drive, Suite 200*
*Columbia, Maryland 21045-2117*

Project Editor/Production Manager: Laura Smearman, NACM
Cover Design: Greg Smearman, H & N Printing & Graphics, Inc.
Typeface: 11/13.5 Times Roman
Composition and Printing: Port City Press, Inc.

Second Edition
The first edition was entitled Credit Management Review and Exam Preparation

© 1992, National Association of Credit Management.
Earlier edition © 1987, National Association of Credit Management

This publication is designed to provide accurate and authoritative information in regard to the subject matter covered. It is sold with the understanding that the publisher is not engaged in rendering legal, accounting, or other professional services. If legal advice of other expert assistance is required, the services of a competent professional person should be sought.

— *From a Declaration of Principles jointly adopted by a Committee of the American Bar Association and a Committee of Publishers.*

Library of Congress Cataloging in Publication Data

Margotta, Maurice H.
      Credit management review and exam preparation

Bibliography:

1. Credit—Management—Examinations, questions, etc.

I. Title
HG3752.5.M37        1992                    658.8'8'076                    88-25505
ISBN 0-934914-82-6

Manufactured in the United States of America.

*To Mom*

*I shall always remember her words of encouragement to be and to do the best you possibly can. Her rich legacy emphasizing the inherent goodness of people and traditional values continues to be a source of inspiration to me.*

# ACKNOWLEDGMENTS

As author I acknowledge with deep appreciation the contributions made to this publication by the following:

Dr. E. Michael Brady, Professor, Human Resource Development, University of Southern Maine, Gorham, Maine. For several years, Dr. Brady and I collaborated on a number of projects while he was director of continuing education programs at the University of Hartford. After he assumed a new position at the University of Southern Maine, we continued to collaborate on projects relating to the affiliation of colleges and universities with professional associations in the business sector.

Cooke O'Neal, former President, National Association of Credit Management (NACM), whose interest in continuing education paralleled mine, provided the enthusiasm and encouragement needed to embark upon the ambitious programs that have moved NACM education light years ahead in a relatively short span of time.

Dr. Ashok Abbott, Assistant Professor of Finance, West Virginia University, contributed to the revision of Chapter 4. Dr. Frederick C. Scherr, Professor of Finance, West Virginia University, collaborated in the revision of Chapters 10 and 11. I appreciate their contributions and assistance.

Dr. Daniel F. Jennings and W. A. Mays, Professor of Entrepreneurship and Strategic Management, Baylor University, contributed material on the "DuPont Systems Applied to National Metals."

I also wish to thank Pam Everett, Executive Secretary, Credit Research Foundation, for producing the final draft revision.

I am grateful as well to the Chief Operating Officers of NACM affiliates and the members of the NACM local committees on education. Don Mosher, President of NACM North Central and Rod Wheeland, Chairman, NACM - Oregon, Inc., contributed ideas, Giulio P. Boeri, NACM Board Chairman 1985-1986 and Clyde E. Williams, CCE, NACM Chairman 1986-1987, merit thanks for emphasizing the importance of NACM's efforts toward providing quality continuing education for all members and for supporting the goals of its education function to achieve this end.

Additional thanks go out to Dr. Walter Hunt who reviewed the final draft and a host of other people too numerous to list here for sharing their ideas, materials and aspirations with me.

Members of NACM's Accreditation Board and National Committee on Education were also most supportive of our efforts to provide a representative review text that would help people brush up and prepare for various examinations related to the professional designations and the CAP and ACAP academic course programs referred to herein which carry credit toward designation requirements.

Maurice H. Margotta, Jr.
Columbia, Maryland

# ABOUT THE AUTHOR

Dr. Maurice H. Margotta, Jr., has held responsible credit management positions for over twenty years. He began his career with Sperry Rand Corporation and subsequently moved on to Litton Industries. While with Litton, he became a member of the faculties of the University of Hartford and other state colleges. For ten years he taught credit and financial management and other subjects, including business ethics. In 1979 the University of Hartford honored him with an academic award for his role as principal founder of the Certified Credit Administrator concept, commonly referred to as the Credit Administration Program (CAP). In 1985 he received their service award for teaching excellence and for having made an outstanding contribution to continuing education. He joined NACM headquarters as Director of Education in January, 1985 and was promoted to Vice President in 1988. In 1989 he was named Vice President of the Credit Research Foundation, responsible for all U. S. education. In 1991 Dr. Margotta was elected to "Who's Who in American Education" for significant accomplishment and leadership.

A member of Phi Delta Kappa, he has authored numerous articles on credit management, finance, and organizational behavior. He was an active member of NACM Connecticut, where he served as a director, chairman of the education committee, and state coordinator of university-based programs. NACM Connecticut presented him with two major awards for his innovative educational initiatives.

Dr. Margotta earned his bachelor's degree from the University of Hartford and a master's degree from the University of Hartford Barney School of Business and Public Administration and another master's degree from Columbia University. He received a Sixth Year Diploma in professional education from the University of Connecticut where he completed pre-doctoral studies and earned a doctorate degree from Columbia University in New York.

# TABLE OF CONTENTS

# INTRODUCTION

This handbook represents a compilation of material that credit managers will find useful in preparing for nationally recognized professional designations of differing levels of education and experience. I have attempted to present it in a comprehensive easy-to-follow format designed to take the mystery out of competency-based testing for practitioners in credit and financial management. Although much of the information presented here is common to all levels of credit expertise, separate sections are devoted to questions and/or answers on the various designations. The questions are similar in form and content to those that have appeared on actual examinations.

Also included are sample test questions and course content applicable to the academic program certificate in Credit Administration (CCA), often referred to as the Credit Administration Program (CAP). Its more rigorous counterpart, the Advanced Certificate of Credit Administration (ACCA), often referred to as the Advanced Credit Administration Program (ACAP), is also offered through the National Institute of Credit (NIC) Collegiate Affiliation network. These certificate programs are offered by colleges and universities chartered by the NIC through its Collegiate Affiliation network. Each program is designed to provide prerequisite knowledge to facilitate meeting requirements for the credit Business Associate (CBA), Credit Business Fellow (CBF) and Certified Credit Executive (CCE) designations.

In addition, many highly experienced as well as business people with less experience in the credit and financial field will find the material contained herein useful as a refresher or informative review. Our aim is to make substantive information enhancing professional competence more accessible to practitioners and others who aspire to a career in credit and financial administration. More and more bankers and financial services people are seeking certification than ever before. This trend is expected to continue well into the year 2000 and beyond.

It should, however, be clearly understood by the reader that career growth hinges on keeping skills at the "cutting edge" through continuing education even after meeting the requirements of a professional designation. The National Association of Credit Management (NACM) requires annual recertification, that is, completion of a designated number of Continuing Education Units (CEU's) to maintain credential certification. This can be accomplished through workshops and other programs offered through the NIC and Credit Research Foundation

(CRF). The CRF, organized in 1949, is the U.S. education affiliate of the National Association of Credit Management. There is also provision for Certified Public Accountants (CPA's) to take courses and participate in local, regional and national seminars to earn Continuing Professional Education (CPE) credit through NACM and CRF. This is made possible through CPE registration authority granted by the National Association of State Boards of Accountancy as a sponsor of continuing education nationwide.

 Registered with the National Association of State Boards of Accountancy as a sponsor of continuing professional education on the National Registry of CPE Sponsors. State boards of accountancy have final authority on the acceptance of individual courses. Complaints regarding registered sponsors may be addressed to NASBA, 545 Fifth Avenue, New York NY 10017-3698, 1-800-CPA-CPE1. Registration No. 90-00039-92

Details are available upon request from NIC, 8815 Centre Park Drive, Columbia, Maryland 21045-2117.

Conscientious review of the material contained herein is intended to help you, the reader, become familiar with the various tests and make it easier to face the actual examinations. Although you may have always studied well and received good course grades, you will find that you invariably remember things best if you have an opportunity to review them before a test. And review is exactly that—it does not require that you study again something which you already know. Accordingly, this book is designed to facilitate getting right to the heart of the matter—those salient points that every credit and financial professional should know and understand.

Finally, do keep in mind that an attitude of enthusiastic interest and a desire to think things out will yield the best results. If you are engaged in self-study, go over the points with which you are having difficulty. If you are enrolled in review sessions, seek help from your peers or instructor on unclear or problem points. If you follow this protocol, you will achieve your goal. I know, because it has worked for hundreds of students who adopted this approach in courses I have conducted on credit and financial management over the years at the university level.

Readers are advised to keep in touch with their local NACM affiliate for current information and notice of any changes in experience or course requirements for the various programs and designations referred to herein.

# PROFESSIONAL DESIGNATIONS

The career designation program is geared toward professionalism in credit and financial management. The primary objective of the program is to assure employers, their customers and fellow designation holders that a CBA, CBF, and CCE has fundamental knowledge to fulfill position requirements. Certified candidates also subscribe to the National Association of Credit Management's Canons of Business Credit Ethics, a copy of which is reproduced in Appendix C.

The specific contents of CBA, CBF, and CCE study materials and examinations are naturally subject to modifications to keep pace with changing emphasis and new techniques in credit management. The overall program is essentially comprised of experience, education, and participation. It includes the successful completion of examinations of increasing complexity and depth. Local study groups may be sponsored by NACM affiliated associations and the National Institute of Credit encourages participation. There are three basic steps to keep in mind: (1) points, (2) requirements and (3) examinations. Brochures are available from the Credit Research Foundation containing instructions. The vehicle to facilitate access and help applicants navigate through the process is the NIC Registration form. This form should be completed and sent in through the local NACM affiliated association. An evaluation of your prior education and course completion is sent to let you know what remaining courses, if any, you need to move on to the next step. From this point forward, the NIC will provide needed guidance to facilitate achievement of your career goals.

# PART ONE

# CURRENT TRENDS IN EDUCATION

This section is an outgrowth of a joint effort with Dr. E. Michael Brady who co-authored with Dr. Maurice H. Margotta, Jr., the article "Toward Certification of the Credit Executive," which appeared in the April 1985 issue of *Credit & Financial Management Magazine*, published by the National Association of Credit Management (the magazine is now entitled *Business Credit*). Copies of the article are available upon request from *Business Credit* magazine, 8815 Centre Park Drive, Columbia, Maryland 21045-2117.

# CHAPTER ONE

# WHY INVEST IN PROFESSIONAL DEVELOPMENT?

Tens of billions of dollars are spent each year by American business to educate employees. Virtually everyone in the workforce, especially those involved in the "information industries," is affected by at least some education or training initiative. Our task here is to provide insight by describing some of the current trends in the continuing growth of business education and discussing how these trends relate to the credit profession. To do this, we shall borrow four ideas from John Naisbitt's popular book *Megatrends*, and add two ideas of our own.

## 1. Short term ←————————→ Long term

One of Naisbitt's most important ideas is that U.S. business and industry, as a whole, is beginning to move from a short-term to a longer-term perspective. "There is unprecedented criticism of American business management today," says Naisbitt. A good deal of this criticism is attributable to the short-term orientation of business. This means there is a tendency to look for quick, expedient answers to complex problems, to value short-term profitability, and for managers to "fast track" their way through numerous positions and companies. Lester Thurow, the noted economist, put it succinctly: "What short-term CEO will take a long-run view when it lowers his income? Only a saint will do that—and there aren't many saints."

A great deal of criticism of education has been voiced in recent years, and some of this is based upon its short-term perspective. For example, we have heard about the so-called "diploma mills" that crank out lots of degrees and crank in high revenues—with no attention to quality or to what their activities mean to the future of their students or the future of society. We've read about colleges and universities that use student athletes for financial or public relations gains, then spit them out onto the streets after their eligibility has expired (often without degrees, and very often without any real education). Many professionals, and I dare say credit managers, have experienced the "quick and dirty" professional seminar, where a full-day of training consists of three coffee breaks, a long lunch, lots of good jokes, plenty of colorful handouts, but not very much substance for the money invested.

Each of us has a lot at stake. Neither business nor education can afford to look only at today. We have to start asking the question: How are our decisions today going to affect us, our organization, our customers, not just next week or next month, but two and five and ten years down the road? Our planning must be on a wider plane.

In terms of business education, asking the following types of questions will help us achieve a longer range perspective:

> What business are we in today? Are we in the railroad business or the transportation industry? Are we in the credit collection business or the financial services business? Are we in the seminar business or the continuing professional development enterprise? In other words, is our thinking narrow or broad?
>
> What business will we be in five years? In ten years? There is an old saying in philosophy to the effect that identity drives action. Who we say we are (and think we are) will go a long way in determining what we do in the world of action.

The important thing is that all of us have to begin to look beyond our noses toward the wider, longer horizon. This is the important message we hear from Naisbitt. We are beginning to think big and long, and that at least is in the right direction.

## 2. Institutional help ←————————→ Self-help

Sir Winston Churchill once said, "Personally, I'm always ready to learn, although I do not always like being taught." Churchill would be glad to know that, in recent times, education has been much more self-help oriented, both inside and outside of industry.

Research on adult learning has shown that when people can participate intimately in the design of their own learning, they learn much more effectively. There should be no surprise in this, since the learning project becomes our own when we help to design it. Finally, after so many years of failure, educators both within and outside of business are beginning to realize this simple truth.

We can see the implications of self-help (self-design) throughout education. Today people can earn both undergraduate and graduate degrees on an independent basis, often with the courses specifically tailored to meet their needs and interests. There continues to be a large number of extension courses (correspondence-type educational programs), and these activities appear to be increasing in the adult education arena. Computer-aided instruction (CAI) is the most important recent innovation to encourage independent learning. Through various educational software packages or specially written programs, employees can achieve new competencies in an efficient way without every stepping into a classroom. In addition to these independent learning initiatives, corporate America has also entered into the self-paced learning programs business, and the NACM, through its National Institute of Credit, offers these programs along with other options. A busy executive can learn to speedread or manage time more effectively by using a "learning package," often consisting of a manual of instruction and an audio tape. In this way, people can learn important skills on their own time, perhaps while driving to work, and certainly at a pace pleasing to them. Also, instructional videotapes are being produced for use in conjunction with personal computers at home.

These trends do not mean that institutions are going to be getting out of the education business. In fact the evidence suggests quite the contrary. What it does mean is that institutions and organizations are becoming increasingly sensitive to the needs of individuals to participate closely in the design and transmission of their own learning.

This theme of self-help or self-directedness is a major megatrend in business education, and it is an idea that will infiltrate several of the other trends we discuss in this article.

### 3. Hierarchies ←——————→ Networking

Both business and education have had ample experience with hierarchical (vertical) organizational structures and decision making. Both have long practiced the classical pyramid theory: information flows from the bottom; decisions flow from the top! Naisbitt tells us that things cannot continue to work this way if our major institutions are going to survive and thrive. Key ideas that were shared at the "Education Update" during NACM's 89th Annual Credit Congress in Washington, D. C., were such critical factors as collaboration, feedback, networking, alliance, and *partnership* between education and business.

No single organization, or type of organization, can invest the tremendous effort required, both now and in the future, to train, develop, educate and certify professionals. Such an effort not only invites, but requires, a partnership between business and education. Each has something very special to give in this relationship, and each has something very special to receive. An example of an exemplary relationship between NACM and higher education is described by this author and Dr. Brady in the article entitled "Toward Certification of the Credit Executive" which appeared in the April 1985 edition of *Credit and Financial Management.*

Simply stated, networks are people talking to each other—sharing ideas, information and resources. In partnership, educators and business professionals can pool their skills and create effective networks of action that can go a long way toward solving many of our current problems.

Consider also that one of the extremely controversial issues in education today is the quality of teachers. This is certainly not due to a shortage of talent in the U.S. It is, however, unequivocally related to the fact that by dangling a sweeter carrot, corporations attract those with the ability to teach and the interest in becoming teachers. The result? This cadre of talented would-be teachers is working for excellence in their companies while making their services as part-time instructors available for both in-house and outside courses.

American business has identified these individuals and is utilizing their services beyond the narrow scope of their job descriptions. The results have been dramatic. For example, some companies, such as the Rand Corporation, award degrees in various technical areas. This has surely raised questions within academic institutions, many of which are no match for corporations that have a great deal of money to allocate to education.

On balance, there is a need to address the extremes between the corporation university and the academic university with corporate linkage. The latter is the alternative that should be more viable and in the best interests of all the participants.

### 4. Either/or choices ←——————→ Multiple choices

We have moved into a period of history in which options are valued. We are indeed seeing this trend in education, training, and certification circles. There are manifestations of this idea to consider seriously:

1. We are finding that there are many ways of acquiring professional training today, including credit and non-credit courses, workshops, conferences, symposia, seminars, and institutes, and within these structures an entire range of curriculum materials exists (films, printed materials, audio and video tapes, and computer aided instruction, as well as more traditional teaching methods.

2. In the area of professional certification, a major focus for NACM, there appear to be a number of possibilities. It is possible to use traditional exams (which test knowledge), assessment centers (which test competency), specified courses or workshops, the portfolio concept of certification, or a combination of options.

The important point to recognize is that many possibilities do in fact exist, and the world of business education and professional certification is not as "black and white" as it may have appeared in the past. NACM is seriously taking the multiple-option trend into account as it designs educational programs for its membership. Emphasis is on providing continuing education for all NACM members and others who aspire to the profession.

### 5. Program-centered education ←⟶ People-centered education

While this is not one of Naisbitt's megatrends, we believe it is no doubt a directive to the future of business education. Unfortunately we have too often designed education and training activities around the needs of something other than the people involved. Organizational structures, or corporate policies, or the latest technical resources have inspired many of our educational programs. But if human resources development is to be taken seriously, we have to put the spotlight on *humans* and not on technology alone.

Is it not people who produce, who respond, who learn? And as another best selling book, *In Search of Excellence*, has clearly suggested, when an organization succeeds, it is primarily because its people have succeeded. It is not so much the size of the corporation that matters but the efforts of small groups within the organization working together to achieve a common goal. It is time that we shifted our priorities away from "subjects" or "technologies" toward meeting the real needs of our most important natural resource—us! We are that which makes it all happen, the movers, the shakers, the doers, the biological equation that must be factored in where it has either been taken for granted or simply omitted. Job descriptions, for example, should switch from being task-centered to human resource-centered.

### 6. Information ←⟶ Knowledge ←⟶ Wisdom

The sixth and final megatrend is perhaps the most subtle. We all know something about the "information age." The point has been driven home time and again as to how our economy has radically shifted in recent times away from manufacturing to service and information industries. But in the meantime, we may have raised information to an altar of worship that it does not, in its own right, deserve. While admittedly information is an important starting point (try to do anything creative or productive without it), we have to move, and ultimately will move, beyond mere information to other more advanced levels of this important resource.

The poet T. S. Eliot once wrote, "Where is the wisdom we have lost in knowledge? Where is the knowledge we have lost in information?"

This remark suggests a hierarchy of value: wisdom is greater than knowledge, which is, itself, greater than information.

In a thoughtful article in *The Futurist*, Richard Bower, the director of the Hubert Humphrey Institute of Public Affairs in Minnesota, said the following about this idea:

> Information is the ore, the sum total of all facts and ideas that are available to be known . . . knowledge is the result of someone applying the refiner's fire to the mass of facts and ideas—selecting and organizing what is useful to somebody . . . wisdom is integrated knowledge . . . that, when applied, make a whole greater than the sum of its parts.

# PART TWO

# NACM
# CERTIFICATION

# CHAPTER TWO

# THE NATIONAL INSTITUTE OF CREDIT

The oldest and broadest based education activity of the NACM is its National Institute of Credit (NIC), organized in 1918. The NIC is the national agency empowered to administer the issuance of professional designations and award certificates and diplomas for various course programs. The Institute is administered by the Credit Research Foundation, U.S. Education affiliate of NACM. Over seventy years after early visionaries founded the National Institute of Credit, it remains the leader in providing access to credit and financial education. The NIC's main objectives are:

1. To establish standards of proficiency and achievement in credit and financial management, and to provide a means for recognition of those who attain the standards, and therefore serve as the national accrediting body for credit and financial courses.
2. To develop and maintain a sound educational program in credit and financial management. This includes certificate and degree programs with a major concentration in credit administration through participating colleges and universities. The collegiate affiliation network consists of over fifty colleges and universities that are chartered by the NIC to offer courses in cooperation with NIC Chapters established at NACM affiliated associa-

tions. A current listing of colleges and universities in the network may be obtained from the Credit Research Foundation.

3. Through local NIC chapters and its affiliation program, to cooperate with institutions of higher education in offering programs of study in credit and financial management. Certificate or degree programs on campus and through local NACM associations are available.

4. To make courses of study available to persons who want to use their discretionary time for personal growth and development. University extension courses through guided independent study and video tapes are examples.

5. To be responsive to the needs of all NACM members, i.e., helping them to position for promotion within the profession and in so doing accelerate their own individual advancement and career growth.

The institute conducts its activities in a number of ways designed to give widest coverage to persons with different educational and business backgrounds. Credit managers who become NACM and CRF members have ready access to the full services of NIC and educational discounts. Non-members are invited to inquire about membership benefits. Contact the Credit Research Foundation, 8815 Centre Park Drive, Columbia, Maryland 21045-2117.

# CREDIT RESEARCH FOUNDATION

The Credit Research Foundation (CRF), the U. S. education affiliate of the National Association of Credit Management, offers formal programs which cover every facet of business credit and financial management. The programs include the Graduate School of Credit and Financial Management, Advanced Credit Executive Studies, Mid-Career School, and the Credit Management Leadership Institute. Information on these offerings and others may be obtained from the Credit Research Foundation, 8815 Centre Park Drive, Columbia MD 21045-2117.

The Foundation also administers the National Institute of Credit (NIC) for NACM. The NIC is responsible for a collegiate affiliation network consisting of more than fifty colleges and universities nationwide. It also administers the professional designation program, i.e., Credit Business Associate (CBA), Credit Business Fellow (CBF) and Certified Credit Executive (CCE). A brochure on the three designations may be requested from the Credit Research Foundation, 8815 Centre Park Drive, Columbia MD 21045-2117.

# CREDIT FOR COURSES

The NIC awards Continuing Education Units (CEU) and Continuing Professional Education (CPE) credits for successful completion of its courses and other courses offered by NACM affiliated associations nationwide.

CEU: The CEU provides individuals with recognition for their efforts to update or broaden their knowledge, skills, or attitudes. Records of CEU's awarded provide a framework within which individuals can develop and achieve long-range educational goals through a variety of available options. Progress toward such goals, at the individual's own pace and possibly planned over a number of years, can be demonstrated and documented by official records of CEU's awarded.

CPE: As an authorized CPE sponsor, certain advanced courses, seminars, and workshops may be taken to meet relicensing requirements of all State Boards of Accountancy. This encompasses learning which contributes to growth in professional knowledge and competence of an individual in the practice of public accountancy, and meets the minimum standards as set forth in the NASBA Standards for formal Continuing Education Programs.

# CHAPTER THREE

# CERTIFICATION

## THE CERTIFICATION PROCESS

For business credit as an applied profession, there are three nationally recognized designations, one for each benchmark level. They are the Credit Business Associate (CBA) for the supervisory level, the Credit Business Fellow (CBF) for the management level, and the Certified Credit Executive (CCE) for the senior management level.

To get started on the career track, there are three simple steps to keep in mind:

1. Career Roadmap Points,
2. Course and/or Experience Requirements, and
3. An Examination.

The certification process begins by registering with the National Institute of Credit (NIC).

## REGISTRATION

To get started, candidates must complete the NIC registration form, a copy of which is shown in Exhibit 3.1. There is a one-time registration fee which covers evaluation, establishment of a permanent record, counseling, and access to programs offered. These services facilitate increasing an individual's contribution to their organization and positions them for further career advancement. Full-time students sponsored by an NACM member receive additional discounts; verification from the collegiate institution of full time status is required. Forms may be

## EXHIBIT 3.1   NIC Registration Form

### NATIONAL INSTITUTE OF CREDIT (NIC)
8815 Centre Park Drive
Columbia, MD 21045

### *REGISTRATION FORM*

EVALUATION REQUEST FOR NIC CREDIT BUSINESS ASSOCIATE, CREDIT BUSINESS FELLOW AND
CERTIFIED CREDIT EXECUTIVE DESIGNATIONS AND THE CREDIT ADMINISTRATION PROGRAM

| | | |
|---|---|---|
| Last Name | First Name | Middle or Maiden Name |

| | | | |
|---|---|---|---|
| Home Street Address | City | State | Zip Code |

| | | |
|---|---|---|
| Firm Name | Job Title | Business Telephone |

| | | | |
|---|---|---|---|
| Business Street Address | City | State | Zip Code |

NACM Affiliated Association you are a member of: _____

Check here if:                    ☐ CRF member                    ☐ CFDD member

Check below the designation or certificate that you wish to be evaluated for:

(The career roadmap progression begins with the CBA)

1. ☐ Credit Business Associate designation (CBA), Plan A
   *Transcripts to be sent by University to NACM affiliate.*

2. ☐ Credit Business Associate designation (CBA), Plan B
   *Include grade reports showing completion of Credit Administration Program Courses with a B average. In addition provide documentation of 3 years credit experience with a current resume.*

3. ☐ Credit Business Fellow designation (CBF), Plan A
   *Transcripts to be sent by University to NACM affiliate.*

4. ☐ Credit Business Fellow designation (CBF), Plan B
   *Include resume showing work history with this form and have University send transcripts to NACM affiliate.*

5. ☐ Certified Credit Executive (CCE)
   *Request application for admission to examination.*

6. ☐ Credit Administration Program
   *(academic program)*

Copies of transcripts from all post secondary institutions where you have completed undergraduate, graduate or continuing education courses are required. Also, include grade reports for any non-credit professional development course which you may wish to have considered.

The non-refundable registration fee of $55.00 covers file set-up, transcript evaluation, work history analysis, record keeping and inquiry responses. Checks are made payable to: National Institute of Credit and mailed with the registration form to your NACM Affiliated Association for approval and submission to NIC Headquarters.

| | |
|---|---|
| Signature of Candidate | Date |

Approved by: _____

| | |
|---|---|
| Chief Operating Officer or designee of NACM Affiliated Association | Date |

REV. 12/91

requested directly from NIC, 8815 Centre Park Drive, Columbia, Maryland 21045-2117.

# APPLICATION

Candidates for certificates and awards are required to complete registration and application forms and return them to their local NACM affiliates with the required fees for recording and forwarding to the NIC. Check with your local NACM affiliate or NIC for the current fee schedule.

Applications for professional designations must include a Career Roadmap, NIC registration form with fee, an indication that official college transcripts are being sent and a resume of experience. (If you are already registered, instructions are furnished by NIC.)

# THE CAREER ROADMAP

The Career Roadmap is the approved vehicle to guide career practitioners toward earning a designation for each skill level from supervisory to senior management responsibility.

Point values are assigned to each of the following major categories which facilitate career progression:

- Work experience and special interest.
- Participation, local and national.
- College and continuing education.
- Special consideration activities.

The Career Roadmap is designed to give better direction to those who would like to become active and academically prepared, and to work toward a credit designation. A point-scoring system is utilized to show both junior and experienced credit managers what it takes to become certified.

Individual roadmaps show NIC the applicant's willingness to participate, share, and lend influence to the credit profession. This point-scoring system is implemented throughout the U.S. via 70 NACM affiliated offices.

There are four basic steps that need to be followed in order to be successful in a credit management career:

1. A mentor should be sought to help set and inspect individual goals (see further discussion on mentoring later in this chapter).
2. Employee performance reviews must include a personal development plan. The individual's Career Roadmap should be incorporated into the annual performance review. Management should be asked to provide the capital budget and time for the individual's plan.
3. Each individual must list the level of credentials preferred or required for their credit management position job description. Once management signs off on the job description, the individual can use the preferred credentials level as a springboard to attending seminars, participating in industry groups, seeking admission to the Graduate School of Credit and Financial Management, and if necessary, attending prerequisite schools first.
4. A goal of scoring at least 10 to 20 points on the individual roadmap each year should be set and a superior should be asked to inspect accomplishments. This motivates management to provide for an employee's personal growth and recognition. Once management is aware of what was achieved, the foundation is in place for building toward future growth.

# CAREER DEVELOPMENT GROUPS

Everyone using the Roadmap needs a vehicle to get to their destination. This means both the credit manager and the company reap benefits going down the same path—the vehicle that NIC has chosen is a Career Development Group located at each NACM affiliate. To participate in a local Career Development Group, a Career Roadmap form must be completed each year and a formal job description submitted which includes the required and preferred credentials, signed off by corporate management (refer to the section on mentoring later in this chapter for an outline of the typical Career Development Study Group).

A sample copy of the Career Roadmap is reproduced in Exhibit 3.2. Career Roadmap forms may be obtained from the local NACM affiliates upon request.

## EXHIBIT 3.2 The Career Roadmap

# National Association of Credit Management
## CAREER ROADMAP OF

Candidate's Name_____S.S. No. _____

Company's Name _____

Company's Mailing Address _____

Candidate's Mailing Address (if different) _____

Candidate's Home Address _____

There are over 600 points available on this roadmap. The following are needed to qualify for credentials.

CBA  50 Roadmap points qualifies participant to apply for admission to the CBA Exam under either Plan A or Plan B.

CBF  100 Roadmap points and receipt of the CBA qualifies participant to apply for CBF exam under either Plan A or Plan B.

CCE  125 Roadmap points qualifies participant to apply for CCE exam.

All candidates must be registered with NIC, have prescribed number of roadmap points and have completed application meeting all requirements for admission to exam. Roadmap points must be "CERTIFIED" by the COO or designee of the local NACM affiliate.

Roadmap Certified by: _____
NACM AFFILIATED CHIEF OPERATING OFFICER OR DESIGNEE

Name of Affiliate: _____

Note 1: Qualification and point value to be determined by COO of NACM affiliate. Submit seminar, course description or request for special consideration to the COO of NACM affiliate along with Roadmap. Complete documentation must be attached.

Note 2: A prequalified seminar is approved by NIC. A local seminar is approved for points by the COO of NACM affiliate.

Note 3: A Task Force is an assignment by National to address specific projects/programs, etc.

# EXHIBIT 3.2 The Career Roadmap (cont'd)

I. WORK EXPERIENCE AND SPECIAL INTEREST

| | POSSIBLE POINTS | MAXIMUM POINTS | TOTAL POINTS |
|---|---|---|---|
| A. WORK EXPERIENCE — Credit Experience | | | |
| _____ | 2 pts. ea. yr. 1st 5 yrs. | 10 | _____ |
| _____ | 1 pt. ea. yr. 6-15 yrs. | 10 | _____ |
| B. SPECIAL INTEREST | | | |
| 1. Serve as Mentor — List Mentee | 5 ea. Mentee | 10 | |
| _____ | | | |
| _____ | | | _____ |
| 2. Mentee Achievement (CBA, CBF, CCE) List Mentee and Achievement | 5 ea. Award | 30 | |
| _____ | | | _____ |
| _____ | | | _____ |
| _____ | | | _____ |
| 3. College Instructor (Business Courses) List Courses Taught and Where | 5 ea. Course | 15 | |
| _____ | | | _____ |
| _____ | | | _____ |
| _____ | | | _____ |
| 4. NIC Instructor — List Courses and Where | 5 ea. Course | 15 | |
| _____ | | | _____ |
| _____ | | | _____ |
| _____ | | | _____ |
| 5. NACM Panelist/Speaker — List Sessions | 3 ea. Session | 15 | |
| _____ | | | _____ |
| _____ | | | _____ |
| _____ | | | _____ |
| 6. Article(s) Published   Include copy of Article(s) | 5 ea. Article | 20 | _____ |
| 7. Special Consideration (See Note 1) | | 5 | _____ |
| Total Points Special Interest and Work Experience  (Add to totals on Page 4) | | | _____ |

II. PARTICIPATION (LOCAL)

| | POSSIBLE POINTS | MAXIMUM POINTS | TOTAL POINTS |
|---|---|---|---|
| A. Local NACM Activity | | | |
| Served on Committee | 3 ea. yr. | 21 | |
| _____ | | | |
| _____ | | | _____ |
| Committee Chaired | 5 ea. yr. | 20 | |
| _____ | | | |
| _____ | | | _____ |
| Industry Trade Group Chair. | | 10 | |
| _____(Industry) | | | _____ |
| Board Member Yr(s) _____ | 3 ea. yr. | 12 | |
| Chief Elected Officer  Yr. _____ | 10 pts. | 10 | _____ |

# EXHIBIT 3.2 The Career Roadmap (cont'd)

## II. PARTICIPATION (LOCAL) (continued)

| | POSSIBLE POINTS | MAXIMUM POINTS | TOTAL POINTS |
|---|---|---|---|
| Attend Local Seminars (within last 5 years) (Sponsored by local NACM or CFDD) | 2 pts. ea. (See Note 2) | 20 | _____ |
| Attend Regional NACM Conference (past 5 years) | 5 ea. yr. | 15 | _____ |
| Regional Conference General Chair Yr. _____ | | 10 | _____ |
| Attend Local Legislative Conference (past 5 years) | 2 pts. ea. yr. | 6 | _____ |
| B. CFDD and/or NIC Organizations Served on Committee(s) | 3 ea. yr. | 21 | _____ |
| _____ | | | |
| _____ | | | _____ |
| Committee(s) Chaired | 5 ea. yr. | 20 | |
| _____ | | | _____ |
| _____ | | | |
| Board Member Yr(s) _____ | 3 ea. yr. | 12 | _____ |
| Chief Elected Officer _____(yr.) | | 10 | _____ |
| Attend Regional CFDD Conference (past 5 yrs.) | 5 ea. yr. | 15 | _____ |
| Regional Conference General Chair Yr. _____ | | 10 | _____ |
| **Total Local Participation Subtotal (Add to total on Page 4)** | | | _____ |

## III. PARTICIPATION (NATIONAL)
Participation points include either NACM or CRF

| | POSSIBLE POINTS | MAXIMUM POINTS | TOTAL POINTS |
|---|---|---|---|
| Attend National Credit Congress (Past 5 yrs.) | 5 ea. yr. | 15 | _____ |
| National Committee Member (NACM/CRF) (List Committees) | 3 ea. yr. | 15 | _____ |
| _____ (yr)_____ | | | |
| _____ (yr)_____ | | | |
| _____ (yr)_____ | | | |
| _____ (yr)_____ | | | |
| National Task Force Groups (List Task Force) (See Note 3) | 2 ea. yr. | 10 | _____ |
| _____ (yr)_____ | | | |
| _____ (yr)_____ | | | |
| _____ (yr)_____ | | | |
| _____ (yr)_____ | | | |
| National Board Member (yrs) _____ | 5 ea. yr. | 20 | _____ |
| National Officer (yr.) _____ | 10 ea. yr. | 10 | _____ |
| Attend National Legislative Conference | | | |
| Years attended _____ | 5 ea. yr. | 15 | _____ |
| National Industry Day Chairman (List Industry and Year) | | 10 | _____ |
| _____ _____ | | | |
| **Total National Participation Points (Add to total on Page 4)** | | | _____ |

# EXHIBIT 3.2 The Career Roadmap (cont'd)

## IV. EDUCATION

| | POSSIBLE POINTS | MAXIMUM POINTS | TOTAL POINTS |
|---|---|---|---|
| A. College Education (Transcripts required) | 5 pts. per 25 cr. hr. | 25 | _____ |
| Master's Degree (Transcripts required) | 5 pts. per 25cr. hr. | 10 | _____ |
| B. NACM schools conducted by CRF<br>Credit Management Leadership Institute (CMLI) Year Attended _____ | | 10 | _____ |
| Mid-Career School   Year Attended _____ | | 10 | _____ |
| Advanced Credit Executive Studies (ACES) Year Attended _____ | | 10 | _____ |
| Graduate School of Credit & Financial Management | 10 pts. per yr. | 30 | _____ |
| School Attended _____ Yr. _____ | | | |
| School Attended _____ Yr. _____ | | | |
| School Attended _____ Yr. _____ | | | |
| C. Programs Approved by NIC — Local Colleges & NACM Affiliates, Teleconferencing and Home Study<br>Credit Administration Program Courses (CAP) | 5 per Course—15 or | 20 | _____ |
| 20 Upon achieving CAP certificate | | | |
| Advanced Credit Administration Program | 5 per Course | 10 | _____ |
| Prequalified Credit Seminars   (See Note 2) | 2 pts. per Seminar | 20 | _____ |

Seminar Name                    Date      Points

_____

_____

_____

| | | | |
|---|---|---|---|
| D. Home Study Courses | (2-5 Points) | 15 | _____ |
| (NIC, AMA, ABA, RMA, etc.) (See Note 1) | | | |

_____

_____

_____

| | | | |
|---|---|---|---|
| E. Credit Research Foundation Meeting Roundtable | 3 pts. per program attended | 12 | _____ |
| F. NACM/FCIB Meeting & Roundtable | 3 pts. per program attended | 12 | _____ |
| **Educational Subtotal  (Add to total below)** | | | _____ |

## V. ROADMAP SUMMARY

| Total Points | | | |
|---|---|---|---|
| | Special Interest/ Work Experience | _____ | From page 2 |
| | Participation (Local) | _____ | From page 3 |
| | Participation (National) | _____ | From page 3 |
| | Education | _____ | From page 4 |
| TOTAL ROADMAP POINTS | | _____ | |

I hereby submit my ROADMAP for NACM Affiliate certification.

Signed_____ Date_____

Roadmap points needed for each designation level are:
- Credit Business Associate (CBA)     50
- Credit Business Fellow (CBF)     100
- Certified Credit Executive (CCE)     125

After registering with NIC and having a Career Roadmap certified with 50 points by NIC, the applicant is ready to be evaluated by NIC for the CBA designation, and if the requirements of Plan A or Plan B (see below) are met, can proceed to take the examination. Registration is processed through the local NACM affiliate to NIC.

# CREDIT BUSINESS ASSOCIATE (CBA) OVERVIEW

Plan A requires satisfactory completion, with a grade average of "C" or better, of seven prescribed courses.

To substantiate satisfactory completion of the prescribed courses, an official transcript from the university should be sent to the local NACM office.

Plan B is an available alternate plan which requires completion of courses that comprise the CAP certificate. A "B" average grade is required, along with an official transcript, and a current resume evidencing three years experience in credit administration.

With 50 Career Roadmap points and fulfillment of requirements of Plan A or Plan B, applicants are admitted to the CBA examination. The examination is administered at the local NACM affiliate office or at the annual NACM Credit Congress. If the latter site is selected, arrangements must be made with NIC 60 days in advance.

Upon successful completion of the examination, a notification is sent which is followed by an engraved CBA certificate forwarded to the applicant's NACM affiliate for presentation at its next meeting.

# CREDIT BUSINESS FELLOW (CBF) OVERVIEW

This next benchmark level requires achieving the CBA designation, 100 Career Roadmap points, and meeting the course or experience requirements under Plan A or Plan B of the CBF designation.

Plan A requires that official college transcripts be sent to the local NACM affiliate office showing satisfactory completion, with a grade average of "C" or better, of nine prescribed courses.

Plan B is an alternative plan which requires meeting the criteria described later in this chapter in the section entitled *The Professional Designations*.

Once the Career Roadmap points and requirements under Plan A or Plan B are met and verified by NIC, applicants are admitted to the CBF examination. Examinations are scheduled for the spring and fall of each year and are taken at local NACM affiliate offices nationwide. Retakes may be scheduled to be taken at the annual NACM Credit Congress.

Upon successful completion of the three-part examination, a notification is sent which is followed by an engraved certificate forwarded to the applicant's NACM affiliate for presentation at its next meeting.

Candidates may now prepare for the CCE designation.

# CERTIFIED CREDIT EXECUTIVE (CCE) OVERVIEW

Plan A requires that an applicant submit an updated Career Roadmap showing 125 earned points and achieving the CBA and CBF designations. The Roadmap is certified by the NACM affiliate and routed to NIC for processing.

Plan B is an available alternative designed for candidates already at the executive level in their careers. It is explained in detail later in this chapter in the section entitled *The Professional Designations*.

# THE CERTIFICATE IN CREDIT ADMINISTRATION PROGRAM

The Credit Administration Program (CAP) leading to the Certificate in Credit Administration (CCA) is as one-year college level course program available to prepare credit and financial people to assume greater responsibility. [CAP or Credit Administration Program is the approved acronym for the CCA (Certificate in Credit Administration) course program.] In so doing, the foundation can be built for moving incrementally upward to National Institute of Credit (NIC) professional designations described herein, i.e., CBA, CBF and CCE.

This particular academic program is therefore designed to provide entry to the Credit Business Associate and Credit Business Fellow designation levels referred to herein.

The concept of the CAP program has been in existence since 1975 where it was field-tested for several years at the University of Hartford. The program is designed to meet the needs of the working credit and financial practitioner. Because an increasing number of career credit people already have a degree or have the equivalent in experience, this route to credentialing is preferred by a wide majority of people surveyed over the years. Studying for the CCA courses therefore avoids redundancy and the program can be completed in one academic year.

The CAP program is available through most NACM affiliates to all colleges and universities affiliated with NIC. The collegiate affiliation process begins at NIC through the NACM affiliate in each area and is coordinated through its education committee chairman. Further information is available directly from the Credit Research Foundation, 8815 Centre Park Drive, Columbia, Maryland 21045-2117.

Nationwide offices of continuing professional development at most colleges and universities, in affiliation with the NIC, offer a number of courses designed to assist candidates in preparing for the Credit Administration Program certificate and gaining admission to exams leading to the Credit Business Associate (CBA) and Credit Business Fellow (CBF) designations referred to earlier. The CAP certificate is the first step in this process.

Only participants who have registered with the NIC and/or enrolled at one of its chapters are eligible to receive matriculation materials and take exams for the CAP. However, approved college and university courses are open to individuals who have not registered with the NIC as yet, but are interested in exploring the Credit Administration Program. Because college courses offered are an enhancement to individual study, the tuition for such courses is in addition to the registration fee with the NIC. Tuition for courses is paid by candidates directly to the provider which may be a university or local NACM affiliated association.

Universities and colleges participate in the Credit Administration program with the cooperation and support of local NIC chapters and affiliates of NACM. Because sufficient lead time is required for new candidates to enroll and receive materials from national headquarters, early registration is advised.

# THE NIC COLLEGIATE NETWORK AS OF 1991

Many colleges in the network offer the Certificate in Credit Administration Program through local NIC chapters (see Exhibit 3.3).

This innovative program fulfills a career development need. John Gardner in his book *Self-Renewal* addressed this kind of issue in referring to the body of custom and "reputable" standards and how new developments often originate outside the area of respectable practice. The land grant college, a profoundly important educational innovation, did not spring from the inner circle of respectable higher education as it then existed—it represented "an impulse from outside that charmed circle." CAP course standards are maintained by NIC's ongoing monitoring of substantive content and quality of instruction. Participants are invited to contact the NIC directly with regard to their experience in the programs.

Four basic courses are offered in the CAP:

1. *Introduction to Credit Management**
2. *Intermediate Credit Management**
3. *Applied Credit Management***
4. *Credit Management Cases*
   * *Introduction to Credit Management* and *Intermediate Credit Management* may be combined into *Credit and Collection Principles.*
   ** *Financial Analysis* is an equivalent for *Applied Credit Management.*

A degree is not required to be admitted to candidacy; however, all candidates must maintain a "B" average to qualify for certification.

# EXHIBIT 3.3 Affiliated Colleges and Universities of NIC

## AFFILIATED COLLEGES AND UNIVERSITIES OF THE NATIONAL INSTITUTE OF CREDIT

| | | |
|---|---|---|
| Rio Salado Community College | Phoenix | Arizona |
| NIC Bakersfield Chapter | Bakersfield | California |
| University of California/UCLA Ext. | Los Angeles | California |
| Southern California Institute of Credit | Los Angeles | California |
| Stanford University | Palo Alto | California |
| Community College of Aurora | Aurora | Colorado |
| Quinnipac College | Hamden | Connecticut |
| Teikyo Post University | Waterbury | Connecticut |
| University of Hartford | West Hartford | Connecticut |
| George Washington University | Washington | D. C. |
| NIC Orlando | Orlando | Florida |
| Pine Mountain Conference Center | Pine Mountain | Georgia |
| Hawaii Pacific College | Honolulu | Hawaii |
| Chicago Institute of Credit | Chicago | Illinois |
| Harper Junior College | Chicago | Illinois |
| Northwestern University | Evanston | Illinois |
| Indiana Institute of Credit | Indianapolis | Indiana |
| NIC Iowa Chapter | Des Moines | Iowa |
| Bellarmine College | Louisville | Kentucky |
| Jefferson Community College | Louisville | Kentucky |
| Maryland Institute of Credit | Hunt Valley | Maryland |
| American International College | Springfield | Massachusetts |
| Detroit College of Business | Dearborn | Michigan |
| Davenport College | Grand Rapids | Michigan |
| Normandale Community College | Bloomington | Minnesota |
| Inver Hills Community College | Inver Grove Heights | Minnesota |
| Mankato State University | Mankato | Minnesota |
| University of Minnesota | Minneapolis | Minnesota |
| North Hennepin Community College | Osseo | Minnesota |
| Dakota County Vo-Tech | Rosemont | Minnesota |
| NIC Kansas City | Kansas City | Missouri |
| St. Louis Community College | St. Louis | Missouri |
| St. Louis University | St. Louis | Missouri |
| NIC Omaha Chapter | Omaha | Nebraska |
| Metropolitan Community College | Omaha | Nebraska |
| Truckee Meadows Community College | Reno | Nevada |
| Dartmouth College | Hanover | New Hampshire |
| Broome Community College | Binghampton | New York |
| New York Institute of Credit | New York City | New York |
| St. John Fisher College | Rochester | New York |
| University of Cincinnati | Cincinnati | Ohio |
| University of Toledo | Toledo | Ohio |
| NIC Pittsburgh | Pittsburgh | Pennsylvania |
| University of Tennessee | Knoxville | Tennessee |
| Dallas Institute of Credit | Dallas | Texas |
| Houston Community College | Houston | Texas |
| Baylor University | Waco | Texas |
| Salt Lake Community College | Salt Lake City | Utah |
| Trinity College of Vermont | Burlington | Vermont |
| Thomas Nelson Community College | Hampton | Virginia |
| Tidewater Community College | Portsmouth | Virginia |
| NIC Central Virginia | Richmond | Virginia |
| Seattle Pacific University | Seattle | Washington |
| Wisconsin Indianhead Tech | Ashland | Wisconsin |
| Marquette University | Milwaukee | Wisconsin |

The above entities comprise the NIC collegiate affiliation network as of March 1, 1991. National Institute of Credit (NIC is administered by the Credit Research Foundation for the National Association of Credit Management.)

# ADVANCED CREDIT ADMINISTRATION PROGRAM (ACAP)

For those credit people at the senior levels, a new advanced program is available (the program is not yet available at all NIC Chapters). The required courses for the Advanced Credit Administration Program (ACAP) are:

## Credit Management Review

An intensive review of those salient points needed to keep up with the state of the art of business credit management. The review reinforces concepts and fundamentals in light of changes to date.

## Credit Management Cases

Selected cases are studied, each in an area the credit executive might expect to encounter in the operating department. Experience and knowledge of the credit function are prerequisite as are the application of industry norms to financial statement analysis.

## Business Finance

Principles of business finance. Topics include: short- and long-term sources of funds, management of financial assets, leverage, dividends, capital building, and financial policies and planning.

## Business and Society

An in-depth study of business ethics and morality. Included are a review of philosophical and phenomenological concepts and their interpretation.

## Credit & Commercial Laws in Review

An overview of laws that the credit executive must be aware of. Areas such as statute of limitations, pre-judgment remedies and limitations of legal referrals are explored. Includes analysis and application of the Uniform Commercial Code.

*Computer Applications*

Fundamental concepts of computer application, use of PC's and selected applications to credit and collection departments.

The advanced program is not available at all NIC Chapters.

For information on recommended textbooks for the above program, contact Education Coordinator, NIC, 8815 Centre Park Drive, Columbia, Maryland 21045.

# THE PROFESSIONAL DESIGNATIONS

## CREDIT BUSINESS ASSOCIATE (CBA)

The Credit Business Associate (CBA) is the supervisory level designation of the National Institute of Credit (NIC). Candidates must register with NIC, complete a Career Roadmap showing attainment of 50 points, and submit an application.

There is a comprehensive examination requirement for the CBA.

To apply, therefore, candidates must provide transcripts showing completion of required courses with a minimum average of "C". There are two plans (A or B) which a candidate may select to follow. The typical required courses for each plan are as detailed below:

### Plan A

- *Economics, Macro*
- *Economics, Micro*
- *Accounting I*
- *Accounting II*
- *Credit and Collection Principles**
- *Financial Analysis***
- *Business Communications*

### Plan B

This alternate plan requires meeting the following criteria:
- Three years' experience in the field of credit.
- Successful completion of the Certified Credit Administrator (CAP) program entailing successful completion of the following

courses: *Credit and Collection Principles\**, *Financial Analysis\*\**, and *Credit Management Cases.*

> \* *Introductory* and *Intermediate Credit Management* are the equivalent of *Credit and Collection Principles.*
>
> \*\* Applied Credit Management is equivalent to *Financial Analysis.*

- Applicants eligible for this alternative must submit a detailed resume and transcripts or grade reports showing that the "B" average requirement for credit management courses was met (official transcripts must be sent from the university to the NACM affiliate office for processing to NIC).

With 50 Career Roadmap points and fulfillment of requirements of Plan A or Plan B, applicants are admitted to the CBA examination. This examination is administered at the local NACM affiliate.

These course requirements may be met by study at local NACM affiliates through a chapter of the NIC, by courses approved by the NIC, or courses offered through a degree-granting college or university. In cases where college work is offered in fulfillment of the requirements, an official transcript must be furnished to the NIC for evaluation (transcripts are to be sent by the college or university to the NACM affiliated association for transmittal to NIC).

College Level Examination Program (CLEP) results are accepted toward non-credit management courses if the grade achieved is "C" or better. Questions in this regard should be directed to the NIC, 8815 Centre Park Drive, Columbia, Maryland 21045-2117.

The NIC keeps records of all registered persons working toward this designation. After individuals have accumulated 50 points and have completed the required course work, they are required to complete an examination for the Credit Business Associate designation and certificate.

## CREDIT BUSINESS FELLOW (CBF)

The next level requires achievement of the CBA designation, 100 Career Roadmap points, and meeting requirements of Plan A or Plan B. The Credit Business Fellow (CBF) is the management level designation of the National Institute of Credit (NIC).

In preparing for it, the student prepares for management levels of credit and financial administration and for assuming greater responsibilities.

Applicants for the CBF designation must qualify as a candidate and pass a comprehensive examination designed to test mastery of the fundamentals of credit and financial management and ability to use these principles in the analysis and solution of current problems. Upon satisfaction of these requirements, the successful candidate is designated as a Credit Business Fellow.

There are two separate plans under which applicants may qualify as candidates for the CBF examination:

## Plan A

The student must a) be the holder of the Credit Business Associate (CBA) designation; b) have three years' experience in credit, financial, or related fields; and c) have successfully completed with an average grade of "C" the requirements stated under Plan A or Plan B, or be currently enrolled in no more than two remaining required courses.

The educational requirements consist of successful completion of required courses. The mandatory courses under Plan A include:

- *Business Law I*
- *Business Law II*
- *Public Speaking*
- *Marketing*
- *Credit Management Cases* (candidates who used this course under Plan B of the CBA may not use it again)
- *Psychology*
- *Management*
- 2 Elective courses from the list below

Some of the elective courses are listed below. Approval of the Director of Education of NIC must be obtained if the student desires to submit any other course as a substitute elective.

- *Accounting (Advanced)*
- *Business Policy*
- *Corporate Finance*
- *Cost Accounting*
- *Financial Management*

- *Credit Insurance*
- *Credit Law*
- *International Marketing*
- *Marketing Management*
- *Organizational Development*

## Plan B

1. Official transcripts showing completion of a master's degree in business or completion of a bachelor's degree in business and a resume detailing a minimum of three years' teaching experience at the college level.
2. A business resume detailing a minimum of five years' of experience in credit management (up to two required courses may be substituted for each year of experience). Experience should be at the management or supervisory levels in the five year count.

Once accepted under Plan A or Plan B, examinations are scheduled for the spring or fall of the year of acceptance. The student may take any or all parts at any sitting, but must pass all three to qualify for the CBF designation.

Requirements referred to herein are as of the date of this publication and subject to change. Changes in the requirements, if any, are intended to keep participants up to date with legal and/or technological changes that affect the profession. The basic principles do remain constant and therefore the material is useful even after changes are made.

## CERTIFIED CREDIT EXECUTIVE (CCE)

## Plan A

1. Applicant submits evidence of having achieved CBA and CBF designations and an updated Career Roadmap showing 125 earned points. The Roadmap is certified by the NACM affiliate and returned to NIC.
2. Upon receipt at NIC, the examination date is scheduled through the local NACM affiliate.
3. Upon successful completion of the examination, a notification is sent which is followed by an engraved certificate forwarded to the applicant's NACM affiliate for presentation at its next meeting.

## Plan B

*This plan is for applicants already at the executive level in their careers.*

1. Completed NIC Registration, Application, and Personal Data forms (see discussion below) should be submitted to the local NACM affiliate for processing to NIC. The registration and application forms are processed by NIC and the Personal Data form is point-scored by the Accreditation Committee. Or, executives may instead complete a Career Roadmap showing 125 points certified by the local NACM affiliate to gain admission to the examination.
2. The weighted Personal Data form score determines whether an applicant is admitted to the examination.
3. If the applicant is not admitted to the examination, a new Application and Personal Data form may be submitted after six months.
4. If the applicant is admitted and passes the examination, notification is sent, followed by an engraved certificate forwarded to the applicant's NACM affiliate for presentation at the next meeting.

## CCE Personal Data Form Instructions:

*(A CCE Personal Data Form is shown in Exhibit 3.4)*

1. Two copies of the Personal Data Form are provided. Candidates prepare one original and make six copies of each page. One copy is kept by the applicant for their file. The original and copies are mailed with a check for the required fees payable to NIC Registrar to: CCE Registrar, NIC, 8815 Centre Park Drive, Columbia, Maryland 21045-2117.
2. Be sure to include all pertinent information on this form. College transcripts must be sent under separate cover by the institution. Information furnished by reference to other sources is not acceptable.
3. If a candidate needs extra space for any question, additional blank sheets are to be used. Each sheet must be identified with the applicant's name and the number of the question to which the information applies.
4. Candidates must provide as much detail as possible. If an applicant cannot state exact dates, "approximately" is used. The use

## EXHIBIT 3.4 CCE Personal Data Form Sample

SAMPLE

## PERSONAL DATA FORM (CONFIDENTIAL)

1.  Total Number of Years in Credit Management _____ (Indicate name of firm[s] on reverse side)

    Total Number of Years in General Management _____ (Indicate name of firm[s] on reverse side)

    Total Number of Years NACM Member _____   CRF Member_____

2.  Member of Which Local NACM Association:_____
    *City and State*

### CATEGORY I - EDUCATION
*(25% of total score)*

3.  Higher Education - College or University training (have the university send official transcripts to NIC)
    *Institution*                      *Date*        *Degree & Major (if no degree please so state)*

4.  Other Higher Education Courses (i.e., technical school and/or correspondence courses - use separate sheet if necessary)

5.  Credit Management Courses, National Institute of Credit (have the university send official transcripts to NIC)
    *Course*                *Date*          *Location*            *Institution*

6.  Credit Management Seminars and Workshops Attended (i.e., CRF, Bankruptcy, etc.)
    *Sponsor & Subject*                 *Date*                *Location*

7.  Holder of NIC Credit Business Associate or NIC Credit Business Fellow Designation

    Credit Business Associate _____        Date Received_____
    Credit Business Fellow _____         Date Received_____

(PLEASE TYPE OR PRINT LEGIBLY)

# EXHIBIT 3.4 CCE Personal Data Form Sample (cont'd)

8.   a.   Candidacy at NACM Graduate School of Credit and Financial Management

Executive Award _____          Date Received _____
Years Completed _____          Campus Location _____

b.   Completion of Advanced Credit Executive Studies Program   Date_____

c.   Completion of Mid-Career School Program
*Session*                          *Date*                          *Location*

d.   Completion of Credit Management Leadership Institute     Date _____

9.   Other Business Management Courses or Other Continuing Education Programs Completed (i.e., AMA, RMA, etc.)
*Sponsor and Course*                    *Dates*                    *Location*

**CATEGORY II - BUSINESS EXPERIENCE**
*(50% of total score)*

10.   List Credit Management Positions Held:

| Title | Number of Employees Supervised | Average Monthly A/R Portfolio Managed | Number of Accounts | Number of Years' Experience |
|---|---|---|---|---|
| 1. |  |  |  |  |
| 2. |  |  |  |  |
| 3. |  |  |  |  |
| 4. |  |  |  |  |
| 5. |  |  |  |  |

# EXHIBIT 3.4 CCE Personal Data Form Sample (cont'd)

11.   Areas of Credit Management in Which You Have Performed

No. of Years

-Assisting in development of credit data processing systems      _____

-Cash Forecasting      _____

-Collection of accounts      _____

-Developing credit department budgets      _____

-Establishing credit lines      _____

-Experience in evaluating customers' financial statements      _____

-Membership on creditor's committee      _____

-Participating in establishing credit policy      _____

-Training credit department personnel      _____

12.   Management Experience Other than Credit Management

| Position | Company | No. of Years |
|----------|---------|--------------|

## CATEGORY III - PERSONAL CONTRIBUTIONS TO IMPROVEMENT OF CREDIT MANAGEMENT
### (15% of total score)

13.   Service/Experience as a SPEAKER on Credit and Financial Management Subjects

| Subject | Dates | Location |
|---------|-------|----------|

14.   Service/Experience as INSTRUCTOR on Credit & Financial Management Subjects (include in-house training and PARTICIPATION in sales meetings)

| Subject | Dates | Location |
|---------|-------|----------|

15.   Published Articles on Credit Oriented Subjects (Title, name of publication and date)

# EXHIBIT 3.4 CCE Personal Data Form Sample (cont'd)

### CATEGORY IV - PARTICIPATION AND SUPPORT OF ASSOCIATION ACTIVITIES
*(10% of total score)*

LOCAL NACM AFFILIATE

16. Elected Offices Held (i.e., President, Vice President, Board Member, Etc.)
    *Position*                                    *Dates*


17. Committee Chairman and/or Member
    *Committee*                          *Dates*          *Chairman or Member*


18. Industry Group Chairman and/or Member
    *Industry Group*                     *Dates*          *Chairman or Member*


19. Regional Credit Conferences Attended
    *Conference*                                 *Dates*


20. Award(s) Received (Check one):
                                         *Award*       *Date*

    Credit Executive of the Year         _____         _____

    Other (Explain) _____


21. Use of Local Association Services
                                                 *Yes*          *No*
    Adjustment Services                          _____          _____
    Collection Services                          _____          _____
    Credit Group Membership                      _____          _____
    Credit Interchange                           _____          _____
    NACM-Business Credit Contributor             _____          _____
    NACM - International (FCIB)                   _____          _____
    Regularly Attend Local Assn. Meetings        _____          _____

## EXHIBIT 3.4 CCE Personal Data Form Sample (cont'd)

NATIONAL ASSOCIATION OF CREDIT MANAGEMENT LEVEL

22.   Offices Held

|   | *Title* | *Name of Committee* | *Date* |
|---|---|---|---|
| A. | | | |
| B. | | | |
| C. | | | |

23.   Committee Chairman and/or Member

|   | *Committee* | *Date* | *Chairman or Member* |
|---|---|---|---|
| A. | | | |
| B. | | | |
| C. | | | |

24.   NACM Credit Congress and International Conferences Attended

|   | *Congress/Conference* | *Date* | *Location* |
|---|---|---|---|
| A. | | | |
| B. | | | |
| C. | | | |

25.   Legislative Conferences Attended:  Washington, D.C., State and Local

*Location*                               *Date*

# EXHIBIT 3.4 CCE Personal Data Form Sample (cont'd)

26. Use of National Services

|  | Yes | No |
|---|---|---|
| Credit Research Foundation Membership | ____ | ____ |
| Credit Management Leadership Institute | ____ | ____ |
| Mid-Career School | ____ | ____ |
| Graduate School of Credit & Financial Management | ____ | ____ |
| Loss Prevention | ____ | ____ |
| CFDD Membership | ____ | ____ |
| NACM-FCIB Membership | ____ | ____ |
| Registered with NIC | ____ | ____ |

### CATEGORY V - GENERAL
(Up to 5 bonus points)

27. Participation in Other Business Organizations (List organization, dates, member or positions held and/or participation)

28. Participation in and Positions Held in Community, Fraternal and Civic Organizations (Indicate dates, organizations and your involvement)

29. Honors Received (List and give date, name of organization)

30. Recertification Credits Earned Through Seminars, Courses, etc. (Indicate the number of Continuing Education Units [CEU's])

    Total Number of CEU's earned _____

    Indicate below and on reverse side where earned

31. Participation Recognition (served as a mentor, speaker, etc.; specify and give dates)

of alphabetical abbreviations for organizations except NACM, NIC, and CRF is not permitted.

5. The Chief Operating Officer of the local NACM affiliated association must sign the form in the space provided.

## Recertification

Candidates are certified for a period of three years and must therefore recertify every three years thereafter until they reach age 60. A CCE Recertification Report is available for this purpose and may be obtained from the NIC. A copy of the CCE Recertification Report is reproduced in Exhibit 3.5.

## Background Information on the CCE

The Certified Credit Executive (CCE) is the highest level professional designation of the National Institute of Credit (NIC) and is intended to signify experience and competence at the senior management level.

## Objectives

The objectives of the CCE designation are as follows:
- To raise professional standards and improve the practice of business credit management.
- To identify and give special recognition to individual credit executives with advanced levels of experience, knowledge, ability, accomplishment, leadership, and contribution in the field of business credit management, as evidenced by the submission of qualifying personal data, transcripts and successful completion of a comprehensive examination. Applications may be supported by either a Personal Data Form or Career Roadmap available from the NIC and local NACM affiliate offices through the United States.
- To enhance recognition of business credit management as an important contributor to company profits, and the business credit executive as a key member of corporate management.
- To assist the entire business community in establishing an objective measure of an individual's knowledge at the senior management level and competence in the practice of business credit management.

## EXHIBIT 3.5 CCE Recertification Report Sample

SAMPLE

# CERTIFIED CREDIT EXECUTIVE
# RECERTIFICATION
### REPORT
*TO BE COMPLETED BY THE CCE*

Name:_____ SSN:_____ - _____ - _____

Telephone:_____ Certification Date: _____

Company: _____ Title: _____

Address: _____

City: _____ State: _____ Zip: _____

NACM affiliate holding membership record:_____

If above affiliate location is different from that at time of
certification, please indicate address at time of last report.

    Affiliate:_____

    City:_____State:_____Zip:_____

This form must be completed and returned to CCE registrar no later than
September 30 prior to recertification date.  The first recertification date
for each CCE is the fourth January 2nd following the date appearing on the
CCE certificate.  After initial recertification, CCEs must recertify at
three year intervals.

☑      6 Points are required to earn recertification i.e., 3 educational
      and 3 participation points (3 educational points = 30 contact
      hours).

☑      All programs and activities to be listed are only those since the
      certification date.

☑      All information requested is to be entered on the form and
      attachments provided where indicated.

Please enclose $100.00 payment for CRF/NACM member Recertification Fee.
**(Sorry, NIC cannot bill you.  All fees must be paid in advance and must
accompany the recertification sheet.)**

☐  My check is enclosed

Date Submitted: _____ Signature: _____

REMIT TO:          **National Institute of Credit**
                 8815 Centre Park Drive
                 Columbia, MD  21045-2117

## EXHIBIT 3.5 CCE Recertification Report Sample (cont'd)

## CERTIFICATION MAINTENANCE CRITERIA

Continuing professional development activities are essential to enable business credit executives to stay at the leading edge of proficiency with rapidly changing economic conditions. Therefore, to retain the Certified Credit Executive designation, CCE recipients must accumulate six professional points each three years and submit a completed CCE Recertification Reporting Sheet to the CCE registrar. Each CCE first reaches the recertification date on the fourth January 2nd following the date appearing on the certificate.

FOLLOWING INITIAL RECERTIFICATION, CCEs MUST RECERTIFY AT THREE YEAR INTERVALS with the CCE Recertification Reporting sheet due by September 30 preceding the recertification date.

Professional points for recertification can be accumulated anytime from the date appearing on the CCE certificate (or from last date of recertification) to the September immediately preceding recertification date. For example, those certified and receiving a certificate dated 1988 file a record of 6 professional points with the CCE registrar by September 30, 1991 and these executives all reach recertification date on January 2, 1992. Any executive receiving the CCE designation in 1989 must file a report on the 6 professional points accumulated by September 30, 1992 and reaches recertification on January 2, 1993.

## LIFE CERTIFICATION

A CCE upon reaching age sixty is certified for life. No further reporting is necessary except to notify the certification registrar.

## PROCEDURES

NIC will mail notices to all CCEs reminding them of maintenance requirements and the CCE registrar will accept at any time a report on maintenance credits for the personal file of each CCE provided the report is for the total 6 professional points.

The Maintenance Reporting sheets must be filed with NIC not less than two months prior to recertification date.

## FEES

For each three year period renewal, a $100 fee will be payable with the Recertification Reporting sheet.

# EXHIBIT 3.5 CCE Recertification Report Sample (cont'd)

*The Accreditation Board has set the following policy for handling loss of certification through failure to meet certification requirements.*

*CCEs certified after August 31, 1988 who do not acquire sufficient CCE maintenance points to achieve recertification on the required date will be notified in writing of suspension from using the CCE designation and will no longer be listed as a CCE in any NACM or NIC publication until such time that the individual:*

*1.   Resubmits to the certification process and successfully meets the criteria for certification by examination or,*

*2.   Acquires make-up points at a cumulative total equal to 2 per year for every year since original date of certification or the last recertification.*

## PROFESSIONAL POINTS ACCEPTED FOR RECERTIFICATION CREDIT

The Accreditation Board has identified a wide variety of educational activities and leadership initiatives through which a certification may be maintained.   A total of 6 points, 3 education points and 3 participation points, is required.

They are listed below by categories.   The Board will continuously review other programs and activities to identify those which, in its judgement, merit inclusion.   Up to 30 hours or three points may be derived from meeting or service activities (Every three years, 30 hours of continuing education plus 30 hours of participation is required for a total of 60 hours or 6 points).

**Points**

I.   **EDUCATION PROGRAMS AND COURSES CATEGORY**

**Continuing Education**
(3 points, 30 hours over three years)

_____   A.   Participation in CRF and NIC approved education programs and programs of allied groups, or programs of degree granting

# EXHIBIT 3.5 CCE Recertification Report Sample (cont'd)

**Points**

institutions of higher education *when the subject matter relates directly to business credit management subjects.* (max. 3 points - CMLI = 1 pt., MCS = 1.5 pts., GSCFM [completion] = 3 pts., ACES = 2 pts.)

_____ B. Participation in educational programs offered by CRF, NIC, CFDD, or FCIB groups and approved luncheon conferences and speeches on credit management topics. (Each 10 hours of instruction = 1 point, total max. 3 points)

_____ C. Participation in other programs and courses that apply to business credit management. (Each 10 hours of instruction = 1 point, total max. 2 points)

_____ D. Completion of home study courses sponsored by a qualified institution applicable to advanced business credit management. (Each approved course = 1 pt., total max. 2 points)

Sponsor: _____

Title of program or course: _____

Number of hours: _____

Location: _____


Sponsor: _____

Title of program or course: _____

Number of hours: _____

Location: _____


Sponsor: _____

Title of program or course: _____

Number of hours: _____

Location: _____


Sponsor: _____

Title of program or course: _____

Number of hours: _____

Location: _____

## EXHIBIT 3.5 CCE Recertification Report Sample (cont'd)

**Points**

Sponsor: _____

Title of program or course: _____

Number of hours: _____

Location: _____

*(Attach program outline, course description, schedule, etc.*
*if other than CRF/NACM/NIC sponsorship)*

II. **PARTICIPATION ACTIVITY OR PROGRAM CATEGORY**

**Points accumulate since date of certification or last**
**recertification. (3 points, 30 hours over three years)**

**Membership**

_____ A. Membership in NACM. (.50 point for each year of membership)

Indicate years of membership by year.

_____

_____

_____

_____ B. Membership in any of the following affiliated organizations:
CRF, CFDD, FCIB (.25 point for each year of membership);

Indicate organization and years of membership by year.

_____

_____

_____

_____ C. Membership in allied societies, e.g., Robert Morris
Associates (RMA), American Banking Association (ABA), etc.
Points accumulate since date of certification or last
recertification. (.25 point during the three year period)

## EXHIBIT 3.5 CCE Recertification Report Sample (cont'd)

Points

Indicate organization and years of membership by year.

_____

_____

_____

**Conventions and Annual Meetings of NACM and its Affiliates**

_____  A.  For attendance at:  NACM Annual Credit Congress and
            Exposition (1 point), Legislative Conference (1 point), NACM
            affiliate Regional Conferences (.50 point), CFDD conferences
            (.25 point), FCIB conferences (.25 point), CRF Seminars and
            Open Regional Meeting (.25 point)

            Identify meetings and years of attendance by year.

_____

_____

_____

**Service as an Officer, Director, Chairman or Committee Member
of NACM, or an NACM Affiliated Organization (A-E)
Service to Allied Societies and Groups (F-G)**

_____  A.  For each year as an officer (.50 point).
_____  B.  For each year as a director (.25 point).
_____  C.  For each year as a chairman of a committee or NIC Chapter
            (.50 point).
_____  D.  For each year as a committee member (.25 point).
_____  E.  For each year as a member of an industry group (.25 point).
_____  F.  For each year as an officer of an allied group (.50 point).
_____  G.  For each year as a board member of an allied group (.25
            point).

Office or position held:  _____

Organization:  _____

Date of service:  _____

# EXHIBIT 3.5 CCE Recertification Report Sample (cont'd)

**Points**

Office or position held: _____

Organization: _____

Date of Service: _____


Office or position held: _____

Organization: _____

Date of service: _____


### Speeches, Instruction, and Other Program Participation in Association Management

_____    A.  Appearance as an instructor at any NACM affiliated organization or CCE study group.  Subject matter must relate to business credit management.  (max. 1 point)

_____    B.  Participation in courses related to business credit management sponsored by the Credit Research Foundation. (max. 3 points)

_____    C.  Participation in courses pre-approved by the National Institute of Credit sponsored by local NACM affiliates. (max. 2 points)

_____    D.  Speeches on business credit management, outside of your NACM affiliate, to organizations other than those mentioned above. (max. 1 point)


Name of program: _____

Sponsor: _____

Length of presentation: _____

Type of involvement (speaker, instructor, panel participant,

etc.): _____

# EXHIBIT 3.5 CCE Recertification Report Sample (cont'd)

Points

Name of program: _____

Sponsor: _____

Length of presentation: _____

Type of involvement: _____


Name of program: _____

Sponsor: _____

Length of presentation: _____

Type of involvement: _____


Name of program: _____

Sponsor: _____

Length of presentation: _____

Type of involvement: _____


*(Attach a copy or outline of speech and copy of program)*


**Published Articles and Other Literary Contributions
to Business Credit Management
Excluding Your Own Organization's Publications**

_____   A.   Each article published including monographs, booklets, newsletters, and contributions to books on credit and financial management subjects, and research conducted in business credit management published and distributed. (max. 1 point)

Publication in which it appeared: _____

Publisher: _____

Date of publication: _____

*(Attach copy if published by other than NACM.)*

# EXHIBIT 3.5 CCE Recertification Report Sample (cont'd)

Points      **Awards Received for Outstanding Accomplishment and Contributions to Business Credit Management**
(max. 1 point per award, max. 1 per year, retroactive 3 prior years)

\_\_\_\_\_      Name of award: _____

Organization presenting award: _____

Date of award: _____

\_\_\_\_\_      Name of award: _____

Organization presenting award: _____

Date of award: _____

\_\_\_\_\_      Name of award: _____

Organization presenting award: _____

Date of award: _____

*(Attach description of each award if other than NACM sponsorship.)*

### Voluntary Community Service

\_\_\_\_\_      Religious, civic, fraternal, or charity work.  Provide details below. (max. .50 point per year)

Describe specific service and dates of involvement:

_____

_____

_____

_____

_____

_____

_____

\_\_\_\_\_      **TOTAL POINTS**

*National Institute of Credit*
*administered by the Credit Research Foundation*
*for and on behalf of the National Association of Credit Management*

## Administration

Administration of the CCE program rests with the Credit Research Foundation (CRF) which operates the National Institute of Credit (NIC) for and on behalf of the National Association of Credit Management (NACM). The qualifications of each CCE candidate are evaluated by the Accreditation Committee of NACM based on a majority vote of at least two-thirds of the committee.

The Accreditation Committee, oversight board for all NIC designations and courses, is responsible for selection of personal data questions as well as the written examination questions and content.

The written examination must be completed in the office of an affiliated association of the NACM or an NIC-approved location. A designated proctor must administer each written examination. The proctor will be the Chief Operating Officer of the affiliated association or a designee. The proctor is required to sign the examination form at the completion of the examination and return it promptly to NIC for grading.

The Accreditation Committee has no intention whatsoever to determine who shall engage in business credit management. If a person is not certified, this does not indicate that the individual is unqualified to be a business credit executive. It does, however, mean that the individual has not fulfilled requirements for the CCE designation, or has not applied for admission to the required examination.

## Eligibility

Members of NACM member companies are eligible for certification under the CCE program.

Application for certification is open to credit executives who have at least six years' management experience, five years of which is within credit management, and who have been with their companies for at least three years. The Career Roadmap or Personal Data form procedures described herein may be used to apply for admission to the examination.

Registration with the NIC is the first step in the review process aimed at guiding applicants toward earning the designation.

## CCE Certification Procedure Overview

Application and NIC Registration forms may be obtained from the NIC or Chief Operating Officers of NACM affiliates, and may be filed with the affiliate at any time. Application forms are supported by the Personal Data form or Career Roadmap as discussed earlier.

After receiving the properly completed Career Roadmap or Personal Data form, the CCE Registrar verifies the prerequisites for eligibility and processes the forms in keeping with the established policy and procedures.

Information obtained on the Personal Data form is evaluated individually by the Accreditation Board. Results of this evaluation are tabulated by the CCE Registrar in accordance with a mathematically weighted scoring system.

Applicants who receive a satisfactory score based on this evaluation of their Personal Data form are notified of admission to the written examination by the National Institute of Credit following review by the Accreditation Committee. The Career Roadmap showing 125 points must be certified by the COO of the NACM affiliate. The Personal Data form is point-scored by the Accreditation Committee. In either case, the number of points determines admission to the examination.

## The CCE Examination

The examination consists of true, false, and/or open-ended questions and essay type questions. Some questions may be required for all candidates. Other questions are categorized to permit candidates a suitable choice of industry-specific questions, depending on their background and experience in specialized areas of credit management, e.g., construction or banking industries.

A typical examination, for example, may cover such subjects as:
- Return on Investment (ROI)
- Credit Policy
- Credit Department Organization and Staffing
- The Selling Side of Credit
- Legal Aspects of Credit
- Financial Statement Analysis
- DSO Formula and its Meaning (Credit Research Foundation's formula)

- Credit Investigation
- Collection Procedures for Profit
- Terms of Sale
- Credit Tools and Their Use to Permit Sales to Marginal Customers
- Business Reorganization, Bankruptcy, and Financial Distress
- Uniform Commercial Code
- Credit Organizations

A candidate who does not qualify for certification because of failure to pass the written examination, but who has completed the Personal Data form or Career Roadmap of the CCE program, may sit once more for the written examination six months from the date of the failed written examination. A candidate who does not meet Personal Data form requirements is encouraged to make reapplication for the CCE designation at an appropriate later date. NIC should be contacted for specific instructions and guidance.

All information pertaining to an applicant's request for accreditation are held in strict confidence by all involved in the accreditation program until the final certification. Certified candidates receive nationwide publicity and recognition.

### Fees

Contact your local NACM affiliate or NIC directly for information on current fees.

### Use of the CCE Designation

The Certified Credit Executive may use the CCE designation with his or her name as a business signature and on business cards.

Certification is for individuals only. The CCE designation may not be used by anyone in a firm other than the person duly certified.

## CANONS OF BUSINESS CREDIT ETHICS

The NIC is interested in the candidate's qualities of character, conduct, and attitudes essential to successful work in credit and financial management. It evaluates these qualities in terms of each candidate's eligibility for a designation. Designation holders subscribe to NACM's Canons of Business Credit Ethics.

A set of "Canons of Business Credit Ethics" has been published by NACM to promote and maintain the highest standards of business conduct and personal performance among its members. Adherence to these canons is expected of all Certified Credit Executives. A copy of the canons has been reproduced in Appendix D.

## STANDARDS FOR ATTAINMENT OF DESIGNATIONS

The possession of any designation from the NIC is recognition that the holder has fulfilled essential technical and educational requirements, has attained prescribed standards, and merits the confidence the public places in the credit profession.

Employers are advised to engage the services of skilled professionals who have received certification. This is of particular importance since business credit is a profession not yet controlled by state boards, so almost anyone who claims to have expertise or knowledge can offer their services to any corporate or organizational entity interested in recruiting qualified people. The credentialed individual, however, has completed educational requirements and extensive instruction in the various facets of credit and financial management.

Credentialing also meets the demands of attorneys and CPA's who need staff to provide credit-related services to their clients. Attorneys and CPA's may earn Continuing Professional Education (CPE) recertification credit through the NIC (see Chapter 2).

## COMMUNICATION

Employment agencies and business and industry groups as well as Chambers of Commerce can be helpful in communicating to companies the need to request specific standards for business credit positions.

## RECOGNITION

Candidates who meet all of the prescribed requirements and pass the examination receive a certificate and are awarded the right to use the designation initials after their names on business cards and stationery. CBF and CCE recipients may purchase a gold pin to wear.

# DESIGNATIONS FACILITATE CORPORATE RECRUITMENT

The NIC, in cooperation with NACM North Central, has made available a software package which links benchmark designation levels to job descriptions. The model job descriptions may be used by corporations to update and standardize their own. By linking CBA to supervisory, CBF to management, and CCE to senior management levels the task of recruiting skilled candidates for credit department openings is simplified. The software may be purchased through NIC. Simply contact the Education Coordinator, Credit Research Foundation, 8815 Centre Park Drive, Columbia, Maryland 21045-2117.

## MENTORING DEFINED

The definition of mentoring adopted by NIC is:

> "a deliberate pairing of a more skilled or experienced person with a lesser skilled or experienced one, with the agreed goal of having the lesser skilled person grow and develop specific competencies."

Refer to Exhibit 3.6 for a chart showing the NIC Mentoring Program.

## MENTORING

NACM affiliates are encouraged by NIC to embrace a "Credit Career Development Group." This is essentially a local network system comprised of members who agree to serve as mentors.

Mentors are usually members who have already earned the CBF and/or CCE designation or members who have served on the affiliate board of directors.

Each mentor should strive to have at least two mentees. The mentees must be recorded or assigned by the local NACM office to facilitate allocation of criteria points for the mentee's professional development.

The group should dedicate an annual starting date (September), establish a cutoff date (June) and plan a recognition meeting.

Group study sessions have proven to be very effective if held in late March or early April to give assurance to those concerned credit people

**EXHIBIT 3.6 NIC Mentoring Program**

# NIC MENTORING PROGRAM

```
┌──────────────────┐        ┌──────────────────┐
│     MEMBER       │───────▷│      MATCH        │
│    REGISTERS     │        │     MEMBER        │
│                  │        │    TO MENTOR      │
└──────────────────┘        └──────────────────┘
        △                            │
        │                            ▽
┌──────────────────┐        ┌──────────────────┐        ┌──────────────────┐
│     MEMBER       │        │     MEMBER        │        │  MEMBER WORKS     │
│  INFORMATION     │        │   ORIENTATION     │        │ THROUGH PROGRAM   │
│    SESSION       │        │                   │        │                   │◁───▷
└──────────────────┘        └──────────────────┘        └──────────────────┘
        △                            │                          △
        │                            ▽                          │
┌──────────────────┐        ┌──────────────────┐        ┌──────────────────┐
│     MEMBER       │        │  DESIGNATION      │───────▷│     LEARNING      │
│    CONTACTS      │        │    PROGRAM        │        │    SESSIONS       │
│  NACM AFFILIATE  │        │    PLANNED        │        │                   │
└──────────────────┘        └──────────────────┘        └──────────────────┘

                                                         ┌──────────────────┐
                                                         │     MENTOR        │
                                                         │  COORDINATES      │
                                                         └──────────────────┘
```

taking the CRF examinations in May. The same should be repeated in September or October in preparation for the November examinations.

## TYPICAL CAREER DEVELOPMENT STUDY GROUP OUTLINE

### Human Resources

Session I
- Introduction
- The Flow of Credit—General Policymaking and Control; Organizing the Credit Department; Day to day Administration; Counseling.
- Theories of Motivation—Theories X, Y and Z; Maslow; Herzberg.
- Organization—Centralization/decentralization; management responsibilities.
- Personnel Administration—Job descriptions; job specifications, staffing steps (hiring, training, delegating, evaluating, terminating).
- Training.

### Credit Management Problems

Session II
- Credit Policy
- Credit Manual
- Systems & Procedures—The Credit File; Automated Systems
- Non-financial Analysis—4C's; Direct and Indirect Investigation; Trade; Bank, RMA principles; Industry Credit Groups

Session III
- Creditor's Interest in Legal Composition—Proprietorship, Partnership, Corporation; Common Stock, Preferred Stock; Parent, Subsidiary, Division; Mergers, Consolidations, Purchase of Assets.
- Assumed Business Names.
- UCC Article 6—Bulk Transfers

Session IV
- Financing Techniques—Factoring, Finance Companies, Leasing, LBO's, Small Business Administration.
- Insurance

Session V
- Financial Statements—Types; Balance Sheet; Income Statement; FASB 95 and Statement of Cash Flows; Trial Balance.
- Accounting Convention

Sessions VI, VII and VIII
- Financial Analysis—Spreadsheets; Common Sizing, Pattern Statements; Ratios; Trend Analysis; Analyses of Debt (Trade, Bank, Bonds, Debentures, Zeros, PIK's, Yield Curves, Etc.) and Equity: Trial Balance Analysis; Analysis by Sales; Budgets and Projections.

Session IX
- Decision Procedures—Credit Approval; Credit Lines.
- Federal and State Regulation.
- Terms of Sale.
- Antitrust and Trade Regulation Laws.

Session X
- Collection Procedures—Principles; Responsibility; Program; Legal Aspects; Claims and Adjustments; Other Collection Problems.

## Legal Aspects of Credit

Session XI
- Property: Real and Personal
- Contract Law: Mutual Assent; Rejection; Counteroffer; Acceptance; Consideration; Competency, Legality; Discharge and Enforcement; Statute of Frauds; Parole Evidence.

Session XII
- Transferring Contract Rights—Assignments.
- Negotiable Instruments—Negotiation; Holder in Due Course.

Session XIII
- Principal and Agent
- UCC Article 7—Documents of Title
- Terms of Sale; Transfer of Title

Sessions XIV and XV
- Bailments
- Security Devices—Guarantees; Mechanics Liens; Bonds on Public Works.
- UCC Article 9—Personal Property Liens; Replevin/Repossession, Auction.
- International Trade
- UCC Article 5—Documentary Letters of Credit

Session XVI
- The Distressed Debtor and Assignments for the Benefits of Creditors.
- Bankruptcy.

It is important to keep in mind that the amount of confidence the individual has when earning credentials, and the respect accorded from upper management are significant. Each individual, however, must start the action on their own behalf.

Concurrent with the above, similar review sessions can be held for those preparing to take the CBA examination.

## Administration of Career Development Study Groups

Each local NACM affiliate may establish a career development committee to oversee workshops and review member applications for the various designations. Applications are subsequently forwarded to the NIC headquarters office in Columbia, Maryland for processing. This procedure is designed to maintain credentialing integrity while affording prospective employers a credentials verification checkpoint. A Career Development Committee will facilitate bringing mentors and mentees together. Mentors help to accelerate advancement of the mentee.

# CONCLUSION

With certification, more credit managers will command higher salaries. Recognition at all levels, i.e., CBA, CBF, and CCE will attract more qualified credit practitioners and encourage individuals to retain their memberships while allowing their companies to benefit from superior performance.

The NACM and CRF as membership associations provide the infrastructure that individuals need to stay current in their profession and network with their colleagues throughout the world.

# PART THREE

# PROBLEM-SOLVING AND REVIEW OF MAJOR TOPICS

The topical information in this discussion is intended to provide an overview to facilitate the review process. This detail is applicable to all examinations administered by the National Institute of Credit.

# CHAPTER FOUR

# FINANCIAL ANALYSIS

In order to review and properly evaluate the data contained in a financial statement, prior to passing on the credit worthiness of a particular account, care must first be devoted to perspective. Details on the character and capacity of a business and its principals must be weighed and consideration given to existing economic conditions. A number of techniques will be presented to assist the credit practitioner in determining whether or not a firm may be extended credit to on a profitable basis.

## FACTORS INFLUENCING ANALYSIS

In addition to a consideration of finances, credit appraisal is dependent upon a number of other influences.

### CHARACTER RATING

The character rating of the company or of the individuals who control the firm being considered for credit is of great significance. Questions to be addressed include: Is the trade reputation a good one, are the principals regarded as honest, hard working people? People and companies take pride in favorable reputations. It takes years to establish a good name and while this does not provide stability in itself, the risk involved in selling a firm enjoying a good moral risk reputation is normally less than that encountered when selling an account of unknown or questionable character.

Care should be given to obtain accurate information on the debtor's integrity and willingness to pay debts when due. The outside interests of principals and their personal habits bear investigation as they relate directly to company management and success.

## CAPACITY

Capacity indicates an ability to perform. It combines both mental and physical abilities and again refers to both the principals of a firm as well as the firm itself. Knowledge, experience and industry of management contribute to capacity. The credit manager must be convinced that an organization is properly managed and in addition to possessing a willingness to perform, it must also have the ability to do so.

## CAPITAL

Capital is an indication of the financial resources which a firm may utilize to conduct its business. This characteristic can be measured in dollars. The analyst, by considering conditions and trends as revealed by financial statements, is able to make a decision on the firm's ability to pay within specified terms.

Individual judgment must be exercised in reviewing the influence of capital. Industry conditions exert a general influence on the financial conditions reflected by businesses. In certain lines substantial investments in fixed assets are necessary while in others the investment in plant and machinery may be minimal. The nature of the business of certain firms may make a relatively large receivables exposure normal and acceptable whereas a similar situation reflected by another organization in a different product line might indicate a danger signal.

A study of industry trends is of importance here. The credit practitioner is particularly interested in determining the progression of working capital, sales, and earnings since these factors heavily influence the final credit decision.

## ECONOMIC CONDITIONS

Economic Conditions influence to some extent the appraisal of the account. General economic conditions, in most instances, influence credit policy. During periods of prosperity the likelihood of a favorable experience with an account in a progressive industry is better than if the industry was in a period of declining sales and lowered profits.

If competition is severe, it may be necessary to grant special terms in specified instances to obtain business. When there is an overabundance of a product or a buyer's market exists, it is generally true that credit must be extended on a more liberal basis in order to obtain a greater share of the market. Conversely when products are in short supply and a seller's market exists, the credit practitioner might want to operate under terms of a more restrictive credit policy.

## INDUSTRY CONDITION

The credit practitioner is interested not only in general economic conditions but also in the specific condition of the industry in which his or her firm is engaged and in the outlook for the various industries sold by his or her organization. Credit decisions, of necessity, commit company funds on either a short- or long-term basis and to perform properly, the credit manager must have a knowledge of existing monetary and banking conditions. This type of information is readily obtained through conversation and correspondence with internal financial personnel, through direct customer contacts, newspapers, and government sources.

Business conditions contribute in large measure to the establishment of credit policy and the alert credit manager is continually aware of the changes that take place in the business environment. The manager is in a position to recommend liberalizing or restricting credit policy because of familiarity with existing conditions.

## SELLER'S INTERNAL CONDITION

The seller is concerned with his own firm's internal condition and relative position in the market. It must therefore be determined whether or not finances are sufficiently strong to assume risks of relatively high degree in order to gain access to a new market. Questions to ask include: Can the seller afford to be selective and assume only the best possible risks because he produces a limited quantity of a product which is in large demand? How great an exposure is a selling organization willing to assume in terms of sales to a single customer? How will requests for extended terms be handled? Competition must be met in many instances but will the granting of lengthy terms impair the seller's own financing ability? The needs of the buyer must also be considered, particularly when it is known that a seasonal problem exists or that a special situation has occurred.

Certainly the credit analyst must be aware of how a policy decision is likely to affect the financial condition of one's own organization or that of the customer. Granting of extra terms may well result in an expanded receivables position or in a need to obtain additional financing. The liberalizing of policy may result in larger bad debt write-offs but a restrictive policy might prove more harmful in that it might tend to impair volume sales and profits.

## METHOD OF OPERATION

Businesses generally are in one of several categories, e.g., retailing, service, or manufacturing. The financial condition reflected by firms in a particular group would normally reflect certain expected conditions. It would be natural to expect that the financial statement of a service account would show considerably less labor expense than that of a manufacturer in that the service account ordinarily would provide intangible services while the manufacturer would be responsible for assembly. In like manner, it might be expected that a service account would turn available capital more actively than a retailer but at the same time, the service account would probably be working on a lesser profit margin.

Good account analysis would include the comparison of an individual statement with a pattern or average statement for the line of business in which the firm under review is engaged. Such a procedure enables the credit manager to weigh the merits of an account with the situation which might be considered typical of the particular industry. It assists in making the credit decision.

## METHOD OF FINANCING

Businesses finance their operations in a number of ways. The method used is sometimes by choice but often of necessity and the type of financing involved has a direct relationship to a firm's financial condition.

A fixed asset expansion may be indicated by a steadily increasing volume and the need for additional production facilities. The manner in which the construction of additional plant space or acquisition of new machinery is handled will have a direct bearing on the financial condition of the organization. If the investment is financed internally it will probably be reflected in a larger slow asset account and corresponding decrease in working capital. If borrowed funds are utilized to accomplish the growth, the long term debt position might increase along with the increase in fixed assets. The principals of the business might invest additional funds or more stock might be sold permitting the financing of the expansion without detriment to working capital.

Operating funds may prove insufficient to cope with a sharply expanding volume and recourse to bank financing or borrowing from factors or finance companies may be necessary to support operations. Such transactions may well result in financial pictures which appear unbalanced. The credit manager must be aware of the effects which different methods of financing have on a financial showing and utilize this knowledge to make a decision.

## SEASONAL FLUCTUATIONS

The number of lines of business which produce income at a relatively steady rate month after month throughout the year is quite rare. Indeed most businesses derive the bulk of their income from one or several seasons in the course of a year. Well known is the local businessperson who waits for Easter, Father's Day, and Christmas, and other than planning for these holidays simply accepts the reduced income generated during the rest of the year.

It is natural to expect that the financial condition of a firm engaged in a seasonal business will show variations from month to month. A cycle usually is set up within a manufacturing organization consisting of a period of preparation, when inventories are built up, a shipping season which sees the inventories converted into receivables, and quite often there is a slack period between seasons when a balance sheet should reflect a rather liquid condition.

A paint manufacturing organization located in the northeastern sector of this country would ordinarily enjoy two busy seasons in the course of a year. The busiest would normally occur in the spring of the year around April-May. Activity would remain at a good level during the summer, although somewhat below that of the spring, and another upsurge should take place in the early fall during September and October. The last months of the calendar year and the early months of the new year are normally slack periods. Most manufacturing concerns have similar cycles although the seasons of greater activity will vary widely with each product line. It is therefore the responsibility of credit practitioner to become familiar with seasonal considerations affecting the product lines that one deals with in order to be properly oriented when reviewing financial information at different times during the year.

## OTHER FACTORS TO CONSIDER

Occasions arise when credit managers may be called on to extend credit in the absence of financial information. Internal conditions may be such that a policy of insisting on statement information before extending credit is not in force.

The credit manager in such as instance is in somewhat of a dilemma when a sizable order is received from a firm which refuses to provide a late financial statement. Refusal to fill the order promptly could well result in the loss of both immediate and continuing profits. Premature acceptance, however, might result in a very slow account or possibly a bad debt loss. Under such circumstances, where company policy permits, the credit manager must rely on non-financial factors in arriving at the credit decision. Such factors include: company and principal history, bank standing, trade standing, and status of financing or factoring arrangement of record.

The history of the concern and background of its principals may be obtained from agency reports. It is important to determine whether or not the firm has a clear record or whether it has in the past become financially embarrassed. The same is true of the principals. Generally, a questionable background is a danger signal and suggests the need for further study. Such investigation may reveal that an insolvency occurred in a period of general depression with considerable progress recorded for many subsequent years. This information would be considered less damaging than the report of an insolvency during a period of relative prosperity. The character of a firm's principals is likewise important. A history of personal bankruptcies, encounters with the law, or other unfavorable information would tend to have a negative effect on the granting of open account credit to the organization with which such an individual was affiliated. Again, other circumstances might permit shipment despite this adverse information.

Bank information is of considerable importance in determining the credit worthiness of an organization. It is wise for a credit manager to establish personal contact with certain bank credit personnel. Many times detailed and valuable information may be obtained by making a visit to the bank or banks of the account under investigation and interviewing the bank officer who handles the account on a face-to-face basis. If a personal call is neither possible nor practical, a telephone call or letter may produce the desired results. In many instances, it may prove best to handle inquiries on a bank-to-bank basis. In this case, the investigating credit manager would ask his or her bank to check with the bank of the account being investigated for detailed information.

Such investigation may provide considerable information of a worthwhile nature. The bank may provide details on the length of the relationship, the basis on which loans are made, and very often may provide at least a general opinion on the financial condition of the firm being investigated. Even when the bank relationship is a non-borrowing one, useful information in the form of average balances, general opinions, and length of relationship, may be forthcoming.

Trade relationships may be determined by obtaining industry group clearance from the Credit Interchange Service of the National Association of Credit Management or some other reliable source. Clearance reports will show how a particular firm is handling its payment with a variety of suppliers. Review of trade information is often a source of good insight as to the financial condition and management of an organization. A clearance report might indicate that a particular firm takes discounts but as a matter of routine, pays in a slow manner where net billings are involved. A trade clearance may indicate that major suppliers are well paid while minor or less important suppliers are given little consideration. The observant credit manager can usually determine the manner in which his or her firm may expect payment from a review of trade experience.

It is often a matter of public record when an organization factors or finances its receivables, inventories, or other assets and the alert credit practitioner should make it a point to contact the source of financing for details and opinion whenever an organization being considered for credit is under review. Factoring organizations, in particular, are helpful in providing close comment on the progress of an account which they service and the information they provide may be of considerable importance in the acceptance or rejection of an order.

Attention should be given by credit managers to their local or regional industry group. Meetings of industry groups permit member credit managers to establish personal contacts with other credit managers servicing the same or similar accounts. Accounts of common interest may be discussed at these industry meetings and questions of general interest may be asked and discussed. The information gathered at such meetings is another important influence on a credit manager's course of action.

Following a review of information from account interviews, public records, newspapers and trade magazines, the decision to sell or not to sell is made in light of existing economic conditions and the seller's credit policy in particular.

The following section will concentrate on analyzing financial information because of its usefulness and desirability in making credit judgments. The credit analyst should nonetheless be aware of the many important non-financial factors such as those outlined above which influence the credit decision-making process.

## DESIRABILITY OF STATEMENT INFORMATION

A financial statement is probably the single most important tool the credit analyst has to work with. Credit managers should, as a matter of routine at regular intervals, seek current financial statements on each of their accounts, whether old or new, gilt-edged or marginal. Conditions constantly change and the facts contained in recent statements permit timely appraisal of current creditworthiness.

The credit practitioner should examine the financial condition of a prospective or established customer in the same manner as a physician examines a patient. Past history should be reviewed for weaknesses. Usefulness of corrective action should be weighed and future planning considered. It is not believed adequate to merely review background information and trade experience. In order to fully protect the investment in receivables of one's firm, the credit manager should examine the condition and trend of a credit seeker and this may be accomplished by reviewing the latest available financial statement of the prospective customer along with earlier financial information. In this manner, a valid judgment of present conditions as well as recent trends may be detected.

A review of operating particulars and balance sheet data should provide answers to the following questions:

1. Is the credit seeking firm in sound financial condition?
2. Will trade indebtedness be repaid in an orderly manner or will slowness develop?
3. Is equity financing adequate or is too much reliance being placed on creditors?
4. Is the firm's capitalization adequate?
5. Are earnings reasonable or do they promise to become so soon?
6. If operations have been unprofitable, are corrective measures underway?
7. Will the extension of credit result in profits or bad debts?

A single balance sheet is of considerable help. It indicates what the financial condition of a firm is at a particular time. If the balance sheet data is fairly close to the date of possible shipment, the decision to sell or not to sell may be based to a large extent on late financial information.

A series of financial statements is even more beneficial because a comparative review of this material permits a determination of trend. A condition regarded as only fair from the review of a single balance sheet might be considered in a somewhat better light if a review of earlier balance sheets indicates that the condition was being corrected. In like manner, a condition such as that of working capital might be regarded as satisfactory from a review of a single financial statement, but if a number of annual statements were available, a sharp decrease in working capital, capable of causing concern, might be revealed.

The credit practitioner should realize that at least a limited amount of trend information may be obtained from a single balance sheet. The presence of an earned surplus would suggest that the overall trend of a firm has been progressive while the presence of a deficit surplus would suggest unprofitable operations. A reserve for income taxes payable or a claim for a tax refund would also provide clues on the operating trend.

## REVIEW OF BASIC ACCOUNTING POLICY AND VALUATIONS

Accounting has been described as a method of collecting, recording, verifying, and presenting financial information. A financial statement consists of a balance sheet, income statement, supplementary data and auditor's comments. In some instances, the amount of financial information submitted for review is somewhat more limited and may be confined to a balance sheet.

The balance sheet lists the assets, liabilities and equity of a business at a given time. Normally the more liquid assets are separated from the other assets of the organization and the more current liabilities from the longer term obligations of a firm. The net difference between the total assets and the total liabilities of a concern represents the equity or net worth of the firm. (See Exhibit 4.1)

An income statement summarizes results of operations for a firm covering a definite period of time. This statement is also called by a variety of other names including the profit and loss statement. The forms in which it is presented differ widely. It is usually desirable to obtain as much information as possible in order that a detailed analysis may be rendered.

Basic information that should be included in an income statement would include: Net Sales, Cost of Goods Sold, Expenses, Pre-Tax and Net Profit figures as well as details on any Extraordinary Profit or Loss. (See Exhibit 4.2)

Financial statements may be presented in a number of ways and in some instances only balance sheet information may be provided. The individual statement is preferred over a consolidated statement which combines the assets and liabilities of the parent and subsidiary while intercompany accounts between parent and subsidiary are omitted. Consolidated statements may disguise flaws in the condition of either parent or subsidiary, and where necessary the credit practitioner should seek both individual and consolidated figures.

## EXHIBIT 4.1 Outline of a Balance Sheet

| *Current Assets* | *Current Liabilities* |
|---|---|
| Cash | Accounts Payable |
| Accounts Receivable | Notes Payable |
| (−) Reserve for Bad Debts | |
| Accounts Receivable (Net) | Bank Loan |
| Inventory | Mortgage (current) |
| Raw Material | |
| Work in Process | Accrued Wages |
| Finished Goods | |
| Total | Accrued Taxes |
| US Govt. Bonds | Other Accruals |
| Marketable Securities | CURRENT LIABILITIES |
| CURRENT ASSETS | |
| TOTAL | Mortgage Payable |
| | |
| *Fixed Assets* | *Slow Liabilities* |
| Land | Capital Stock |
| Buildings | Capital Surplus |
| Machinery & Equip. | |
| Furniture & Fixtures | Earned Surplus |
| (−) Depreciation Reserve | |
| | NET WORTH |
| Other Assets | |
| | LIABILITIES & |
| TOTAL ASSETS | NET WORTH |

Occasionally in connection with proposed mergers or new financing, the credit analyst may encounter a pro forma statement and should be familiar with it. A pro forma statement is not an actual picture of a firm's financial condition but rather is a projection which attempts to reflect what effect certain proposed financing or merger plans will have on condition.

Balance sheets in many instances will contain footnotes which, generally speaking, fall into two categories. The first entails items which do not readily lend themselves to numerical balance sheet or profit and loss items and would include specifics on contingent liabilities, pending litigation, and the like. The other type of footnote usually explains in

## EXHIBIT 4.2  Outline of a Profit and Loss Statement

*Gross Sale*
  (−) Sales Discounts
     Sales Returns and Allowances
          subtotal

*Net Sales*
Cost of Goods Sold:
     Inventory (beginning of period)
  (+) Purchases
          subtotal
     Total Inventory Available for Sale
  (—) Inventory (end of period)

*Gross Profit*
  (−) Selling Expenses
     General Expenses
     Administrative Expenses
          subtotal

*Net Operating Profit*
  (+) Other Income
  (−) Other Expenses

*Net Profit*

*(Note: If a Profit and Loss Statement is drawn up on a manufacturing concern, another cost "Labor and Factory Overhead," is included in Cost of Goods Sold. This reduces the Gross Profit figure.)*

some detail the qualifications set forth in the scope and opinion paragraph of the auditor's certificate. The credit analyst must consider this data in conjunction with the regular financial presentation in arriving at a decision.

## CERTIFICATION

Independent certified public accountants express opinions on statements which they have audited in the form of a report which accompanies the financial statement. In their certificates, the auditors express an opinion which may or may not be qualified. This certificate should be read by the credit analyst because it provides information on the scope of the audit and will reveal any deviations from normal procedure. It must be remembered, however, that management is responsible for the financial statement and the accountant is only liable for his opinion of the statement.

## ACCOUNTING CONVENTIONS

Accountants in preparing financial statements must make certain assumptions and adopt certain procedures. The judgment factor is introduced when the accountant decides which method to utilize in depreciating fixed assets and in determining what valuation method to use on inventories. Variations between the economic value of items included in a financial statement and their actual cost are attributable to accounting conventions. More detailed information on accounting conventions is available from the American Institute of Certified Public Accountants.

## VALUATIONS

The valuation placed on inventories and the methods in which assets are depreciated have an important influence on the final result produced by an organization during a given time period. The credit practitioner should therefore become familiar with these effects as they will have direct bearing on interpretation of the data included in a financial report.

### Inventory Valuation

The Profit and Loss Statement includes in its figures the dollar value of inventory at the beginning of the period and the dollar value of inventory remaining, or not used, at the close of the same period. It is apparent by inspection of the format of the Profit and Loss Statement that the reported cost of goods sold can be affected by the valuation placed on these inventories.

Several methods of inventory valuation can be used to influence reported operating results, and ultimately the amount of profits subject to income taxation. The following valuation methods are acceptable to the accounting profession and to the Internal Revenue Service.

## Last-In-First-Out

Abbreviated LIFO, this method permits inventory to be valued for costing purposes at the price last paid for similar material or goods.

In a period of rising prices, this procedure enables management to hide a portion of profits. For example, if material had cost $2 per unit at the time it was bought, but had since gone up in price to $2.50, a charge of $2.50 for cost of goods could be made against the selling price when the completed product had been sold. Profit would be understated by $.50 and costs would be overstated by the same amount.

During a time of declining prices, this method overstates profit. If it is assumed that the goods of the previous example bought at $2 can be purchased for $1.50 when the completed product is sold, then the charge to cost of goods is $1.50. Since the material had been bought at a higher price, costs are understated and profit is overstated by the difference.

## First-In-First-Out

The FIFO method of inventory valuation has the opposite effect on reported earnings. It says that the cost of materials charged against a sold article shall be equal to the price paid for the oldest such material on hand at the time the sale is made.

For example, if successive unit prices of materials purchased over a period of time were: $1.75; $1.80; $1.90; $1.80; $1.50; $1.60; . . . then the cost of material for the first unit sold would be $1.75; for the second, $1.80; for the third $1.90; and so on. In effect, costs and profits would be affected directly by the prices of material on hand the greatest length of time, or "first-in.'

During a period of rising prices, the FIFO method understates costs and overstates profit, while the reverse effect is obtained in a period of declining material cost.

It should be noted that these two methods are acceptable for valuation purposes in tax reporting and are acceptable by CPA's in financial reporting and if one of these methods is consistently followed, there is no distortion.

## Cost or Market, Whichever is Lower

Conservative accounting practice prefers this method. Inventory value is set at the lowest possible figure for, theoretically, this method discounts any market rises but fully accounts for decreases in inventory prices.

Insofar as productivity analysis is concerned, this method of inventory valuation inflates the apparent cost of materials which have been converted and sold and tends to understate earnings. Other less common valuation systems include average cost and base stock methods.

# DEPRECIATION

Just as the method of inventory valuation has a direct effect on the Profit and Loss Statement, so does the method chosen to provide for the replacement of fixed assets. Amounts charged to depreciation are direct reductions of Profit and are included in costs.

## Straight Line

This is the simplest way to calculate depreciation. Salvage value is deducted from the cost of a fixed asset and the remainder pro rated over its useful life.

This method makes several assumptions about costs which are not borne out by the facts. The usefulness of a machine is hardly the same during its tenth year as when it was new. A constant charge for the wear and tear of the machine, therefore, does not reflect the true situation.

The styles, capacities, and capabilities of machines change over the years and so do their prices. Consequently, a depreciation reserve set up to replace a machine ten or twenty years hence is neither adequate nor realistic. (For specifics on the various methods permitted, consult the IRS for information on changes brought about by the Tax Reform Act of 1986.)

## Additional Reserves

Methods of depreciation permitted by the IRS usually allow companies to regain a good part of the cost of fixed assets in a relatively short period of time. This invariably provides for internal generation of funds for expansion, or for replacement of obsolete equipment. Because of sweeping changes brought about by the Tax Reform Act of 1986, the IRS and/or your tax accountant should be consulted in this regard.

While some financial relief is given to companies, the allowable charges may be insufficient to preserve the capital of the firm. Therefore top management may decide to set up special reserves to provide for replacement of capital equipment.

## STATEMENT LIMITATIONS

It must be remembered that considerable judgment is reflected in the picture projected by a financial statement and this reflects the thinking of the management, directors, or accountants of the firm who may have either conservative or rather liberal business leanings. Assets are not necessarily reflected at their true economic value. Buildings may be worth considerably more or less than the dollar value at which they are carried. Depreciation charges may be low in comparison to replacement costs.

A financial statement is a reflection of values for an operating business. In many instances realizable proceeds from a liquidation of such a business would be considerably below the asset value shown on a current statement.

Financial information is often filed in an incomplete manner. An accountant's report may be lacking or figures may be submitted in the form of estimates. Profit and loss details may be withheld or footnoting may not be detailed. Proper analysis requires a complete presentation and every effort should be exerted to obtain the detail necessary for a complete examination. While it is true that considerable information may be garnered from the review of a balance sheet alone, a clearer understanding of a given situation will undoubtedly result from an examination of the entire financial presentation.

The trend of a business is best determined by a review of two or more consecutive financial statements although certain trend information may be obtained from a single balance sheet. It would for instance be possible to determine if overall progress has been recorded by reviewing the earned surplus position and profitability in the most recent period. This can be determined by an examination of the income tax liability.

Consideration must be given by the credit practitioner to the worthiness and capability of the individual who prepared the financial statement. A statement prepared by a Certified Public Accountant who has spent years in obtaining training and experience would be given greater credence for credit purposes than one prepared internally by a firm's staff or official and it would have much greater impact than mere estimates. As a practical matter, however, it is a question of making use of what is available. Financial information is not always readily provided by customers who are guarded about releasing information.

Despite the presence of a number of flaws in financial statements, their value to the creditor in providing an answer to the question of acceptability of an account is considerable. The understanding and proper interpretation of financial statements will provide the practitioner with the ability to render a proper and prudent credit judgment.

# CHAPTER FIVE

# UNDERSTANDING FILINGS OF THE UCC

A working knowledge of how to file the UCC-1 and related documents is as important to career credit and financial people as understanding the general ledger is to an accountant.

We have, therefore, included a "how to" section on initiating UCC filings.

## INTRODUCTION

The Uniform Commercial Code (UCC) is a body of laws created by the National Conference of Commissioners to standardize the many complex individual state laws dealing with rights and responsibilities of buyers and sellers in commercial business. The continuing growth of interstate commercial business necessitated the formation of these mutually accepted laws.

In 1942, a board of nationally prominent judges, lawyers, and law instructors assisted by the American Bar Association compiled the first draft of the Code. This draft was approved and the UCC was available for use in 1952.

Pennsylvania was the first state in the union to adopt the Code in July 1954. Massachusetts was the second state to utilize it in October 1958. Today, there are 49 states plus the District of Columbia which have adopted the Code. The exception is the state of Louisiana which has to date adopted only portions of the UCC. For specifics, refer to the NACM's *Credit Manual of Commercial Laws* which is updated every year, with each new edition published in January.

# ARTICLES AND GENERAL PROVISIONS

The UCC is made up of ten articles:
- Article 1—General Provisions. Deals primarily the purposes and policies of the Code.
- Article 2—Sales. Covers transactions in goods.
- Article 3—Commercial Paper. Replaces the Negotiable Instrument Law.
- Article 4—Bank Deposits and Collections. Similar to items governed in Article 8.
- Article 5—Letters of Credit. Covers instruments used by financial institutions such as banks.
- Article 6—Bulk Transfers. Refers to the Uniform Fraudulent Act.
- Article 7—Warehouse Receipts, Bill of Lading, and other Documents of Title. Brought about by the consolidation of the Uniform Warehouse Receipt Act, Uniform Bills of Lading Act, and the Uniform Sales Act.
- Article 8—Investment Securities. Deals with the laws governing a negotiable instrument used with securities.
- Article 9—Secured Transactions, Sales of Accounts, Contract Rights, Chattel Paper. Formed to regulate security interest in personal property and fixtures, sale of accounts receivable, contract rights, and chattel paper.
- Article 10—Effective Dates and Repealer. Contains the background laws used to create the Uniform Commercial Code.

# OBJECTIVES OF THE UNIFORM COMMERCIAL CODE

The three main objectives of the UCC are as follows:

1. To simplify, clarify, modernize, and make uniform the laws governing commercial transactions.

2. To facilitate the continued expansion of commercial practice with the absence of confusion and with ease of conformity.

3. To promote uniformity among various jurisdictions.

The UCC article most widely used by businesses is Article 9, which deals with secured transactions. The primary reason for a business to use this article is to record its "security interest" or the right to secure payment or performance of an obligation. It must be filed with the Secretary of State, Town Clerk, or County Clerk.

There are three major types of UCC forms: The UCC-1 or Financing Statement, see Exhibit 5.2; the UCC-3 or Financing Statement Change Form, see Exhibit 5.3; and the UCC-11 or Information and Copy Request Form, see Exhibit 5.4.

The UCC-1 or Financing Statement is the formal presentation for filing a security interest. The general requirements are listed in Exhibit 5.1. When filled out, it should contain all the necessary information for the Secretary of State, Town Clerk, or County clerk to record a security interest for a fee. The form asks for the debtor's name and address, the secured party's name and address, time and date as recorded by the filing officer, a description of what is to be covered, the signatures of both parties, and, on some forms, included is a space for an assignment.

Most states have their own approved UCC forms, but will generally accept original security agreements for filing—provided that all necessary information has been supplied. Penalty fees for filing a nonstandard form may range anywhere from $2 to more than $10 for filing, or may be rejected. Filing fees vary from state to state. Check NACM's *Credit Manual of Commercial Laws* for the latest information. To keep abreast of the various state fees, you should obtain a copy of the annually published *Uniform Commercial Code and Related Procedures Manual* (available from the NACM Publications Department), which gives a listing by state of each state's requirements for filing.

The UCC-3 or Financing Statement Change Form must always refer to an original financing statement by file number and date and place filed. The form is used primarily for changes. The general requirements

## EXHIBIT 5.1   Financial Statement: General Filing Requirements

1. Financing statement must contain:
   a. Name and address of secured.
   b. Name and address of debtor.
   c. Describe types of items of collateral. (It is wise to be very detailed.)
   d. If timber or crops, describe real estate and name of record owner or lessee where same are growing or are to be grown.
   e. If proceeds or products of the collateral are claimed, it should be so noted in the financing statement.
   f. Financing statement should be signed by debtor and secured in all cases except when:
      • Collateral is subject to a security interest in another jurisdiction.
      • An accompanying legal document supporting the financing statement has been duly signed by debtor and secured. You are urged to use the standard UCC forms.
   g. Original secured need not sign when:
      • Financing statement is assigned and same is indicated on statement. The party to whom interest is assigned must sign.
      • The names and addresses of the assignees are indicated on the financing statement.
2. Financing statement

are listed in Exhibit 5.5. This form is used primarily for changes. The form contains space to provide information on:

*Continuation.*   When the original financing statement goes over the five-year period. Example: A seven-year contract for equipment.

*Termination.*   The secured party no longer claims an interest. Example: A paid-in-full account. In some cases, the UCC-1 provides the termination.

# EXHIBIT 5.2 UCC-1 or Financing Statement

### PLEASE TYPE THIS FORM

UNIFORM COMMERCIAL CODE — FINANCING STATEMENT    FORM UCC-1    STATE OF CONNECTICUT

UCC-1 REV. 2-80

**INSTRUCTIONS**

1. Remove Secured Party and Debtor copies and send other 4 copies with interleaved carbon paper to the Secretary of the State. Enclose filing fee.
2. If the space provided for any item(s) on the form is inadequate the item(s) should be continued on additional sheets, preferably 8" x 10". Only one copy of such additional sheets need be presented to the filing officer with a set of four copies of Form UCC-1. Long schedules of collateral, indentures, etc., may be on any size paper that is convenient for the secured party. Do not attach to UCC-1 form.
3. If collateral covers timber, minerals including oil and gas or accounts financed at the wellhead or minehead, this financial statement shall show that it covers this type of collateral, shall recite that it is to be filed in the real estate records and the financing statement shall contain a description of the real estate.
4. When a copy of the security agreement is used as a financing statement, it is requested that it be accompanied by a completed but unsigned set of UCC-1 forms, without extra fee. Do not attach to UCC-1 form.
5. At the time of original filing, filing officer will return third copy as an acknowledgment. At a later time, secured party may date and sign Termination Legend and use third copy as a Termination Statement.

This Financing Statement is filed with Office of The Secretary of the State, Uniform Commercial Code Div., 30 Trinity St., Hartford, Conn. 06115

| Name and Address of Debtor *(Or Assignor)* | Name and Address of Secured Party *(Or Assignee)* | For Filing Officer *(Date, Time, Number)* |
|---|---|---|
| | | |

1. This financing statement covers the following types (or items) of property *(Describe)*

2. (If collateral is crops) the above described crops are growing or are to be grown on (describe real estate above or on separate sheet).
3. (If applicable) the above goods are to become fixtures on (describe real estate above or on separate sheet) and filing statement is to be filed for record in the real estate records.
    (If debtor does not have an interest of record) the name of the owner is _____
4. ☐   (If products of collateral are claimed) products of collateral are also covered.
    _____ Number of additional sheets presented.    ☐ Debtor is a transmitting utility as defined in 42a-9-402 Conn. General Statutes.

| WHICHEVER IS APPLICABLE | Signature of Debtor *(Or Assignor)* | Signature of Secured Party *(Or Assignee)* |
|---|---|---|

# EXHIBIT 5.3 UCC-3 or Financing Statement Change Form

UCC-3 NEW 5/82

### STATE OF CONNECTICUT
### — UNIFORM COMMERCIAL CODE—
STATEMENTS OF CONTINUATION, PARTIAL RELEASE, ASSIGNMENT, ETC. - FORM UCC-3
### IMPORTANT! READ INSTRUCTIONS ON BACK BEFORE FILLING OUT!

This statement is presented to THE SECRETARY OF THE STATE for filing pursuant to the Uniform Commercial Code.

| 1. DEBTOR(S) *(last Name)* AND ADDRESS | 2. SECURED PARTY(IES) AND ADDRESS(ES) | FOR FILING OFFICER *(Date, Time, Number, and Filing Office)* |
|---|---|---|
| | | |

This statement refers to original Filing Statement No. _____ Dated _____ 19 ___

A. ☐ CONTINUATION - The original financing statement between the foregoing Debtor and Secured Party, bearing the file number shown above, is still effective

B. ☐ PARTIAL RELEASE - From the collateral described in the financing statement bearing the file number shown above, the party releases the property indicated below.

C. ☐ ASSIGNMENT - The Secured Party certifies that the Secured Party has assigned to the Assignee whose name and address is shown below, secured Party's rights under the Financing Statement bearing the file number shown above in the property indicated below.

D. ☐ TERMINATION - The Secured Party certifies that the Secured Party no longer claims a security interest under the financing statement bearing the file number shown above.

E. ☐ AMENDMENT - The financing statement bearing the above file number is amended as set forth below:

| BY: _____ | BY: _____ |
|---|---|
| Signature(s) of debtor(s) *(Only on amendments)* | Signature(s) of secured party(ies) |
| DATED: | DATED: |

## EXHIBIT 5.4 UCC-11 or Information and Copy Request Form

**REQUEST FOR COPIES OR INFORMATION.** Present in DUPLICATE to Filing Officer, Secretary of State, Connecticut.

| Debtor | Party requesting copies or information | For Filing Officer use: |
|---|---|---|
| | | |

FILING OFFICER: ☐ Please furnish certificate showing whether there is on file as of _____, 19___ at _____ .M. any presently effective financing statement naming the above debtor, and if there is, give date and hour of filing of each such statement and names and addresses of each secured party named therein. FEE $6.00

☐ Please furnish copies of the following. Enclosed is the fee of $3.00 for the first three pages of each statement plus $3.00 for the fourth and each additional page of each statement.

| FILE NUMBER | DATE AND HOUR OF FILING | NAME AND ADDRESS OF SECURED PARTY |
|---|---|---|
| | | |
| | | |
| | | |
| | | |
| | | |

Secretary of the State

ORIGINATOR—RETAIN FOR YOUR RECORD

By: _____
Signature of Filing Officer

STANDARD FORM—UCC-11 REV. 7-76
UNIFORM COMMERCIAL CODE

*Partial Release.* A partial release discharges interest only on certain items. Example: A financing company buys a deal from a bank for only a portion of the equipment covered.

*Assignment.* Secured party assigns the rights to a third party. Example: A broker sells a deal to a finance company to be funded. The finance company now becomes the secured party.

*Amendment.* When collateral is added or changed. This must be signed by the debtor. Example: You have serial numbers on equipment already filed.

The UCC-11 form or Financing Statements Information and Copy Requisition form is used to obtain copies of already filed UCC's or to find out how many other filings are recorded on a given company.

## CHECKLIST PRIOR TO FILING

Contained herein is a checklist (Exhibit 5.6) to be used when you are preparing a UCC form for filing to avoid delays and rejections. The form also stresses the necessity of thoroughness.

To keep track of what was sent for filing, where it was sent and when, a control log can be created. Exhibit 5.7 shows a sample control log. All the necessary information for the proper follow-up is

## EXHIBIT 5.5 Financing Statement Changes: General Filing Requirements

**1. Continuation**
   a. Must state original financing statement is still effective.
   b. Must identify the financing statement by file numbers.
   c. Must be signed by secured party.

**2. Partial Release**
   a. List description of collateral to be released.
   b Name and address of debtor.
   b. Name and address of secured.
   d. The file number of financing statement.
   e. Must be signed by secured.

**3. Assignments**
   a. May be done on financing statement with either a part or all of rights.
   b. By filing a separate written statement of assignment, in which case secured must sign and include the following:
   - Name of debtor and secured of record.
   - File number, date of filing of financial statement being assigned.
   - Name and address of assignees.
   - Description of collateral being assigned.

**4. Amendments**
   a. May be done on financing statement with either a part or all of rights.
   b. Must specifically identify the financing statement being amended.
   c. If collateral is being added, the amended financing statement is effective as to the added collateral, only from the filing date of the amendment.

**5. Termination**
   a. Must be identified by file number.
   b. If signed by other than secured of record, accompany with assignment signed by secured stating his transfer of interest.

## EXHIBIT 5.6 Checklist for Preparing a UCC Form for Filing

1. Be sure you have correct spelling of debtor's name as well as secured party's name.
2. Be certain that you are using proper addresses for debtor and secured party.
3. When describing what is covered, be as precise as possible.
4. Enter debtor's and secured party's names at bottom of form for signature.
5. Investigate the validity of the debtor's name and address.
6. Send in filing as soon as possible to reserve position on claim.
7. Be sure the form was signed by both the debtor and the secured party.
8. Refer to the *Uniform Commercial Code* section in NACM's *Credit Manual of Commercial Laws* to determine where to file—i.e., state, town, county. If in doubt, call the Secretary of State.
9. Use the approved state forms whenever possible to expedite recording and save penalty fees for use of non-standard forms.
10. Refer to NACM's *Credit Manual of Commercial Laws* to determine the correct filing fee. If in doubt, call the Secretary of State. If the enclosed fee is incorrect, the form will be rejected and returned.
11. Determine if goods are fixtures or farm goods in order to file in the proper place.

written in: debtor's name, where filed—state, county, or town; what type of UCC form—UCC-1, UCC-3, or UCC-11; the fee for filing; and the date it was sent for filing. When you receive your acknowledgment copy with the filing notation, you can write the date in and file it with the customer's folder.

To keep track of the length of coverage on secured items (which is five years), an index card file system can be used to monitor the duration time. Some accounts may have to be secured for more than five years. Extended coverage is obtained by filing a Continuation Statement where the original Financing Statement was filed.

**EXHIBIT 5.7 Sample UCC Filing Log**

| Name of Debtor | Place Filed | Form Fee | Date Sent | Date Received |
|---|---|---|---|---|
|  |  |  |  |  |
|  |  |  |  |  |
|  |  |  |  |  |
|  |  |  |  |  |
|  |  |  |  |  |
|  |  |  |  |  |
|  |  |  |  |  |
|  |  |  |  |  |
|  |  |  |  |  |
|  |  |  |  |  |
|  |  |  |  |  |

### EXHIBIT 5.8  UCC Record System

Expiration [5 yrs from recorded date]

Name and Address of Debtor _____

_____

| | | |
|---|---|---|
| Terms _____ | Filed | Date Recorded |
| | State _____ | |
| A/C No. _____ | Town _____ | |
| | County _____ | |

On the card you can list debtor's name and address, account number, terms of contract, where and when it was filed, and the expiration time. File the cards by month and year the expiration will occur (Exhibit 5.8).

For more detailed information on the Uniform Commercial Code, refer to NACM's *Credit Manual of Commercial Laws* updated annually and published each January.

# CHAPTER SIX

# DECISION-MAKING FOR THE CREDIT MANAGER

It is the nature of credit department activity that credit managers and support personnel must make decisions every day. This entails the analysis of all information available on accounts and deciding on the best possible course of action based upon this information. There are sound techniques to assist credit managers in this problem-solving, decision-making process. These are tried and tested processes which assist the credit manager most in problem-solving activities.

Behind every decision, there is often a background of unclear and distantly seen ideas—of notions discarded in despair because they were found to be unmanageable—of acceptance, rejection, and correction.

Credit managers who find themselves rushing upon problems unprepared don't know when to attack the problems, grasp the problems, or avoid the problems. They don't know how far they can hope to go in solving problems.

Effective credit managers take the steps necessary to bring about achievement of their goals. They define their problems, gather and consider the pertinent facts, and formulate sound decisions. In so doing, they weigh many intangibles and calculate imponderables. The examination of all pertinent facts is an important part of the process. It is therefore very important to arrive at a decision about granting or denying credit after a close and critical analysis of the problem, aided by the resources within the decision maker and others' knowledge that can be assessed. (See Exhibit 6.1)

To be effective, credit managers are well advised to develop "problem awareness," i.e., the ability to look for possible signs of dispute so that obstacles can be nipped in the bud early in the process.

The problem-solving process consists of identifying and defining the problem, getting the facts, weighing alternatives, making the decision, and following up. The following discussion will examine each step in the process.

# IDENTIFYING AND DEFINING PROBLEMS

To accurately determine what the problem is and classify it according to priority, ask questions such as:

- Is it my problem?
- Has anything similar ever happened before?
- Should I handle it alone?

If the situation is complicated, break it down to essentials and in so doing eliminate associated problems, fears, and wants, proceeding to the point where you arrive at a pertinent question free of extraneous detail. Once your mind is free from time-consuming issues and from wandering off to detours of fears and wishes, the problem may well solve itself.

To facilitate defining the problem also consider whether it's a people problem or a situation problem. If a people problem, define it further. If a group problem, get the group involved and, if they are uniquely qualified, utilize their technical knowledge. If the figures just don't add up to a credit approval decision and all other factors have been evaluated, then it becomes a situation problem and the group need not be approached. Here the judgment call rests with the credit practitioner.

# GETTING THE FACTS

Now that you have a feel for the dimensions of the problem the stage is set for asking the questions who, what, when, where and why to ensure that you have all of the facts. This means questioning yourself and other people who have the answers.

## EXHIBIT 6.1 The Process of Analysis

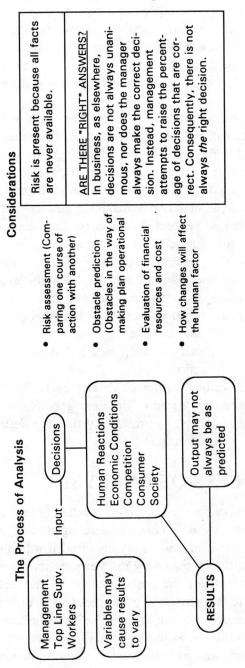

**Considerations**

Risk is present because all facts are never available.

ARE THERE "RIGHT" ANSWERS? In business, as elsewhere, decisions are not always unanimous, nor does the manager always make the correct decision. Instead, management attempts to raise the percentage of decisions that are correct. Consequently, there is not always *the* right decision.

- Risk assessment (Comparing one course of action with another)
- Obstacle prediction (Obstacles in the way of making plan operational)
- Evaluation of financial resources and cost
- How changes will affect the human factor

**The Process of Analysis**

Management
Top Line Supv.
Workers

Input — Decisions

Human Reactions
Economic Conditions
Competition
Consumer
Society

Variables may cause results to vary

Output may not always be as predicted

RESULTS

It helps to jot down what you know about the problem, i.e., everything that did or did not happen. This contributes to your arriving at a prompt solution. Asking questions is an ongoing process in fact gathering. In so doing, however, be sure to record incremental details, even a summary of a telephone call is useful. For this purpose, writing on the inside file jacket or use of a telephone call record sheet will suffice.

Having analyzed a particular problem, the credit manager arrives at a judgment about it, the evaluation. The credit manager has isolated the facts needed to reach a solution. These facts are weighed carefully, being certain that the credit manager has discovered what was needed and whether it is satisfactory and not merely adequate. Care must be exercised to avoid jumping to conclusions, e.g., because the last-column facts are not what was expected or wanted, they are totally unacceptable. This is the time for deliberation and thinking in terms of alternative possibilities. The credit manager is not paid to reject orders, hence, it is important to find ways to approve even the most marginal of accounts. Naturally, if a marginal account is approved it must be carefully monitored to ensure that payments are being made on a timely basis in keeping with the terms of sale extended.

While making an analysis, keep in mind that the end result is a recommendation for action.

Pause at each critical center to determine if there are facts that will help to make the decision. The manager invariably works with probabilities, i.e., what is the probability that the desired results will take place for a given decision?

# THE PROCESS OF ANALYSIS

Society has guides for the acceptable conduct of business. The expectations of society are becoming more stringent and less tolerant of deviation. The credit manager may also find it difficult to adhere to legal requirements that may vary in interpretation from year to year. Particularly difficult for the credit manager is the task of balancing responsibilities to the individual employees and to the company. However, if management does not take the initiative in attempting to discover its responsibilities, society will usually impose the responsibilities upon the company and its management through the law. What credit managers do in terms of day to day activities is legally driven, e.g., the Uniform Commercial Code, bankruptcy laws, and a host of other commercial laws including the Bankruptcy Laws. Refer to NACM's *Credit Manual of Commercial Laws* for detailed information in this area.

# WEIGHING ALTERNATIVES

Imagination is always needed from the beginning to the end of the problem-solving process. It enables us to determine what new information is available to ascertain the connection between facts, and how to weigh and consider data to arrive at a decision. Generally, there are several ways to solve a given problem. You try them out and then choose the course of action that appears most likely to get results.

Each completed analysis yields data for one decision. You then decide on the basis of the possibilities revealed. Consciously make it a point to steer clear of being rigid in your thinking. The effective credit manager adapts to new situations; changes departmental plans to satisfy realigned territories, markets, or competitive conditions; substitutes one credit analyst for another or one training program for another; rearranges the way the credit function is run; provides time for on-the-job training; and encourages people to attend external education programs which also provide an excellent opportunity for networking.

You should think of every possible repercussion before you go forward with your decision. Exercise care that this decision is consistent with others you have made. Do, however, remember that to grow personally and professionally, you must take risks.

# MAKING THE DECISION

By now you have considered all the available facts and pertinent points of view. The burden of making a decision is not transferable. It is therefore very important to obtain as much support as possible early in the decision-making process. Be wary of last ditch solutions. Delay is a decision. Doing nothing is a decision. Whether you make the decision or not, the decision is always made.

## FOLLOW-UP

Evaluate the effect of your decision. Consider making any corrections necessary if something has occurred which you did not foresee or if something has occurred which changes the complexion of the situation.

Using the five-step approach referred to above will invariably result in better decisions, signaling to top management that the credit manager is indeed a creator of profits. In the final analysis your supervisor may conclude that credit and financial people are the best salespeople the organization has.

## SETTING UP AND ORGANIZING A CREDIT DEPARTMENT

### Structure

1. Determine overall objectives, purposes, and desired results.
2. Assign activities necessary to accomplish above.
3. Set a grouping of activities.
4. Tie major function into a framework.
5. Adopt techniques for putting structure into effect:
   - Utilize existing staff.
   - Improve immediately.
   - Monitor and fine tune, phase in.

### Staffing

1. Ensure that authority is equal to responsibility.
2. Screen and select on the basis of:
   - What must be done.
   - Standards to meet.
   - Time frame.
   - Career path.
   - Company growth expectations, i.e., assure performance with plans.

### Training

1. Impart objectives and establish performance measurement.
2. Develop policy and procedure manuals.

3. Hold meaningful performance appraisals to help department and other staff find best ways to meet mutual needs.
4. Continue training to enhance performance.
5. Give financial and non-financial recognition.
6. Set controls to insure the department meshes will with other units to achieve optimal results.

# ADVANTAGES TO THE COMPANY WITH A CREDIT DEPARTMENT

- Increased sales and profits vis-a-vis specialized department manned by skilled people.
- Quality enhancement through timeliness, thoroughness and closer attention to detail.
- Greater volume of accounts can be handled, potential problems anticipated with less effort and expense.
- Corporate creditability and image improves once the credit department is operational.

# CHAPTER SEVEN

# HUMAN RELATIONS IN CREDIT MANAGEMENT

Human relations in credit is certainly no different from its application to any other facet of business administration. However, the behavioral side of the credit manager's responsibility is particularly important since there is daily interaction with both employees and with customers. There must be some familiarity with this aspect. Therefore, because this is a very important area, enough detail is included herein to facilitate answering test questions referred to in Chapters 9 through 12.

The intent therefore is for you to learn to apply the concepts by answering the questions and going over the answers. It should not be necessary to reread material contained in several textbooks.

Human relations entails communication, work groups, conflict management, and leadership.

## COMMUNICATION

The communication process is upward, downward, horizontal, and can also take the form of the ever-present grapevine. Presented herein are those aspects every career professional must be aware of to succeed.

Communication in general is viewed as a transfer of meaningful information to others. More specifically, there is interpersonal communication which is the interaction between you and another individual. A very important factor in this process is listening. The better you are at listening, the more you are likely to retain information. Studies reveal that most business people retain only 25% of the information imparted to them. Improvement of listening skills would undoubtedly increase this percentage.

Particularly important to the communication process is feedback. Feedback flow of information is from one individual back to the other, from the receiver to the sender.

Finally, there is nonverbal communication which is the conscious or unconscious behavior on the part of an individual (the sender) when it takes place before another individual (the receiver) and is taken in by the mind of the receiver either consciously or subconsciously.

Credit managers encounter different communications patterns within various organizations. Although there are many patterns and the experts have made extensive studies of each pattern, our review will focus on the most common communication patterns. This focus recognizes the impact communication has on the accuracy and speed of the message, the performance of the individual or group, and satisfaction of employees and customers.

## Downward Communication

Downward communication is the transmission of information from higher to lower levels in the organization. The flow of downward information is determined by the chain of command within an organization which has a hierarchical structure.

## Upward Communication

This is the transmission of information from the lower levels in the organization to the top. The flow from lower to top levels is not as obstacle-free as from top to lower levels. Excellent companies provide for an upward communication system to complement a downward system.

## Horizontal Communication

Horizontal communication, also called lateral communication, is the formal transmission of information across company units on the same level. Among the methods to facilitate this form of communication are committee meetings attended by individuals from other departments and dissemination of written reports.

## The Grapevine

The grapevine is the informal channel of communication resulting from interaction between co-workers, acquaintances, and friends in organizational units. Although not officially sanctioned by the formal organization, the grapevine does exist and can be used effectively as a supplement to the formal channels. It can also be an excellent source for monitoring employee satisfaction.

# MOTIVATION

The formal credit department work group stems essentially from the overall organizing function of management. Such groups are usually defined by prescribed relationships between employees and an organizational plan aimed at achievement of specific goal objectives. From this, informal work groups take shape because the employee has a need to interact and associate with other employees who have common interests, a need for belonging, and an encompassing need to fulfill social needs.

Credit managers are responsible for understanding human behavior, creating the proper climate, and applying motivational techniques to lead their people toward maximum productivity. A credit manager must be able to translate employee needs into positive goals by integrating these needs with the goals of the credit department and the company. It is very important to provide people with an opportunity to satisfy their needs through understanding and motivational techniques.

Undertaking and motivating credit people requires a basic understanding of human behavior and motivation. It is an area where the measure of the credit manager's leadership ability is put to the test.

Credit department employees are confronted with daily problems, obstacles, and challenges. Consequently, even the best performers may lose enthusiasm, get into a rut, or lose the job satisfaction derived from their work. The credit manager must understand and be sensitive to ameliorate potential problems that may result from inattention to individual needs or wants.

To motivate others, credit managers must be able to satisfy their people emotionally. This requires concern and skill. For example, over and above the effort a credit practitioner gives to the job, that person has a reserve amount of energy that can be given if there is motivation to do so. There is no rational way to force a person to give this reserve ability and energy; however, it is usually given willingly if time and effort have been given to motivate the individual, i.e., instill the will to go the extra mile.

Enthusiasm cannot be purchased . . . you can't buy loyalty nor the devotion of hearts and minds. Those qualities have to be earned by the effective credit manager. Helping others to uncover and utilize their full range of talents is a privilege and responsibility of leadership.

Employee involvement enhances morale and enables employees to bring their personal goals into harmony with organizational goals. Listed below are suggested ways to accomplish this.

  a. Make your people aware of and encourage their input into goal objectives.
  b. Respect the efforts and abilities of each member of your staff.
  c. Give praise as deserved to show appreciation.
  d. Be open to suggestions and encourage new ideas and/or ways to improve existing ways of doing things.
  e. Decide promptly . . . don't keep your people waiting or guessing.
  f. Convey your interest in helping others to advance their careers.
  g. Share your knowledge and encourage people to feel they are working with you, not under you.
  h. Let each person know where they stand, whether they are static or capable of moving ahead.
  i. Strive constantly toward better methods and ways to benefit both the individual and the company.
  j. Consciously work to instill in your people a feeling of security.

Finally, keep in mind that you have to give respect. Cooperation and mutual trust are important considerations in human relations. Let your people know the way it is, level with them and foster ways to encourage working as a team. People are individuals and not objects to be molded into something they are not. Always recognize their individuality and channel their talents toward the long range goals of the department and the company. By giving people what they want and need emotionally, they will give you what you want and need. Always keep foremost in mind that people want recognition and always hunger for appreciation.

The excellent companies have come to realize that their human resources are their most important corporate asset. We therefore acknowledge that a company is only as good as its human resources.

The Credit Research Foundation (CRF) can recommend reading material and courses in the area of human resource development to those interested in pursuing further study in this subject.

Another related, important area to consider is business ethics. The CRF is an advocate of adherence to a code of business ethics. The National Association of Credit Management (NACM) has published its "Canons of Business Credit Ethics" which is available upon request or may be purchased as a plaque ready to hang. (A copy of the canons is reproduced in Appendix D.)

# CHAPTER EIGHT

# EFFECTIVE CREDIT DEPARTMENT LETTERS

## INTRODUCTION

Effective communications are designed to provoke action. It is neither practical nor appropriate for a collection follow-up to plead, beg, or excessively use words such as please, thank you, hopefully, possibly, or respectfully.

For years the National Institute of Credit (NIC) has required candidates for the Credit Business Associate (CBA) designation to complete a course in Business Communications. While this section represents only a small fraction of such a course, it is important for credit people to be familiar with what constitutes an effective letter within the context of credit and collections.

The sample letters on the following pages (see Exhibits 8.2 through 8.8) have been tried and tested. They are quite useful and may be adopted with some modification for your own use.

These sample letters are included to familiarize you with effective business credit written communication which is part of the designation tests and mid-term or final exams offered through the NIC.

Also provided herein is a sample copy (see Exhibit 8-1) of the "Guide Letter Instruction Sheet." which can serve as an aid in initiating preformatted letters such as those included in this chapter for use on a word processor. The form has provisions for variables, extra messages, the name of the person who will sign the letter and number of copies. Each form is initiated by the originator of a particular follow-up letter and turned over to those responsible for word processing.

# EFFECTIVE USE OF COLLECTION FOLLOW-UP LETTERS

In credit management, customer follow-up letters constitute a request for action. This form of communication requires attention to known experience with the customer and appropriate planning.

For a collection follow-up letter to be effective, it must be designed to provoke action on the part of the recipient. The letters should always be sent to the proper contact person—never have a letter sent to "Accounts Payable" or "Accounting" or a department name.

Today, virtually all follow-up letters are preformatted. But it is a good idea to have several variations of format in each series of letters, i.e., early stage, middle stage, and last stage. Sample follow-up letters at each stage are contained in this chapter, see Exhibits 8.2 through 8.8. These sample letters are intended to serve only as guides and of course should be edited as necessary to fit the given situation.

It is imperative that we keep in mind the objective to retain customer goodwill while attempting to collect amounts owed. But there is one rule which must never be broken—"be sure to do what you state you will do" in your letters.

The usual progression is from the first mild reminder to a more directed reminder, followed by a forceful letter and then to a final demand. Remember the rule—that when you send a "final demand" letter, it is intended to be final and must be the last letter sent from your office. This letter should be sent via certified mail, return receipt requested. Any letters sent after your final demand letter would be from an outside collection agency or an attorney. Some firms prefer to have the credit manager make a personal visit if the dollar amount warrants it.

In addition to collection follow-up, there are occasions when it is prudent to send a customer relations letter. Customer relations letters are recommended in situations involving overpayment, unauthorized deductions, unearned discounts, returned merchandise, and damage claims.

To summarize, the format of your letter should fit the individual customer. Also, always remember to do as stated in the letter and to never send another follow-up message after the "final demand" letter. The follow-up process requires having a good follow-up system to ensure that if no response is received, the next letter is sent on a timely basis. A good follow-up system is linked to good communications and information on payments received. Such a system will avoid the possibility of sending a letter to someone who has already paid. The only possible excusable exception would occur when the incoming payment and outgoing letter cross in the mail.

Courses in business communications are offered through the NIC and in cooperation with those colleges and universities within the NIC nationwide network. The courses cover oral presentations, report writing, preparing proposals, listening skills, speech-giving, visual aids, and more.

## EXHIBIT 8.1  Guide Letter Instruction Sheet

Dept. _____ Letter _____ Date _____
Customer's Name:

_____

Address: _____

_____

City: _____ State _____ Zip _____
Attention: _____
Invoice, Credit Memo, Check Information, or P.O. #
(List information as it is to appear on letter to be typed.)

_____

_____

_____

_____

Other Fill-ins:

_____

Signature by: _____
Branch Copy: _____
Other Copies: _____

**EXHIBIT 8.2 Credit Letter #1**

May 4, 199X

Mr. John Doe
ABC Corporation
Main Street
Hartford, CT 06101

Dear Mr. Doe:

We call your attention to an unpaid balance which is comprised of the following:

| INVOICE DATE | PURCHASE ORDER # | INVOICE NO. | INVOICE AMOUNT |
|---|---|---|---|
| 0/00/00 | 0000000 | 0000000 | $000.00 |

If you have not already done so, please process the above for payment. If there are any problems causing a delay in payment, contact me immediately. Thank you.

Very truly yours,

Bill Smith
Credit Department

## EXHIBIT 8.3 Credit Letter #2

May 4, 199X

Mr. John Doe
ABC Corporation
Main Street
Hartford, CT 06101

Dear Mr. Doe:

No doubt our previous letter escaped your attention; otherwise we are sure you would have sent us your check for the following items:

| INVOICE DATE | PURCHASE ORDER # | INVOICE NO. | INVOICE AMOUNT |
|---|---|---|---|
| 0/00/00 | 000000 | 000000 | #000.00 |

Won't you please cooperate by sending us a check today to pay up your account.

Bill Smith
Credit Department

**EXHIBIT 8.4  Credit Letter #3**

May 4, 199X

Mr. John Doe
ABC Corporation
Main Street
Hartford, CT 06101

Dear Mr. Doe:

On several occasions we have reminded you of the items which make up your past due balance.

If uninterrupted service is to continue, it is imperative that you send us your check for $000.00 immediately.

We are confident that we can count on your cooperation; please do not disappoint us.

Very truly yours,

Bill Smith
Credit Department

## EXHIBIT 8.5　Credit Letter #4

May 4, 199X

Mr. John Doe
ABC Corporation
Main Street
Hartford, CT 06101

Dear Mr. Doe:

We have tried to handle your account in the most courteous manner possible. You have received several letters concerning the past due balance of $000.00.

Because we have received no reply, we have only one alternative left; your account will be turned over to our attorneys to effect payment in whatever manner they deem necessary unless your check is received in this office by 00/00/00. The entire situation now rests in your hands.

Very truly yours,

Bill Smith
Credit Department

## EXHIBIT 8.6  Credit Letter #5

INVOICE #: 00000
DATE: 00/00/00
AMOUNT DUE: $000.00

Mr. John Doe
ABC Corporation
Main Street
Hartford, CT 06106

Dear Mr. Doe:

Although prior notices and demands have been made for payment of your past due balance shown above, our records indicate you have not paid the amount due.

To avoid court action, full payment of the amount due must reach this office within ten (10) days from the date of this letter. Your check or money order should be forwarded in the enclosed, self-addressed return envelope.

Otherwise, ten (10) days after the date of this letter, and with no further notice to you, we will have no alternative but to enforce collection as provided by law.

Very truly yours,

Bill Smith
Collection Department

## EXHIBIT 8.7  Credit Letter #6

May 4, 199X

Mr. John Doe
ABC Corporation
Main Street
Hartford, CT 06101

Dear Mr. Doe:

Your check #0000 dated 0/00/00 in the amount of $000.00 was returned to us marked "Insufficient Funds."

To clear this item from your account and avoid further action, we must have a certified check by return mail. Your immediate action will be appreciated.

Very truly yours,

Bill Smith
Credit Department

**EXHIBIT 8.8 Credit Letter #7**

May 4, 199X
INVOICE #: 00000
DATE: 00/00/00
AMOUNT DUE: $000.00

Mr. John Doe
ABC Corporation
Main Street
Hartford, CT 06106

Dear Mr. Doe:

Although we try to maintain good relations with all of our customers, occasionally unexpected situations may occur. Please accept our apologies for whatever inconvenience you may have experienced. In order to rectify the situation to your satisfaction, we are notifying the people responsible.

Should you have any questions in the future, please feel free to contact this department as we would be glad to provide service to a good customer. Your patience in this matter has been greatly appreciated.

Very truly yours,

Bill Smith
Credit Department

## PART FOUR

# REVIEW OF EXAMINATION QUESTIONS AND ANSWERS

Questions have been selected which will test and explain concepts related to each area of importance.

NIC strives to ensure that each examination is fairly graded. Multiple choice questions are graded by key or by computer. Essay and objective answers are distributed to graders who are responsible for reading and interpreting each question. The grader assigns points to each answer by comparing it to a grading key which contains important concepts that should be included in each answer and the points allocated to each concept.

The multiple choice questions are usually graded with a curve so that a score of 75% can be earned with less than three fourths of the questions answered correctly. This is done by adding a "rigor factor" of several points to your score on a given set of multiple choice questions. For example, a score of 35 correct out of 50 multiple choice questions may be adjusted by adding a 4-point "rigor factor." The revised grade is 39 out of 50 or 78%. This allows you to miss some questions with no penalty.

Every question should be answered on the examination. Consider that even if you do not fully understand a multiple choice question, there is a 25% probability of guessing the right answer and these odds can be improved by eliminating at least one obviously incorrect choice.

Finally, questions that are not answered correctly by 60% of the test-takers are not counted toward the final grade. Consequently, no one is penalized for a question that most candidates do not understand.

# CHAPTER NINE

# The CBA Examination Questions and Answers

## INTRODUCTION

Following is a sample Credit Business Associate Examination which contains typical questions and answers usually found on the examination.

You will note a variety of questions including those which are open ended and even a case study.

Do not limit yourself to the questions on this sample examination; it will be useful to review all of the questions and answers contained in this book. Also, please note that Chapter 12 contains questions and answers which may apply to any or all examinations, so you should also benefit from reviewing all of the sample questions in Chapter 12.

To maintain the integrity of examinations, questions will change from time to time as deemed necessary, but the format does remain virtually the same.

# SAMPLE

## Credit Business Associate Examination

NAME: _____

Important Notice:

## PART I

Read the questions carefully and answer each one thoroughly and concisely. You have up to three hours to complete the exam, however, you may leave as soon as you have finished. Turn in all scratch sheets to the proctor with the completed exam. No books or reference materials are allowed in the examination room.

1. List the three types of credit.

_____ _____ _____

2. What are the three C's of Credit?

_____ _____ _____

3. List two characteristics of a marginal account.
    (1) _____
    (2) _____

4. Define the terms below:
    (a) Business Credit _____

    (b) Consumer Credit _____

    (c) Private Credit _____

    (d) Public Credit _____

(e) Secured Business Credit _____

(f) Unsecured Open Account Credit _____

(g) Investment Credit _____

(h) Revolving Charge _____

(i) Terms _____

(j) Creditor _____

5. What is the purpose of the NACM?

_____

_____

6. What is the purpose of a credit policy?

_____

_____

7. What is "Account referral?"

_____

_____

8. What is an industry credit group?

_____

_____

_____

9. What is the FCIB?

_____

_____

_____

10. Name three business entities.

(1) _____

(2) _____

(3) _____

## PART II

## Business Equipment Corporation

Frank Mann and three cohorts formed a partnership to distribute business equipment. Each individual invested $25,000 to get the company started.

Frank and Steve, one of the partners, had experience selling office equipment for a large manufacturer, from eight to twelve years. Frank, in anticipation of becoming a business owner, took courses in small business management. The combined talent and know-how of the partners was certainly noteworthy to banks and other credit grantors. They incorporated under the provisions of subchapter S for tax purposes.

The partners obtained exclusive dealership arrangements from several manufacturers of office equipment. Growth was planned to coincide with increasing sales and cash flow. Therefore the company's first year was not expected to be profitable, but the business would survive.

The partnership team worked hard and put in long hours. By the end of the third year the net worth of the firm increased from $100,000 to $250,000 from retained earnings. Each partner was allowed to draw enough money to cover living expenses.

In time, one of the partners relocated to a different area and sold his quarter interest. The remaining partners bought him out at the book value of his ownership interest.

One year later the company's net worth increased to $500,000. Another partner decided to leave, even though the business was growing. Frank and Steve decided to acquire his interest.

The entire business was now in the hands of the two individuals with the greatest sales experience. Volume expanded and growth continued at a rapid pace. The increased sales credited larger receivables and bigger inventories. This meant increased current liabilities, and the business was now handling sales volume greater than normal for its net working capital and tangible net worth.

Care had to be exercised, since there were more receivables with slow payments and thus a greater potential for bad debt. Inventory losses from dropping values could spell disaster. Cash flow might not be adequate to meet accounts payable on a timely basis.

Several months into the new fiscal year with prior year sales at 1.5 million, the business began to encounter trouble. Half of the receivables were running 90 or more days past due, sales were off, and inventories increased, leading to declines in price.

The partners met with their bankers to decide on a solution to their crisis. They discussed which would be the better solution: an infusion of cash from a bank loan or to file for bankruptcy. A reorganization under Chapter 11 of the bankruptcy code was considered and eventually ruled out. The bankers recommended asset based financing. Under their proposal the bank would take over the company's receivables and provide a revolving line of credit. The cost was high—prime rate plus three points—however, it seemed to be the best available alternative.

The business survived and although profits were less, within two years the ailing firm was healthy once again. To ensure that this continued, a credit manager was hired and marginal accounts were very closely monitored.

By the end of that fiscal year, Frank bought Steve out and became the sole owner of the company. He subsequently met with his credit manager to discuss sales policy and they agreed on parameters that would create more sales. The business was now strong enough to take over its own receivables, so Frank notified the bank accordingly.

Business Equipment Corporation is now a thriving business with 40% of its accounts classified as marginal. Credit and sales interact frequently and when there is a disagreement, Frank makes the final decision.

1. What should have been done sooner in terms of bringing in new sales?

2. Should the company have resisted having the bank take over its receivables?

## Answers to
## Credit Business Associate Examination
### PART I

1. List three types of credit. (Any three of the five listed are okay)
   Business Credit, Export Credit, Agricultural Credit, Investment Credit, Consumer Credit.
2. What are the three C's of Credit?
   Character, Capacity, Capital.
3. List two characteristics of a marginal account.
   Slow Pay, Unsatisfactory Finances.
4. Define the terms below:
   (a) Business Credit: Business to business credit where the product is sold for resale.
   (b) Consumer Credit: Credit used by banks and businesses to encourage consumer sales.
   (c) Private Credit: Refers to business credit, agricultural credit, investment credit, consumer credit, and bank credit.
   (d) Public Credit: Refers to granting credit to city, county, state and federal government agencies.
   (e) Secured Business Credit: Security obtained under article 9 of U.C.C.
   (f) Unsecured Open Account Credit: Credit granted by a supplier selling to a business for processing or resale.
   (g) Investment Credit: Placement funds in productive assets to earn a profit.
   (h) Revolving Charge: Where customer makes a minimum monthly payment on account due.
   (i) Terms: Payment due in 30, 60 or 90 days.
   (j) Creditor: The entity extending credit to a debtor.
5. What is the purpose of the NACM?
   To serve the interests of practitioners and provide assistance and guidance in solving common problems and issues.

6. What is the purpose of a credit policy?
   To have a framework for consistent credit decisions directed toward attaining corporate goals.
7. What is "Account referral"?
   Referral to a third party when usual collection procedures fail to obtain the payment due.
8. What is an industry credit group?
   Groups that are organized to serve those members within a particular industry. They exchange information in writing or verbally.
9. What is the FCIB?
   FCIB is the international credit association arm of NACM.
10. Name the three business entities.
    (1) Proprietorship, (2) partnership, (3) corporation.

## Answers to Credit Business Associate Examination

## PART II

1. Once the receivables growth became evident, the partners should have brought in a credit manager. If they were not sure, a consultant could have been employed.
2. Not unless they had other sources of revenue to get them over the crisis. Asset based financing is expensive but does serve a purpose.

# CHAPTER TEN

# THE CBF EXAMINATION QUESTIONS AND ANSWERS

## INTRODUCTION

The Credit Business Fellow examination is the management level test designed to measure the level of skill mastery on the part of the applicant in relation to job requirements. Practitioners at this level in their careers should be familiar with the concepts and principles contained in the examination.

## CBF TYPICAL EXAMINATION QUESTIONS & ANSWERS

### PART IA—CREDIT & BUSINESS LAW

Directions:  Indicate whether each of the following statements is TRUE or FALSE.

1. *Stare Decisis* is the doctrine whereby lower courts are required to follow precedents set by higher courts.

2. One is entitled to an "equitable" remedy only when there is not adequate remedy "at law."
3. Partners are not entitled to extra compensation unless the partnership agreement so provides.
4. A foreign corporation is one incorporated in a state other than the one in which it is doing business.
5. 'Capital Stock" means the net assets of the corporation.
6. In case of dissolution, the first obligation of a partnership is distribution of accumulated profits, if any.
7. A limited partnership is one in which each of the limited partners is not liable beyond the amount of his or her investment.
8. 'Ultra-Vires" means legal acts of a corporation, with its chartered powers.
9. A corporation that controls the operations of another corporation through stock ownership is called a holding company.
10. All partners are the agents for the partnership and the general rules of agency govern that relationship.
11. A partnership can consist of one or more corporations.
12. A voting trust where shareholders transfer their shares to a trustee for the purpose of electing directors is illegal.
13. The board of directors can set up committees consisting of some of its members to whom some of the board's powers can be delegated.
14. Dividends of the corporation may be paid out of available cash even if such dividend will leave the corporation without sufficient assets to meet its outstanding liabilities.
15. A partnership is a legal entity and thus pays federal income taxes at the same rate as that of a corporation.
16. Every stockholder of every corporation organized in the United States is entitled to preemptive rights when new stock is issued.
17. A corporation pays no taxes but each shareholder pays taxes on his or her share of the income in each year.
18. Upon the death of any partner, his or her estate can appoint an individual to act as the replacement partner in the partnership.
19. Whether a corporation may elect to be taxed as a partnership is a matter of the law of the state that issued the certificate of incorporation.

20. A corporation, being a creature of state, is subject to the withdrawal of its corporate charter at the whim of that state.
21. Every partner has a right to formal accounting of the affairs of the partnership at reasonable times.
22. All corporations are subject to regulation by the Securities and Exchange Act.
23. Unless an agent is authorized to sign his principal's name to a negotiable instrument the principal is not bound.
24. An agent can commingle his principal's money with his or her own so long as he or she keeps careful record.
25. A third party who discovers that the agent has acted for an undisclosed principal may sue the undisclosed principal.
26. If an agent is a minor, the third party can disavow the contract before the agent reaches his majority.
27. An agency contract need not be in writing to be enforceable.
28. Any person who holds himself out as an agent is never liable to the third party, even if he or she in fact was not the agent for the principal.
29. A principal may ratify the acts of an agent, even if the agent acted originally outside the scope of his or her authority.
30. Every employee of a company is an agent.
31. Any information given to an agent is imputed to the principal.
32. A principal has the duty to indemnify the agent for any expenses in carrying out the agency duties.
33. An agent warrants to third persons that he or she has the authority to represent the principal with regard to the particular transaction.
34. Death of either principal or agent terminates the agency even though the agency agreement has not expired in accordance with its terms.
35. An agent may enter into a contract where he or she advises the third party of his or her agency status but will not name the principal.
36. One who holds a security interest in personal property has absolute title in the property until the debtor pays the total purchase price.
37. Generally, after a secured creditor forecloses and sells collateral, any surplus will belong to the debtor.

38. The docketing of a judgment with the county clerk constitutes a lien on any real property of the debtor located in that county.
39. Inventory is classified by the UCC as an "intangible."
40. The only method of perfecting a security interest in inventory is by filing a UCC financing statement.
41. One can perfect a security interest in accounts receivable either by filing or possession.
42. A UCC financing statement generally need not be renewed for five years.
43. The UCC has been adopted by every state in the United States plus the District of Columbia.
44. Under the UCC, one can repossess collateral without notice to the debtor, so long as no breach of the peace is required.
45. Anyone purchasing inventory in the ordinary course of business takes such inventory free and clear of any security interest of the secured party.
46. A security agreement is required even though a standard form of financing statement has been properly filed to perfect a security interest in the other.
47. In order for a consignment sale to be effective against the creditor of the buyer, a seller must usually file a UCC financing statement.
48. No distinction is drawn by the revised UCC between "accounts" and "contract rights" and a security interest in one is a security interest in the other.
49. Under the 1972 revision of the UCC, a security interest in collateral constitutes a security interest in the proceeds of that collateral unless specifically excluded in the security interest.
50. A landlord's lien has priority over a perfected security interest in machinery located on the landlord's property unless the statute granting such landlord's lien provides otherwise.
51. A Federal Tax Lien has priority over a perfected security interest in inventory from the moment the lien is filed.
52. When real property is sold "subject to" the mortgage, the buyer is personally responsible for payment of the underlying debt that is secured by the mortgage.
53. A debtor may renounce his right to notice of sale of the collateral in the security agreement and prior to default.

54. A has a perfected security interest in X's inventory. B subsequently perfects a security interest in X's accounts. B will have priority as to X's accounts in any dispute with A.
55. Failure to comply with the foreclosure provision of Article 7 of UCC may result in the secured party's inability to obtain a judgment against the debtor for any deficiency.
56. Warranties of title are impled in sales contracts.
57. A contract entered into between a minor and an adult is voidable.
58. A sale made "as is" and "with all faults" is sufficient to disclaim a warranty of title.
59. Article 9 of the UCC applies to sales of personal property.
60. The risk of loss is always on the buyer whether the sale is "a sale on return" or "sale on approval" transaction.
61. Title passes when the parties to a sale specifically express an intention that such title pass.
62. A buyer generally has the right to inspect goods upon delivery.
63. All contracts for the sale of goods must be in writing to be enforceable.
64. In order to establish fraud, a misrepresentation has to be material.
65. Every seller of goods, unless disclaimed, makes a warranty that it transfers good title.
66. An exclusion or modification of the warranty of fitness for a particular purpose must be in writing.
67. To disclaim the warranty of merchantability, under the UCC, one must mention merchantability, and in the case of a writing, the disclaimer must be conspicuous.
68. An offer which can only be accepted by performance of a particular act is called a unilateral contract.
69. An offer to purchase 500 yards of wool piece goods six months from the contract date at a "reasonable price" is too indefinite to result in an enforceable contract.
70. A newspaper advertisement by a department store is generally held to be an offer that can be accepted by the customer.
71. Generally, a counter offer in a negotiation for a personal service contract is a rejection of the original offer.
72. If a court finds that the consideration exchanged between the parties is unequal, it will not enforce the contract.

73. An uncle's promise to pay $500 to his niece "in consideration of love and affection" is binding.
74. A contract entered into by an adjudicated insane person is void even if the other party was unaware of the adjudication.
75. All contracts forbidding competition are illegal restraints of trade and are thus void.
76. Silence in certain situations where the party has a duty to speak may constitute fraud.
77. An oral contract not to be performed within one year may be enforceable if there are witnesses to the agreement.
78. An assignee of a contract takes it subject to all defenses that existed against the assignor at the time of the assignment.
79. If, after a contract is made, its performance becomes illegal, both parties are discharged from the contract without damages to either party.
80. A guaranty of the debts of another must be in writing to be enforceable.
81. A written agreement pursuant to which the purchase of goods agrees to purchase the entire output of the seller is unenforceable by reason of "indefiniteness."
82. The doctrine of Promissory Estoppel has been used by the courts to enforce promises of contributions to charitable organizations where consideration cannot be found.
83. A voidable contract is a contract that never existed.
84. Under common law, an acceptance that changes the terms of the offer creates a contract, but only with respect to the terms that are agreed upon.
85. In most states, the making of a contract on Sunday is unlawful and will not be enforced.
86. Under the UCC, a writing signed by any one of the parties to the contract will be sufficient to satisfy the Statute of Frauds.
87. In order to negotiate bearer paper, it is necessary for the transferor both to endorse and deliver the instrument to his or her transferee.
88. A bank may refuse to certify a check of its customer even though there are sufficient funds in the account.
89. A promissory note payable on the maker's "21st birthday" is payable at a definite time and the note is negotiable.

90. Where the terms of an instrument are ambiguous, handwritten terms control typewritten terms.

91. A holder in due course takes the instrument subject to all defenses that were available against the transferor.

92. X, a holder in due course, transfers the instrument to his daughter, Y, as a Christmas gift. Y is a holder in due course.

93. The Bankruptcy Code does not permit the filing of an involuntary Chapter 11.

94. One must allege and prove that an act of bankruptcy has been committed in order to successfully file an involuntary petition in bankruptcy under the Bankruptcy Code.

95. A trustee's powers are equal to the powers of a Debtor-in-Possession.

96. To confirm a plan of arrangement, creditors holding 50% in number and amount of claims must consent.

97. A creditor's committee must serve without compensation and the members must bear their own expense.

98. A discharge in bankruptcy discharges a husband's obligation to pay alimony.

99. A suretyship arrangement always involves three parties: the creditor, the debtor, and the surety or guarantor.

100. A guarantor or surety is entitled to be subrogated to the rights of the creditor after the surety has made good on the obligation.

101. An individual who has made a false oath on his or her bankruptcy schedules may not receive a discharge in bankruptcy.

102. The trustee may avoid a fraudulent transfer under the Bankruptcy Code or under any state statute.

103. A reclaiming creditor's rights are subject to the rights of a buyer in the ordinary course.

104. A bank's right of set-off is a common law right and therefore can receive a discharge.

105. Under the Bankruptcy Code, both an individual and corporation can receive a discharge.

106. The state court administering an assignment for the benefit of creditors has no power to issue a discharge to the debtor as that would usurp the power of the federal court.

107. Generally, an out-of-court settlement is binding on only those creditors who consent to compromise their debts in writing.

108. Creditors extending unsecured credit to a debtor-in-possession are administration creditors and would have prior rights to distribution of assets over prebankruptcy creditors in the event of a liquidation.

109. If a debtor is unable to obtain credit, the court, after notice of a hearing, may grant a new creditor a lien prior to that of existing creditors.

110. In a contract for goods "FOB New York," the risk of loss passes to the buyer when the seller delivers the goods to a carrier in New York.

111. A seller has a right to stop goods in transit upon discovering a buyer's insolvency.

112. A sale to a third person of specific goods that the seller has agreed to sell to another person in another contract is a form of anticipatory breach.

113. A buyer who receives nonconforming goods may refuse to bring the package indoors and any damage to the goods caused by inclement weather will be the responsibility of the seller.

114. A seller who seeks to reclaim goods from an insolvent buyer is subject to the rights of a bond fide purchaser for value.

115. A holder cannot be a holder in due course if he or she has knowledge that the drawer of the check is an infant.

116. A draft is an instrument whereby the third party creating it orders another party to pay money to a third party.

117. Whether an instrument is negotiable or nonnegotiable depends upon the intent of the party issuing the instrument.

118. An instrument that is not negotiable is interpreted under the general rules of contract law and not under the UCC.

119. A note payable in Mexican pesos at a bank in Austin, Texas, is not negotiable.

120. A draft payable upon "X's death" is negotiable since X's death is certain.

121. An instrument "payable to A or B" requires the endorsement of both A and B.

122. A holder in due course takes the instrument subject to the defense of failure of consideration.

123. A maker of a note who files a petition in bankruptcy will not receive a discharge of the debt if the note is held by a holder in due course.

124. A check can be presented only for payment and not for acceptance.

125. An instrument payable "on demand" may be presented within a reasonable time after an endorser signs it.

126. Under the UCC, a payee may be a holder in due course.

127. If X purchased an instrument for value payable "20 _____ after day," X would not be a holder in due course.

128. Under the UCC, a bank might rightfully dishonor a check if not drawn on its printed form.

129. All endorsers warrant that all signatures are genuine or authorized on the instrument.

130. An instrument "payable to John Jones" is not negotiable.

131. The attempt by an endorser to limit the negotiation of an instrument further is unenforceable.

132. Endorsers are liable generally in the order in which their signatures appear on the instrument.

133. Notice of protest is required only where the dishonored instrument is drawn in or payable in a foreign country.

134. A party who endorses "without recourse" is not liable on the instrument as an endorser or for breach of warranty.

135. One who signs an instrument as an accommodation endorser nevertheless incurs the same liability to subsequent holders as it does to any other endorser.

136. The relationship of a bank to its depositor is one of debtor-creditor.

137. Failure to accept a draft when it is due is a dishonor.

138. Unless a note provides for interest at a given rate, the note bears interest at the legal rate from the date of issuance.

139. A blank endorsement is a waiver of all defenses to the instrument.

140. A "cashier's check" and a "bank draft" are synonymous.

141. The holder of a negotiable promissory note is not affected by the maker's bankruptcy.

142. Even though one party to a contract clearly expresses his or her intention not to perform, the other party must await the scheduled time for performance under the contract before bringing suit.

143. A buyer may revoke his or her acceptance of goods if he or she was unaware of the nonconformity at the time of the acceptance and reasonably notifies the seller of his or her revocation.

144. 'Bill Smith" is an example of a blank endorsement.

145. A check is a draft drawn on a bank and payable on demand.

146. For an instrument to be negotiable, the amount to be paid thereunder must be certain, including the amount of all interest and charges.

147. The liability of the drawer of a check is primary and the holder may proceed against him or her directly.

148. The maker of a note is a secondary party and must receive notice of dishonor before he or she can be held liable on the instrument.

149. Notwithstanding the filing of a petition, a creditor having a security interest in the debtor's accounts receivable may collect the accounts by notifying the account debtors of his or her interest with obtaining the permission of the Bankruptcy Court.

150. A discharge in bankruptcy discharges a claim for damages arising in an auto accident that has to be reduced to judgment.

## PART IA—ANSWERS TO CREDIT & BUSINESS LAW QUESTIONS

| | | | | | | | | | |
|---|---|---|---|---|---|---|---|---|---|
| 1. | T | 31. | T | 61. | T | 91. | F | 121. | F |
| 2. | T | 32. | T | 62. | T | 92. | T | 122. | F |
| 3. | T | 33. | T | 63. | F | 93. | F | 123. | F |
| 4. | T | 34. | T | 64. | T | 94. | F | 124. | T |
| 5. | F | 35. | T | 65. | T | 95. | T | 125. | T |
| 6. | F | 36. | F | 66. | T | 96. | F | 126. | T |
| 7. | T | 37. | T | 67. | T | 97. | F | 127. | T |
| 8. | F | 38. | F | 68. | T | 98. | F | 128. | F |
| 9. | T | 39. | F | 69. | F | 99. | T | 129. | T |
| 10. | T | 40. | F | 70. | F | 100. | T | 130. | T |
| 11. | T | 41. | F | 71. | T | 101. | T | 131. | T |
| 12. | F | 42. | T | 72. | F | 102. | T | 132. | T |
| 13. | T | 43. | F | 73. | F | 103. | T | 133. | T |
| 14. | F | 44. | T | 74. | T | 104. | F | 134. | F |
| 15. | F | 45. | T | 75. | F | 105. | F | 135. | T |
| 16. | F | 46. | T | 76. | T | 106. | T | 136. | T |
| 17. | F | 47. | T | 77. | F | 107. | T | 137. | T |
| 18. | F | 48. | T | 78. | T | 108. | T | 138. | T |
| 19. | F | 49. | T | 79. | T | 109. | T | 139. | F |
| 20. | F | 50. | T | 80. | T | 110. | T | 140. | F |
| 21. | T | 51. | F | 81. | F | 111. | T | 141. | F |
| 22. | F | 52. | F | 82. | T | 112. | T | 142. | F |
| 23. | T | 53. | F | 83. | F | 113. | F | 143. | T |
| 24. | F | 54. | F | 84. | F | 114. | T | 144. | T |
| 25. | T | 55. | T | 85. | F | 115. | T | 145. | T |
| 26. | F | 56. | T | 86. | F | 116. | T | 146. | F |
| 27. | T | 57. | T | 87. | F | 117. | F | 147. | F |
| 28. | F | 58. | F | 88. | T | 118. | T | 148. | F |
| 29. | T | 59. | F | 89. | F | 119. | F | 149. | F |
| 30. | F | 60. | F | 90. | T | 120. | F | 150. | T |

## PART IB—CREDIT & BUSINESS LAW

1. **Q.** What constitutes interstate business?
   **A.** Business conducted by two (2) or more parties in different states.
2. **Q.** Can officers and/or shareholders of a corporation be held personally liable for the debts of the corporation?
   **A.** Officers and/or share holders of a corporation may not be held personally liable for the debts of the corporation unless:
   (1) they have signed a personal guarantee
   (2) the corporate veil can be pierced under state law
3. **Q.** Can a company legally charge any rate of interest on past due accounts, and why or why not?
   **A.** No. Most state laws prohibit assessment of interest or late charges on past due account balances unless the customer has agreed to such charges in writing, and then such charges must be at the rate allowable by prevailing law in the state where the customer is domiciled.
4. **Q.** In its collection process is it legal for a company to use stationery of a fictitious in-house law firm or collection agency, and what are the general rules regarding this practice?
   **A.** Such practice would be illegal and improper in most states. This type of activity is deceptive and misleading. Most states have adopted statues which would make is unlawful.
5. **Q.** What is an "Assignment for benefit of creditors?"
   **A.** This is the voluntary transfer of all or substantially all of a debtor's property to another person or persons in trust for the purpose of liquidating the property and/or collecting monies to pay creditors under applicable state laws.
6. **Q.** Is a parent company responsible for the debts of a subsidiary?
   **A.** The law generally considers the parent and subsidiary as separate entities, with no intercompany liability for debts. However, a parent may guarantee the obligations of a subsidiary by way of a Corporate Guarantee to a creditor.
7. **Q.** What documents that are issued by an independent auditor or accountant is the principal means by which a creditor evaluates the risk of doing business with someone seeking credit?

**A.** A financial statement consisting of a balance sheet and profit and loss statements, and a certificate of opinion.

**8. Q.** What is the basic objective of the Uniform Commercial Code?

**A.** To make the law of commercial transactions simple, clear, modern and uniform under one statute. The code deals with such subjects as sales, secured transactions, commercial paper, bulk sales and other matters.

**9. Q.** Person as defined in article 1 of the Uniform Commercial Code refers only to _____?

**A.** An individual or organization which includes a Corporation, Partnership, Trust, Estate or Government.

**10. Q.** What is the statute of limitations?

**A.** A law which limits the length of time within which an action for breach of any contract must be commenced.

**11. Q.** How does Regulation B of the Equal Credit Opportunity Act effect grantors of business credit when an application for credit is not accepted?

**A.** They are not required to notify the applicant of the reasons for non-acceptance unless he/she requests in writing such advice within 30 days after oral or written notification that adverse action has been taken.

**12. Q.** List one advantage and one disadvantage to the debtor and the creditor of an assignment for the benefit of creditors.

**A.** It is relatively less expensive than a formal bankruptcy filing, but it does not discharge debtor from his debts (or any other reasonable advantage and disadvantage).

**13. Q.** What is the statute of frauds?

**A.** A law which requires certain specific kinds of contracts to be in writing, and in the absence of a writing such contracts are generally not enforceable.

**14. Q.** What remedies does the seller have upon learning that a buyer is insolvent?

**A.** Where the seller discovers buyer's insolvency after buyer has received possession of the goods. Seller may reclaim the goods upon demand made within ten (10) days after buyer received the goods. In addition, if buyer misrepresented its solvency within three (3) months of the delivery of goods, seller may reclaim the goods at any time.

## Legislation

**15. Q.** How does the "Fair Debt Collection Practices Act of 1977" apply to collection of a commercial debt, one business collecting from another?

**A.** It does not apply. This act primarily covers consumer type transactions in which goods are purchased for personal, family or household purposes.

**16. Q.** What is the Sherman Antitrust Act and how does it affect American businesses?

**A.** The Act prohibits contracts or conspiracies between persons who attempt to restrain or monopolize free trade or commerce between states and/or countries.

**17. Q.** How do industry trade groups operate within the guidelines of the Sherman Antitrust Act?

**A.** Members of a credit group may discuss and/or exchange past (A/R) experience on customers only. Such discussion and/or exchange of information cannot include price, discounts or terms of sale on any future transaction(s) or any agreement to fix prices, terms, customer lists or similar matters.

**18. Q.** What is the Robinson-Patman Act and how does it affect American business?

**A.** This act prohibits any person(s) or business(es) from discriminating in price between different purchases of goods of like quality when the transaction(s) involve interstate commerce and such discrimination substantially lessens competition or may create a monopoly.

## Contracts

**19. Q.** Does a partnership require a written contract between the partners before it can legally transact business, and why or why not?

**A.** No, a written contract is not required. The only requirement is mutual consent by all the parties to form a partnership and agreement on the basic terms. Each person must give his/her consent; he/she cannot be made a partner by the action of another party.

20. **Q.** What are the basic legal requirements of a contract?
    **A.** 1. An offer must be extended and accepted;
    2. All involved parties must be competent.
    3. The subject of the contract must be legal.
    4. Consideration may be required under state law; depending on the contract it may have to be in writing.

21. **Q.** Name reasons that a contract can be invalidated.
    **A.** Fraud, mutual consent by all parties, etc.

22. **Q.** Under the law of contracts, how may an offer be made?
    **A.** Orally, in writing or by some act which may be interpreted as an offer.

23. **Q.** Under the law of contracts, how long does an offer that has been properly communicated continue?
    **A.** Until it is revoked, rejected or accepted within a specified period, or lapses after a reasonable period of time.

24. **Q.** How may a contract be discharged?
    **A.** By performance, breach, agreement, alteration or by operation of law.

25. **Q.** List two (2) or more types of contracts that are required to be in writing.
    **A.** Assignment of wages, sale of land or an interest therein, and contracts for sale of goods if the value is at least $500.00.

26. **Q.** What does the law require in order for an agent to sign for his/her principal and the principal to be bound by that signature?
    **A.** The agent must be duly authorized. Must be an act of *principal* granting or implied granting authority.

27. **Q.** When a buyer discovers upon delivery of goods that the goods do not comply with the requirement of the purchase contract, what rights does the buyer have with respect to the goods?
    **A.** 1. Buyer may reject all of the goods.
    2. Buyer may accept all of the goods.
    3. Buyer may accept any commercial unit or units and reject the balance of the goods.

## Sales

28. **Q.** Under the terms of F.O.B. sales, when does title pass from the

seller to the buyer?

**A.** Unless otherwise expressed, title to the goods sold F.O.B. passes to the buyer on delivery to the carrier, or at the point to which seller agrees to pay freight charges.

## Negotiable Instruments

**29. Q.** You receive a check marked "in Full of Account" which does not in fact pay the entire balance due of a liquidated and undisputed account. By accepting and depositing the check, are you prevented from moving to collect the remaining balance? (Please give full explanation.)

**A.** If no *bona fide* dispute exists as to the amount due, you may keep the check and pursue collection for the balance. If a dispute exists state law is in conflict. In some states, such as New York, the creditor can endorse the check "Under Protest" or "Without Prejudice" which will reserve his rights against the debtor. In other states if the check is deposited, an accord and satisfaction results.

**30. Q.** What is the basic rule of assignment concerning the assignee taking a negotiable instrument?

**A.** That the assignee takes it subject to the same defenses and limited to the same rights as the assignor.

**31. Q.** What is a "holder in due course?"

**A.** A "holder in due course" is a person who takes a negotiable instrument (a) for value, (b) in good faith, (c) without notice that the negotiable instrument is overdue, has been dishonored or that there are any valid defenses against the negotiable instrument.

**32. Q.** With respect to a negotiable instrument or check, what rights does a "holder in due course" have?

**A.** A "holder in due course" takes the negotiable instrument or check, free from all claims on the part of any person, and defenses of any party to the negotiable instrument or check with whom the holder has not actually dealt except for defenses set forth in Article three (3) of the UCC.

**33. Q.** What is the liability of any person who endorses a negotiable instrument or check by simply endorsing the negotiable instrument without specifying any limitation on the endorsement?

**A.** Endorser agrees that upon dishonor of the negotiable instrument or check and appropriate notice, the endorser will pay the instrument in accordance with the terms of the instrument, and will make payment to the holder of the instrument or to any subsequent endorser of the instrument.

**34. Q.** Although state statutes may differ in detail, what is the common principle that applies to "Bad Check Laws?"

**A.** A person or firm who knowingly makes and/or negotiates a check for which there are insufficient funds, is guilty of a crime, and may be subject to civil penalties under the state law where the person/firm resides.

## Bulk Transfers

**35. Q.** Under the Uniform Commercial Code (UCC), what is a bulk transfer?

**A.** This refers to a transfer of a substantial part of or all of the material and/or inventory in bulk and not in the ordinary course of the transferor's business.

**36. Q.** Describe in general the requirements of the bulk transfer section of the Uniform Commercial Code.

**A.** The bulk transfer section requires the transferor in a transfer subject to the act, to provide to the transferee a schedule of all property transferred and a list of all existing creditors of the transferor. The list and schedule must be maintained for six months by the transferee. The transferee must give notice of the proposed transfer to all of the creditors appearing on the list provided by the transferee.

**37. Q.** What is the effect of failing to comply with the bulk transfer section of the Uniform Commercial Code?

**A.** Creditors of the transferor may still pursue the transferor for the transferor's debts. In addition, in the absence of compliance, the transfer is ineffective with respect to any creditor of the transferor who did not receive the required notice of the proposed transfer. As a result, such a creditor of the transferor seeking to satisfy an obligation of the transferor could attach the transferred property in the hands of the transferee for a period of six (6) months after the transfer.

## Secured Transactions

**38. Q.** Under the Uniform Commercial Code, how long does a UCC-1, Financing Statement, remain in effect after its filing date?

**A.** A UCC-1 remains in effect for five years from date filed, then it must be renewed.

**39. Q.** Under the Uniform Commercial Code, in what types of collateral may security interests be granted (name at least four or more)?

**A.** Inventory, accounts receivable (proceeds from sale of goods), equipment, fixtures, crops and deposit accounts.

**40. Q.** Under article 9 of the Uniform Commercial Code, what generally determines priority among conflicting perfected security interests in the same collateral?

**A.** Time of perfection.

**41. Q.** What is a security interest?

**A.** An interest in personal property or fixtures which secures payment or performance of an obligation.

**42. Q.** How does one obtain information of existing lienholders?

**A.** A UCC-11 search request, UCC Div.

**43. Q.** How can a secured party protect his security interest against the claims of third parties?

**A.** By taking possession of the collateral or by filing notice that he has a security interest in the property covered by the security agreement with the appropriate filing officer.

**44. Q.** Why is the ability of a materialman, contractor or subcontractor to obtain a lien important?

**A.** It may provide him with security which will allow him to consider extending credit.

**45. Q.** What is a security interest under the UCC?

**A.** A lien interest in personal property or fixtures which secure payment or performance of an obligation.

**46. Q.** What are the requirements for creating a valid security agreement?

**A.** 1. Either the collateral is in the possession of the secured party, or debtor has signed a security agreement which contains a description of the collateral; and

2. Value is given or has been given; and

3. The debtor has rights in the collateral.

**47. Q.** What is the most common method used for perfecting a secured party's security interest in the collateral?

**A.** Filing a Financing Statement.

## Bankruptcy

**48. Q.** Explain the difference between a voluntary and an involuntary petition for bankruptcy.

**A.** A voluntary petition is filed by a person/company seeking relief from creditors under the Bankruptcy Act. An involuntary petition is filed by three or more creditors who have claims against the debtor amounting to a total of $5,000 or more. If the total number of creditors is less than 12, any one creditor may file the involuntary petition.

**49. Q.** Who may serve on a creditor's committee in a bankruptcy proceeding?

**A.** Usually a creditor's committee consists of the seven largest unsecured creditors, however the court may change the number of committee members to insure fair representation of all creditors. Separate committees of other interested parties such as equity holders may also be formed.

**50. Q.** Under Chapter 11, how long does the debtor have to file a plan of reorganization with the court?

**A.** Chapter 11 of the Bankruptcy Act requires a debtor file a plan of reorganization within 120 days after filing the petition in bankruptcy. After 120 days, anyone can file a plan unless the court grants the debtor an extension.

**51. Q.** Can anyone other than the debtor file a plan of reorganization with the court?

**A.** Yes, a plan of reorganization can be filed by a creditor's committee or trustee in bankruptcy after 120 days of filing the petition, unless the court grants the debtor an extension.

**52. Q.** As an alternative to bankruptcy, what are the advantages of a voluntary "out-of-court" settlement?

**A.** There are several advantages to this type of proceeding; it is not encumbered by court proceedings, no court costs are involved, and the debtor stays in business with a better chance of becoming a more stable customer.

**53. Q.** Under Chapter 7 of the Federal Bankruptcy Act, how long must a debtor wait after discharge to file bankruptcy again and obtain another discharge?

**A.** Six (6) years.

**54. Q.** Under the Bankruptcy Act, what is a discharge?

**A.** A discharge releases the debtor from all debts that arose before the date of the order for relief.

**55. Q.** What is the purpose of an Automatic Stay under the Bankruptcy Code?

**A.** To protect the debtor from actions of his creditors in order to prevent any creditor from obtaining special advantage.

**56. Q.** What is the impact caused by filing of a bankruptcy petition with respect to efforts by *secured* creditors to collect unpaid debts from a debtor?

**A.** The bankruptcy act contains an automatic stay which prohibits any party, whether secured or unsecured, from commencing or continuing any act to obtain collection of an obligation.

**57. Q.** What is the impact caused by filing of a bankruptcy petition with respect to efforts by *unsecured* creditors to collect unpaid debts from the debtor?

**A.** The bankruptcy act contains an automatic stay which prohibits any party, whether secured or unsecured, from commencing or continuing any act to obtain collection of an obligation.

**58. Q.** What are the elements of a preference, or preferential transfer under the Bankruptcy Code?

**A.** 1. The transfer to or for the benefit of a creditor;
2. A transfer for or on account of an antecedent debt owed by the debtor before the transfer was made;
3. A transfer made while the debtor was insolvent;
4. A transfer made within ninety days of the date of filing of the bankruptcy petition or if the creditor is an insider, a transfer within one year before the date of the filing of the bankruptcy petition; and
5. A transfer that enables the creditor to receive more than the

creditor would receive if the debtor were in a Chapter 7 liquidation, or if the transfer had not been made.

**59. Q.** If a bankruptcy court determines that a transfer before filing of the bankruptcy petition is a preference, what is the impact of that determination on the transfer?

**A.** The debtor, or the trustee in bankruptcy for a debtor, may recover the transferred property or the value of the transferred property from the person or entity receiving the transfer.

**60. Q.** Does bankruptcy always mean business failure? Explain.

**A.** No. Many over-leveraged firms remain operationally viable and are accounts of importance before the filing, during the procedure and after a successful reorganization.

## LEGAL CASE STUDY

Ajax Sporting Goods, Inc. opened its sporting goods store in a major metropolitan area in 1980. Ajax financed its operation in part through a line of credit in the maximum amount of $50,000 with Big Bank. Big Bank's line of credit was secured by a properly executed and perfected security interest in accounts receivable. In January 1984, Ajax borrowed an additional $10,000 from Small Bank, and did not provide to Small Bank a security interest of any kind related to the loan. In addition, in early 1984 Local Bank loaned Ajax $20,000, also without security. Local Bank, however, obtained a written guaranty from Mr. Risk, President of Ajax guarantying repayment of the loan by Ajax. By June 1, 1984, Ajax was insolvent, and on January 1, 1985 Ajax filed a voluntary Chapter 11 bankruptcy petition.

**1. Q.** On September 20, 1984, Ajax paid in full a long overdue loan received by Ajax from a Finance Company at the time Ajax commenced its business. What effect will the bankruptcy petition have on this repayment?

**A.** No impact, because the repayment occurred outside the preference period more than ninety days before filing of the bankruptcy petition.

**2. Q.** On November 15, 1984, Small Bank obtained from Ajax a perfected security interest in Ajax's inventory to secure repayment of Small Bank's $10,000 loan. What is the impact of the bankruptcy filing on this transaction?

A. The perfected security interest amounts to a transfer within ninety days of the bankruptcy petition. The transfer satisfies the other elements of a preference and therefore the debtor in possession or the trustee in bankruptcy may void the transfer of the perfected security interest to Small Bank.

3. **Q.** On December 1, 1984, Rocket Corporation which had three months earlier sold $5,000 worth of tennis rackets to Ajax, received payment in full of the $5,000 bill for the tennis rackets. The next day Rocket delivered $3,000 worth of additional tennis rackets to Ajax, and agreed to allow Ajax to pay for the tennis rackets in sixty days. What is the impact of the bankruptcy proceeding upon the $5,000 payment?

   **A.** The $5,000 payment was within the ninety day preference period, and satisfies the other requirements of a preferential transfer. Without the additional facts, the debtor or the trustee in bankruptcy could recover the $5,000 payment from Rocket.

4. **Q.** On August 15, 1984, Ajax repaid to Mr. Risk a $5,000 loan which Mr. Risk had made to the company three years earlier. What is the impact of the bankruptcy upon this repayment?

   **A.** Mr. Risk is an insider because of his position as an officer of the company. The preferential transfer period for transfers to insiders is expanded from three months to one year. Therefore even though the transfer occurred more than three months before the bankruptcy petition was filed, the transfer did occur within one year before the filing of the bankruptcy petition, and the debtor or trustee may therefore recover from Mr. Risk the repayment he received.

5. **Q.** On September 1, 1984, Local Bank received a $10,000 payment against the loan obligation owed by Ajax to Local Bank, which obligation was guaranteed by Mr. Risk. What is the impact of the bankruptcy proceeding upon this payment?

   **A.** Ordinarily this repayment more than three months before the bankruptcy proceeding was filed would not be a preference. The preference statute however provides that a transfer to or for the benefit of an insider, which occurs within one year of the bankruptcy petition, may be recovered. Because Mr. Risk had guaranteed the obligation owed to Local Bank, the payment to Local Bank was a transfer for the benefit of Mr. Risk, an insider. Therefore since that transfer occurred within one year of the date of the bankruptcy petition, the debtor or the trustee may recover the transfer from Local Bank or from Mr. Risk.

# CBF EXAMINATION TYPICAL QUESTIONS & ANSWERS

## PART II—CREDIT MANAGEMENT PROBLEMS

### Questions

1. Ratios show the financial relationship that exists among various items taken from the balance sheet and operating statement for any one year. They are used by a credit analyst to help determine the financial strength of customers. Describe how the following ratios can be used. (15% of score)
   a. Working capital turnover.
   b. Days sales to current debt.
   c. Inventory to working capital.
   d. Current debt to net worth.
   e. Current assets to current debt.
2. Answer each of the following questions. (15% of score)
   a. What would a negative or low working capital position indicate?
   b. What purpose does a comparison of year-end balance sheets over a period of years serve?
   c. A good accounting system includes five control documents, one of which is a deviation analysis. Name the other four.
   d. Indicate whether all or some of the following items should appear in the financial data section of projections or forecasts.
      (1.) Sources and applications of funding.
      (2.) Capital equipment list.
      (3.) Balance sheet.
      (4.) Break-even analysis.
      (5.) Pro-forma cash flow analysis.
      (6.) Deviation analysis.
      (7.) Historical records (if any).

**e.** Indicate whether this statement is true or false:
Together, the income statement, cash flow, breakeven analysis, and balance sheet provide a comprehensive model of the operations, liquidity, and the past and near future of the business.

**f.** What is the item on a balance sheet that generally includes all debts that fall due within the coming year?

**g.** Re:   liabilities and stockholders' equity. Are both sides always in balance? If yes, what is listed in each column?

**h.** Customers are usually given 30, 60, or 90 days in which to pay. Because some customers fail to pay, in order to show the A/R figure on a balance sheet realistically, what must be taken into account?

**i.** On a financial statement, current and long-term liabilities are added up and listed under what heading?

**j.** To help you interpret the current position of a company, what ratio is more helpful than the dollar total of working capital?

**3. a.** Discuss why a profit and loss statement should be submitted along with balance sheets. Also, name six of the basic ingredients contained in a P&L statement (one ingredient is net income after taxes, or final net profits).

**b.** Recognizing that net worth is equity, that is, the owner's share of the business, indicate on what side of the balance sheet this is listed and why. (15% of score)

**4. a.** In which of the current assets are credit managers particularly interested above all others and why? (15% of score)

**b.** Name the four balance sheet elements of primary concern to credit managers.

**5. a.** From the balance sheet for Alta Industries, calculate each of the ratios selected below and indicate if the result is acceptable. (For example, if a result is 3.1 and the industry average is 2.1, obviously 3.1 is quite acceptable.) (30% of score)

Estimated Industry Average

| | |
|---|---|
| • Current assets to current liabilities | 2.82 |
| • Liquid or quick ratio | 1.1 |
| • Debt to net worth | a) 40.7 or b) 78.1 |
| • Fixed assets to net worth | 25.4 |

**b.** What does each of the below ratios measure?   (10% of score)

Current assets to current liabilities
Liquid or quick ratio
Debt to net worth
Fixed assets to net worth

### BALANCE SHEET OF ALTA INDUSTRIES
#### Sales—$1,287,000; Net profit—$48,000

| Assets | | Liabilities | |
|---|---|---|---|
| *Current:* | | *Current:* | |
| Cash | $ 53,000 | Accounts payable | $ 54,000 |
| Accounts receivable | 150,000 | Accruals | |
| Inventory | 191,000 | (taxes, etc.) | 51,000 |
| | | Note payable—bank | |
| | | (current portion) | 10,000 |
| | | Total current | |
| Total current assets | $394,000 | liabilities | 115,000 |
| | | | |
| *Fixed:* | | Long term | |
| Real estate and | | Note payable—bank | |
| fixtures | 295,000 | (less current portion | |
| Less depreciation | | shown above) | 91,000 |
| reserve | 122,000 | | |
| | $173,000 | Total liabilities | $206,000 |
| | | **Stockholders' Equity** | |
| | | Capital stock | 149,000 |
| | | Retained earnings | |
| | | beginning of year | |
| | | Surplus, end of year | 48,000 |
| Total assets | $567,000 | Total | $567,000 |

6. Below are several common ratios used by credit managers to analyze accounts. Describe briefly how each ratio can be used and why.

*Example*: Quick Ratio

This can be used to measure dollar investment in liquid assets required to cover current debt. Liquid assets offer greater protection to short term creditors since inventory is not easy to evaluate because of age, price fluctuations, shrinkage, etc.

a. Debt to equity.
b. Current debt to net worth.
c. Asset turnover.
d. Return on sales.
e. Return on investment.

7. Dating and cash discounts can affect margins of profit. The invoice date and terms of sale are as shown below. Indicate the last date for taking the cash discount on each of the following.

*Example*:

| Date of Invoice | Terms of Sale |
| --- | --- |
| September 13 | 3/20, EOM |

Answer: October 20

| Date of Invoice | Terms of Sale |
| --- | --- |
| a. October 12 | 2/10, EOM |
| b. June 29 | 1/10, EOM |
| c. July 29 | 3/10, EOM |
| d. November 4 | 2/10, EOM |
| e. May 5 (goods rec'd May 15) | 3/10, n/30, ROG |

8. a. Credit risks require appraisal by the credit manager or his/her designee. Name two of the three general areas from which the credit manager can obtain information on a new customer account.

   *Example:* One of the three areas in question is business history and background of customer account.

   b. Other than what is mentioned in Questions 6 & 7, what else must the credit manager look for? List at least four.

   *Example:* Evidence of dishonesty.

9. Prepare in account format a balance sheet for Frank's Supply as of June 30, 1987.

| | |
| --- | --- |
| Accounts Payable: | $ 100.00 |
| Accounts Receivable: | $ 400.00 |
| Cash: | $2,720.00 |
| Delivery Equipment: | $1,000.00 |
| Notes Payable: | $ 400.00 |
| Office Equipment: | $1,200.00 |
| Frank Alta, Capital: | $4,820.00 |

**10.** The following financial statements reflect financial relationships for the calendar years 1986 and 1987.

   **a.** In the columns shown at the right, calculate sources and uses of funds for the calendar year ending 12/31/87.

   **b.** Use any additional calculations you deem necessary, then determine profitability, financial efficiency, and indicate your decision on how to handle the account.

| | 12/31/86 | 12/31/87 | Use | Source |
|---|---|---|---|---|
| Cash | $ 68,500 | $ 34,900 | | |
| Accounts Receivable | 694,600 | 786,300 | | |
| Inventory | 612,400 | 654,600 | | |
|   Current Assets | 1,375,500 | 1,475,800 | | |
| Fixed Assets | 412,400 | 419,600 | | |
|   Total Assets | $1,787,900 | $1,895,400 | | |
| | | | | |
| Accounts Payable | $ 504,900 | 685,200 | | |
| Due Banks | 40,200 | 70,000 | | |
| Accrual and Taxes | 22,800 | 44,200 | | |
|   Current Liabilities | 567,900 | 799,400 | | |
| Long-Term Debt | 60,000 | 40,000 | | |
| Common Stock | 500,000 | 500,000 | | |
| Earned Surplus | 660,000 | 556,000 | | |
|   Total Liabilities and Capital | $1,787,900 | $1,895,400 | | |
| | | | | |
| Net Working Capital | $807,600 | 676,400 | | |
| Days Sales Outstanding | 35.1 Days | 44.6 Days | | |
| Inventory to Net Working Capital | 76% | 94% | | |
| Fixed Assets to Net Worth | 36% | 40% | | |
| Total Debt to Net Worth | 54% | 80% | | |

## Part II Credit Management Answers

1. How the ratios can be used:
   a. Working capital turnover. To determine the number of dollars in net sales a company receives for each dollar of working capital. Or reduction of working capital signals instability of the company or measures adequacy of working capital.
   b. Days sales to current debt. To determine the number of days sales required to pay present liabilities. Or to learn how liquid the company is.
   c. Inventory of working capital. To determine if company is carrying enough inventory to meet customer requirements. A low ratio indicates that the company is not carrying enough to meet demand and vice versa.
   d. Current debt to net worth. To determine how much owner owns vs. how much creditor owns. For example, if 200% is 2:1; for every dollar that owner has, the creditor owns $2, hence the creditor has greater risk than the owner. Or simply to determine if the company has enough of its own money in the business to pay current bills.
   e. Current assets to current debt. To determine company's ability to meet current obligations. Or to evaluate working capital relationships.

2. a. A major danger signal, a company with this kind of working capital position is said to be illiquid, i.e., suffering from a liquidity problem. With owner's equity less than debt, creditors, in effect, "own" the business and bankers would be reluctant to loan any more.
   b. It will highlight trends and spotlight weak areas.
   c. (1) Balance sheet.
      (2) Breakeven analysis.
      (3) Income statement.
      (4) Cash flow.
   d. All should appear in financial data section of projections or forecasts.
   e. True.
   f. Current liabilities.
   g. Yes. In liabilities column, all debts due under stockholders

equity, list the amount stockholders would split up if company were liquidated at its balance sheet value.

  **h.** A provision for bad debt.

  **i.** Total liabilities.

  **j.** Current assets.
     Current liabilities.

**3. a.** Because they will help to assess the customer's progress or lack of it.

    (1) Sales.

    (2) Cost of goods sold.

    (3) Gross profit.

    (4) Operating expenses.

    (5) Operating income or earnings (including adjustments).

    (6) Net income before taxes.

  **b.** Shown on the liability side of balance sheet because the business owes the owner that much.

**4. a.** Cash on hand and in the bank, because this is what customer uses to pay his bills. If total cash position is very light—e.g., $5000 out of combined current assets of $75,000—then obviously customer is operating with an imbalanced condition with most of the current assets in inventory and A/R.

  **b.** (1) Assets

    (2) Liabilities

    (3) Net worth or equity

    (4) Working capital

**5.**

$$\frac{\text{Current Assets } 394,000}{\text{Current liabilities } 115,000} = 3.42\% \ (2.82)$$

$$\frac{\text{Liquid assets } 203,000}{\text{Current liabilities } 115,000} = 1.76\% \ (1.1)$$

$$\frac{\text{Current liabilities } 115,000}{\text{Net worth } 361,000} = 31.8\% \ (40.7)$$

$$\frac{\text{Total liabilities } 206,000}{\text{Net worth } 361,000} = 57\% \ (78.1)$$

$$\frac{\text{Fixed assets } 173,000}{\text{Net worth } 361,000} = 47.9\% \ (25.4)$$

**6. a.** Debt to equity: shows the relationship between total creditor's interest and the owner's. It is an indicator of the customer's ability to leverage, and of relative investment made in the business by owners and creditors.

**b.** Current debt to net worth: shows the relationship between creditor's current funds and owner's investment. It raises the question of whether the customer has enough of their own money in the business to pay current bills.

**c.** Asset turnover: shows the number of times all assets are turned over during the year. It tells the credit manager how well the firm is utilizing the assets (opportunity use).

**d.** Return on sales: measures profitability. As profit increases, the degree of risk lessens.

**e.** Return on investment: measures the amount of money earned in relation to the investment. It helps evaluate management efficiency and the demonstrated ability to generate additional capital.

**7. a.** October 12                    2/10, EOM
Answer: November 10

**b.** June 29                          1/10, EOM
Answer: August 10

**c.** July 29                          3/10, EOM
Answer: September 10

**d.** November 4                       2/10, EOM
Answer: December 10

**e.** May 5 (goods rec'd May 15)       3/10, n/30, ROG
Answer: May 25

**8. a.** 1) Financial worth, 2) Paying record through trade and book references.

**b.** 1) Lack of business experience, 2) Bad location, 3) Insufficient capital, 4) Loose credit practices.

9.

FRANK'S SUPPLY
JUNE 30, 1987

| ASSETS | | LIABILITIES | |
|---|---|---|---|
| Current Assets: | | Current Liabilities: | |
| Cash | $2,720 | Accounts Payable | $100 |
| Accounts Receivable | 400 | Notes Payable | 400 |
| Total Current Assets | $3,120 | Total Current Liabilities | $500 |
| | | | |
| Delivery Expense | $1,000 | CAPITAL | |
| Office Equipment | 1,200 | Frank Alta, Capital | $4,820 |
| Total Plant Assets | $2,200 | | |
| | | TOTAL LIABILITIES | |
| TOTAL ASSETS | $5,320 | AND CAPITAL | $5,320 |

10.

| | 12/31/86 | 12/31/87 | USE | SOURCE |
|---|---|---|---|---|
| Cash | $ 68,500 | $ 34,900 | $ | $ 33,600 |
| Accounts Receivable | 694,600 | 786,300 | 91,700 | |
| Inventory | 612,400 | 654,600 | 42,200 | |
| Current Assets | $1,375,500 | $1,475,800 | | |
| Fixed Assets | 412,400 | 419,600 | 7,200 | |
| Total Assets | $1,787,900 | $1,895,400 | | |
| | | | | |
| | | | | |
| Accounts Payable | $504,900 | $685,200 | $ | $180,300 |
| Due Banks | 40,200 | 70,000 | | 29,800 |
| Accrual and Taxes | 22,800 | 44,200 | | 21,400 |
| Current Liabilities | $567,900 | $799,400 | | |
| Long-Term Debt | 60,000 | 40,000 | 20,000 | |
| Common Stock | 500,000 | 500,000 | | |
| Earned Surplus | 660,000 | 556,000 | 104,000 | ___ |
| Total Liabilities and Capital | $1,787,900 | $1,895,400 | $265,100 | $265,100 |
| | | | | |
| Net Working Capital | $807,600 | $676,400 | | |
| Days Sales Outstanding | 35.1 Days | 44.6 Days | | |
| Inventory to Net Working Capital | 76% | 94% | | |
| Fixed Assets to Net Worth | 36% | 40% | | |
| Total Debt to Net Worth | 54% | 80% | | |

# CBF EXAMINATION TYPICAL QUESTIONS & ANSWERS

## PART III—HUMAN RELATIONS IN CREDIT MANAGEMENT

### Questions

1. Interpersonal communications is particularly important in credit and financial management. Communicating with employees, other managers, and customers is estimated to occupy between 50% and 90% of a manager's time. Several different communication systems exist in an organization, that is, downward, upward, horizontal or lateral, and grapevine. Give an example of how you use each system to achieve your goal objective. Be specific.
   a. Downward communication
   b. Upward communication
   c. Horizontal or lateral communication
   d. Grapevine
2. "Change" often causes conflict. Successfully managing change increases the likelihood that positive benefits will result from conflict. How does a manager manage change to achieve positive benefits?
3. Personal and organizational goals: It has been suggested that as an individual interacts with an organization, these interactions should contribute to maintaining a sense of personal worth and importance. Others say that personal goals in harmony with organizational goals are important to satisfaction and improve productivity. How can you apply this knowledge to your department's goals of increased productivity and worker satisfaction?
4. Motivation is particularly essential in the credit function because highly motivated employees can bring about substantial increases in performance and substantial decreases in problems such as absenteeism, turnover, tardiness, strikes, grievances, and so forth.

## CASE STUDY - THE CREDIT ADMINISTRATOR

Frank Snow is age 45 and has been with Regal Wax Company for 20 years. He is in a top-paying credit administrator's position, a role he had held for 15 years. Frank is active socially and shows interest in most employee activities. He is friendly and well liked by all employees, especially younger ones, who often seek his advice. He is very helpful to them and never puts them off. When among these employees, he never speaks negatively about the company.

Frank's shortcoming, as his boss Bill Lange sees it, is his tendency to spend too much time talking with other employees. This causes Frank's work to suffer and consequently hinders the output of others. Whenever Bill confronts Frank with the problem, Frank's performance improves for a day or two, then he tends to slip back into his habit of storytelling and interrupting others.

Bill considered having Frank transferred out of the Credit Department to a job where he would have less opportunity to interrupt others. However, Bill concluded that he needs Frank's experience, especially since he has no replacement for Frank's job.

Frank is secure in his personal life. He owns a nice house and lives comfortably. His wife works as a bank loan officer, and their two children are grown and away from home. Bill has sensed that Frank feels that he is as high as he'll ever go in the company. This doesn't seem to bother him since he feels comfortable and likes his job.

  **a.** What would you do to attempt to motivate Frank if you were Bill Lange?

  **b.** Suppose Bill could transfer Frank, would you recommend that he do it? Why?

## PART III—HUMAN RELATIONS IN CREDIT MANAGEMENT

**Answers**

**1. a.** Transmitting information from higher to lower levels of the organization. This system does not facilitate immediate direct feedback.

  **b.** Communication originates at lower levels and flows to the top. Communication from bottom does not flow as freely as communication from the top.

  **c.** Formal communication across organizational units of the same approximate level. Interdepartmental committee meetings and distribution of written reports are common methods for facilitating horizontal communication.

  **d.** This channel results from the contacts between friends or acquaintances in various organizational units. The grapevine generally is not sanctioned as a part of the formal organizational structure, but it always exists.

2. Manager is to act as counselor in helping the participant(s) reach an acceptable solution. The approach is to build trust, discussing upcoming changes, involving employees in making changes, making sure the changes are reasonable, avoiding threats, following a sensible time schedule, and implementing the change in the most logical place.

3. Motivate people by showing how the department goals are in harmony with their own. For example, if they achieve or exceed goal expectations regularly, recognition will follow in terms of appropriate rewards, and their career goals will mesh with departmental goals. The employee must value the rewards that are being offered.

4. a. Appeal to Frank's ego and tell him that he is looked up to by other employees . . . or that in this position he can have a very positive or negative effect on younger employees. Appealing to him to set a good example will stimulate his pride and ego and may turn him around.

   b. First try the above. If it doesn't work, then consider transferring Frank. However, every attempt should be made to correct the problem before doing this.

The examination will also include reference to motivation and performance, work groups, communication, the Hierarchy of Needs Theory, the Motivation/Hygiene Theory, Expectancy Theory, Management by Objectives, Staffing, Leadership Styles, Types of Rewards, and Pay as a Motivator. Most college textbooks on *Introduction to Management* cover these topics in detail.

Readers may contact the National Institute of Credit for a list of recommended readings if more information is required.

# CHAPTER ELEVEN

# THE CCE EXAMINATION QUESTIONS AND ANSWERS

## INTRODUCTION

The Certified Credit Executive (CCE) designation is designed to measure understanding of concepts and principles at the senior management level. The level of difficulty exceeds that of the CBA and CBF.

A sample CCE exam has been reproduced below to give you a feel for how the exam is constructed. It would be beneficial to review the sample exam as well as the typical questions and answers which follow the actual sample exam.

**SAMPLE
CCE CERTIFIED CREDIT EXECUTIVE
EXAMINATION**

NAME & TITLE: _____

COMPANY: _____

ADDRESS: _____

PROCTOR FOR EXAM: _____ DATE: _____

This examination is to be completed at one sitting in the office of an affiliated association of the National Association of Credit Management.

A minimum of three hours should be allowed for completion of the examination.

The individual supervising the examination is to sign above in the space marked "Proctor for Exam."

The examination is in three parts:

Part I.　True or False: Place an "X" in the appropriate space for each of the questions.

Part II.　Essay Questions: Use the blue book provided to answer these questions. Be sure your name is on the book cover. Answer any *three* groups of questions from the five groups. Answer *all* parts in each group that you choose. Be sure to indicate the number of the question beside each of the answers.

Part III.　Credit Case Study: Use the enclosed book to answer this question.

- Answers must be legible and written in ink.
- Your book and this examination must be returned to the proctor at the conclusion of the examination.

## PART I

## TRUE OR FALSE QUESTIONS

**T　　F**

_____ _____ **1.** When examining a P&L statement internally, it is standard practice to express each individual item as a percentage of net sales.

_____ _____ **2.** Gross margins vary from industry to industry but within any particular line there usually exists only a small difference between margins obtained by a successful and unsuccessful operation.

_____ _____ **3.** Individual items on the balance sheet will vary considerably with the season, with volume increases and decreases, with collections and payments and with the ordinary daily activities of a business.

**T**    **F**

\_\_\_\_  \_\_\_\_   **4.** Usually a steady volume increase is desirable as it is an indication of growth and progress. As with most other factors, sales must be considered in light of both economic and industry conditions.

\_\_\_\_  \_\_\_\_   **5.** The net worth figure shown on a trial balance is not current. It usually reflects the position at the previous fiscal period or at the date of the latest available balance sheet.

\_\_\_\_  \_\_\_\_   **6.** An inventory estimate may be provided by management on the basis of visual inspection or other casual review of merchandise.

\_\_\_\_  \_\_\_\_   **7.** Working capital requirements are best determined by drawing up a cash forecast to cover a specific period of time, normally a year.

\_\_\_\_  \_\_\_\_   **8.** Among the requirements for setting up a cash forecast are:
- an estimate of volume month by month
- cost information on materials, labor and overhead which may be set up as a percentage of sales
- an estimate of monthly inventory purchases

\_\_\_\_  \_\_\_\_   **9.** The liquidity of assets is the convertibility of their value into cash.

\_\_\_\_  \_\_\_\_  **10.** As a firm finances its operations with larger amounts of short term liabilities, profits tend to increase, but so does the risk of technical insolvency.

\_\_\_\_  \_\_\_\_  **11.** In the absence of agreement one way or the other, partners are entitled to receive nothing for extra services rendered.

\_\_\_\_  \_\_\_\_  **12.** To obtain an interest in a firm, a limited partner invests only money and has no say in management.

\_\_\_\_  \_\_\_\_  **13.** Presentment for payment may be made only to the person primarily liable on the instrument.

**T**　**F**

14. If a negotiable promissory note is conditionally delivered, and the condition fails, the maker is not liable to any subsequent holder.

15. Under the UCC, a signature on an instrument which does not clearly indicate it is made in some other capacity, is an endorsement.

16. Where a sight draft is payable at a bank, and the creditor learns that the person to make payment has no funds there to meet it, the creditor is excused from presenting the draft, and may proceed to enforce his legal rights.

17. As between the immediate parties, even a negotiable instrument must have consideration to support it.

18. "William Smith" is an example of a qualified endorsement.

19. A trade acceptance may be discounted at the seller's bank.

20. A straight Bill of Lading is non-negotiable.

21. When a check is negotiated by blank endorsement, all real and personal defenses are waived.

22. "Dishonor" consists in non-payment of a bill or note.

23. Post-dating a check renders it not negotiable.

24. A bank draft is a cashier's check.

25. A sale induced by fraud is voidable by the party who suffered the fraud.

26. A corporation that controls the operations of another corporation through stock ownership is called a holding company.

27. Members of the Board of Directors are expected to act within the doctrine of "The Prudent Man."

28. In the absence of an agreement to the contrary, a partnership is dissolved by the death of a partner.

29. "Capital Stock" means the net assets of the corporation.

**T      F**

____   ____   **30.** A partner's interest in a partnership is susceptible to being seized under legal process.

____   ____   **31.** The effect of stopping goods in transit is to extend the seller's lien to goods that are not in the seller's possession.

____   ____   **32.** A mistake by one party as to the quantity of raw materials does not affect the sale agreement.

____   ____   **33.** A promise to do what one is already obligated to do constitutes consideration.

____   ____   **34.** Title passes immediately to the buyer under a sale or return agreement.

____   ____   **35.** A provision in an acceptance that payment be made in cash usually adds a new term.

____   ____   **36.** Title to future goods passes upon execution of a value contract for sale.

____   ____   **37.** An offer, once it has been communicated, can be withdrawn.

____   ____   **38.** A *lis pendens* puts creditors on notice that there is a pending legal action, yet to be decided.

____   ____   **39.** When there have been prior dealings between merchants, the offeree's silence may constitute an acceptance.

____   ____   **40.** An "acceleration clause" in a note or security agreement gives the holder of the obligation the right to demand full payment at any time before due date if he so desires.

____   ____   **41.** Upon agreeing to pay for goods in full at the time of sale, payment is a condition that takes precedence over the seller's duty to deliver.

____   ____   **42.** Usually, misrepresentation has to be material in order to avoid a contract.

____   ____   **43.** If a payment is made beyond the Statute of Limitations, the debtor can be sued.

____   ____   **44.** Consideration in a contract to sell goods has to be in the form of money.

**T     F**

___  ___  **45.** "Issue" is the first delivery of a instrument complete in form, to an individual who takes it as a holder.

___  ___  **46.** When the drawer of a check stops payment, he is thereafter discharged of all liability on the check.

___  ___  **47.** A certificate of deposit is a certificate by a depositor that he has deposited a certain sum of money with the bank.

___  ___  **48.** Every negotiable instrument is payable at the time fixed therein plus three days of grace.

___  ___  **49.** "Pay to Susan Akins (signed F. Moore)" is an example of a qualified endorsement.

___  ___  **50.** A due bill is a bill of exchange which has become due.

## PART II
## ESSAY QUESTIONS

- Answer any *three* groups of questions from the five groups below.
- Answer *all* parts in each group that you choose.

### GROUP A

1. Why is the Credit Manager concerned with the legal composition of a business?
2. What is the purpose of Chapter 11 under the Bankruptcy Code?
3. What are the debtor's rights under Chapter 11?

### GROUP B

4. Give an example of a contractual lien.
5. Give five of the ten articles of the Uniform Commercial Code (UCC).
6. What is a mechanic's lien designed to accomplish?
7. If there is a provision in the contract against filing of a mechanic's lien, what is the effect?

8. What is the name of the federal act that applies to bonds accompanying contracts awarded pursuant to invitations for bids issued on and after October 25, 1935?

## GROUP C

9. What is the largest single cost item for most banks?
10. Why don't corporations issue more equity?
11. Why is the rating a firm receives on a new bond issue important?
12. The expected cost of bankruptcy is said to depend on two things. What are they?

## GROUP D

13. Thinking in terms of mergers and acquisitions, indicate at least three ways to acquire another company.
14. One of your slow pay accounts was acquired by a prominent corporation. Will your account improve from a credit standpoint? Explain.
15. Balance sheet entries have a plus or minus effect. Indicate opposite each entry whether the effect was plus or minus.
    a) Net worth a/c credited _____
    b) Liability a/c credited _____
    c) New worth a/c debited _____
    d) Asset account credited _____
    e) Asset account debited _____
16. Indicate two examples of contingent liability.

## GROUP E

17. Give a brief explanation of each of the following:
    a) The Sherman Act
    b) The Clayton Act
    c) The Robinson-Patman Act
18. If a marginal account shows a bankruptcy in its credit history should credit be denied? Why?
19. What is a "Promissory Note"?
20. Why are ratios used in financial statement analysis?

## PART III

## CREDIT CASE

## REGAL BUSINESS MACHINES, INC.

Regal Business Machines, Inc. was a division of Mann Corporation responsible for sales of used business machines received as trade-ins through Mann Corporation sales. The credit manager is Morgan Kenney.

While most of the used machines were sold outright, about 25% were leased to customers that preferred this option.

All credit analysts at Regal were responsible for lease sales in their geographic area of responsibility.

Morgan Kenney, upon reviewing a detail of accounts receivable from analyst Louise Den, noted that several of her past due accounts were lease sales, i.e., the salesman delivered the machines and arranged to heave a leasing company pay Regal and contract with the customer to make monthly payments.

Concerned, Morgan spoke to Louise who assured him that she approved the orders only upon receipt of the purchasing order form from the leasing company.

Morgan then asked if purchase requirements had been met prior to her approval. Louise did not understand. Morgan then picked up a purchase order and pointed to a clause standard on all leasing company purchase orders, i.e., "this P.O. is issued subject to meeting all of our requirements indicated below." Louise seemed confused. Morgan then pointed to the "requirements below":

1. First and last payment
2. Signed agreement
3. UCC 1

In addition, he asked to see all of her lease accounts. This was not readily apparent since three other leasing companies were used in the past. Upon review, Morgan discovered that 85% of the leasing company invoices were past due.

Louise obviously did not differentiate between regular and leasing company purchase orders. Although in her role for five years, apparently no one had told her otherwise and Morgan simply assumed that she knew better.

1. What must be done to rectify the problem?
2. Should Morgan terminate Louise?

## SAMPLE CCE EXAMINATION
## ANSWERS
## PART I

| | | | |
|---|---|---|---|
| 1. | T | 26. | T |
| 2. | T | 27. | T |
| 3. | T | 28. | T |
| 4. | T | 29. | F |
| 5. | T | 30. | T |
| 6. | T | 31. | T |
| 7. | T | 32. | T |
| 8. | T | 33. | F |
| 9. | T | 34. | T |
| 10. | T | 35. | F |
| 11. | T | 36. | F |
| 12. | T | 37. | T |
| 13. | F | 38. | T |
| 14. | F | 39. | T |
| 15. | T | 40. | F |
| 16. | T | 41. | T |
| 17. | T | 42. | T |
| 18. | F | 43. | T |
| 19. | T | 44. | F |
| 20. | T | 45. | T |
| 21. | F | 46. | F |
| 22. | T | 47. | F |
| 23. | F | 48. | F |
| 24. | F | 49. | F |
| 25. | T | 50. | T |

## GROUP A—ANSWERS

1. Because it is important to know about 1) the continuity of the business, 2) the capital-raising potential, and 3) the liability of the principals.
2. To reorganize and rehabilitate a debtor whereby all parties of interest are dealt with in a fair and equitable manner.
3. 1. The debtor-in-possession has the right to operate the business inside the ordinary course of business.
   2. The debtor-in-possession has all the rights and power of a trustee with limited exceptions.
   3. The debtor-in-possession has the exclusive right to file a plan of reorganization within the first 120 days after filing the bankruptcy petition.

## GROUP B—ANSWERS

4. Assume this buyer XYZ Co. orders 200,000 bolts from your company to be delivered at 20,000 per month for ten months. XYZ takes delivery on and pays for 120,000 bolts over a period of six months. XYZ also pays for 10,000 more bolts in advance. But in the seventh, eighth, nine and tenth months, XYZ does not take the other 80,000 bolts, even though they paid for 10,000 of them, you (the seller) have suffered damage. These damages constitute a claim against XYZ Co. The contractual lien allows you to have a lien on all the bolts still in your possession even though 10,000 of them are already paid for. Hence a lien is granted by the buyer to the seller on goods that have been paid for but are still in seller's possession.
5. 1. General provisions
   2. Sales
   3. Commercial paper
   4. Bank deposits and collections
   5. Letters of Credit
   6. Bulk transfer
   7. Warehouse receipts, B/L's, and other proof-of-title documents
   8. Investment securities
   9. Secured transactions

10. Effective date and repeals
6. To secure to the materialman compensation for work and labor performed or material furnished for construction, repair or alteration of a building or improvement.
7. A number of states held that such a clause does not preclude the principal contractor from claiming a lien but applies only to subcontractors and materialmen; the states are Arkansas, Idaho, Illinois, Massachusetts, New York and Washington.
8. The Miller Act

## GROUP C—ANSWERS

9. The cost of funds, mostly interest on deposits, plus borrowed funds.
10. They have not needed new equity.
Equity is expensive to issue.
There is a management preference on earnings per share.
11. Because it affects the interest rate the firm must offer.
12. The probability that bankruptcy will likely occur.
The cost of bankruptcy if it does occur.

## GROUP D—ANSWERS

13. a) Leveraged stock
    b) Exchange of stock
    c) Cash or short term financing
    d) Long-term financing
    e) Equity-financing
14. Yes. Because the surviving company assumes liability for debts of the companies party to the acquisition.
15. a) Increase
    b) Increase
    c) Decrease
    d) Decrease
    e) Increase
16. a) Pending lawsuits
    b) Possible additional taxes for prior years. These are not liabilities in fact, but liabilities may result because of existing circumstances.

## GROUP E—ANSWERS

17. a) Sherman Act—prohibits contracts, combinations and conspiracies in restraint of trade.

   b) Clayton Act—intended to correct defects in the Sherman Act, and to supplement it by granting certain administrative agencies power to stop violations of the law before an offense has occurred.

   c) Robinson-Patman Act—is an amendment to the Clayton Act and provides that it shall be unlawful for any person engaged in commerce to discriminate in price between different purchasers of like grade and quality of goods.

18. Usually no. Because the record since the bankruptcy should determine current credit worthiness.

19. "An unconditional promise in writing made by one person to another, signed by the maker, engaging to pay on demand or at a fixed or determinable future time, a sum certain in money to order of bearer."

   For a past due account it is a way to obtain written acknowledgement of the debt and by postponing the due date transfers the account from Accounts Receivable to Notes Receivable.

20. To measure relationships between balance sheet items and profit and loss detail. Ratios are often used to aid in the appraisal of financial data preliminary to determining a customer's financial strength.

# CCE EXAMINATION TYPICAL QUESTIONS & ANSWERS

Below are typical questions and answers which are likely to appear on the CCE examination.

1. **Q.** What is a mechanic's lien designed to accomplish?

   **A.** A mechanic's lien is used to secure compensation for labor and materials purchased for construction, repair, or alteration of a building or improvement.

2. **Q.** What is the liquidity of a particular asset?

   **A.** The liquidity of an asset is the convertibility of an asset into cash. The closer an asset is to being converted into cash during the normal course of business, the higher is its liquidity.

3. **Q.** What is the difference between a general partner and a limited partner with respect to the firm's management decisions?

   **A.** A general partner is part of the firm's management and has a say in the firm's decisions. A limited partner has no such say in management decisions.

4. **Q.** Describe the effects on the possibility of insolvency if a firm finances with short-term debt rather than equity.

   **A.** Short-term debt financing must be refinanced each time it comes due. If the firm is unable to refinance, perhaps due to poor financial results, it may face insolvency. The same is not true for equity. Thus, using more short-term debt financing increases insolvency risk.

5. **Q.** Give two of the requirements for a negotiable instrument, as defined by the Uniform Commercial Code.

   **A.** Any two of the following are correct:
   1. The instrument must be in writing.
   2. The instrument must be an unconditional promise to pay a certain sum of money.
   3. The instrument must be payable on demand or at a specified time.
   4. The instrument must be payable to order or bearer.

6. **Q.** What type of ratios measure the productivity of the firm's various types of assets?

   **A.** Turnover ratios measure the productivity of the firm's assets in producing sales. Any turnover ratio is computed by dividing the year's sales by the book value of the asset. Higher ratios generally indicate higher asset productivity; however, turnover ratios which are too high indicate overtrading.

7. **Q.** Give the two basic requirements for a firm to be creditworthy.

   **A.** Ability to pay and willingness to pay.

8. **Q.** What is the purpose of the control function in managing a credit department?

   **A.** The purpose of the control function is to see that a credit department performs according to its planned objectives and strategy.

9. **Q.** Give two objectives that the credit manager should keep in

mind when performing collections from customers.

**A.** Any two of the following are correct:
1. Proceed systematically with collection effort.
2. Get the customer to discuss the matter.
3. Get the money.
4. Preserve customer goodwill.

**10. Q.** When exchanging credit information, the credit manager must be concerned with possible actions by the debtor for libel. Give and explain one of the two defenses to the charge of libel.

**A.** Either of the following is correct:
1. Truth.   Truth is a complete defense if all statements made are true (not if part is true and part is untrue).
2. Privileged communications.   These are statements made to another person who has a similar interest in the debtor, such as another creditor. However, if the communication is shown to be malicious, this defense can be overthrown.

**11. Q.** Give one source of industry ratios for comparison purposes.

**A.** Any of the following three is correct:
1. Robert Morris Associates (*Annual Statement Studies*)
2. Dun and Bradstreet (*Key Business Ratios*)
3. If the seller has a large number of customers, ratio information may be extracted from its customer database.

**12. Q.** Under the antitrust statutes, granting different terms of sale to customers purchasing the same product is legal under some circumstances. Give and briefly discuss one such circumstance.

**A.** Either of the following is correct:
1. When the buyer is receiving an equivalent product or service from another seller who has granted these terms (the "meeting competition in good faith" defense).
2. When the costs of the sale are lower for that particular customer (typically because of differences in shipping costs—the "cost justification defense").

**13. Q.** Are corporations primarily regulated by state or federal laws? Explain your answer.

**A.** Corporations are primarily regulated by state law. While the Constitution outlines the corporate form of organization, its rights and powers are generally restricted by the laws in the state in which it is incorporated; it is a "foreign corporation" in other states.

**14. Q.** When prices are falling, which inventory valuation method— LIFO or FIFO—overvalues inventory? Explain your answer.

**A.** The answer is LIFO. In a falling market, the LIFO method (in which the last units of inventory are removed first in accounting for inventory value) leaves older merchandise in the inventory's accounting value. In a falling market, this older inventory is overvalued, since it can be purchased currently at a lower price.

**15. Q.** Explain the use of the cost of capital in making credit management decisions.

**A.** The cost of capital is the seller's weighted-average cost of funds; it is the average return required by the seller's suppliers of capital. In credit management, the cost of capital is used in allowing for the time value of money for credit decisions which involve investment in assets.

**16. Q.** Give an advantage and a disadvantage of informing the customer of his or her credit line.

**A.** Advantages. Any of the following is correct:
1. Revealing the credit line allows an opportunity to discuss the customer's credit position.
2. Revealing the credit line reduces the difficulties that occur when an order is held because the credit line is insufficient.

The disadvantage is that customer goodwill may be lost, as the customer may view a relatively low credit line as a lack of confidence in management's ability to run the firm.

**17. Q.** A firm increases cash by $10,000, decreases accounts receivable by $40,000, and increases short-term borrowings by $25,000. What will be the change in net working capital resulting from these actions?

**A.** Increases in assets increase net working capital; increases in liabilities decrease net working capital:

| | |
|---|---:|
| Effect of change in cash: | +$10,000 |
| Effect of change in receivables: | −$40,000 |
| Effect of change in short-term borrowings: | −$25,000 |
| Change in net working capital: | −$55,000 |

**18. Q.** Which of the following most nearly represents the meaning of an auditor's certificate containing an unqualified opinion? Why?

   a. The auditor has reviewed the accounting data but has not made any internal or external checks to assess its validity.

   b. The auditor has assessed that the accounting data conform to generally accepted accounting principles. External and internal checks have been performed to assess this.

   c. The auditor has assessed that the accounting data are representative of the true value of the firm, should the firm or its assets be sold.

   **A.** The answer is *b*. Alternative *a* is incorrect; rendering an unqualified opinion requires internal and external checks. Alternative *c* is incorrect in that the auditor certified to accounting procedures, not market value. Alternative *b* most nearly describes the auditing process which results in an unqualified opinion.

**19. Q.** Explain the financing technique called "factoring without recourse."

   **A.** This technique is equivalent to the sale of accounts receivable assets as soon as they are generated via sales. The factor checks credit, makes credit-granting decisions, and purchases the resulting receivables. The factor bears all bad-debt and slowness costs in this arrangement.

**20. Q.** Explain the effects of a subordination arrangement on a debtor's creditworthiness.

   **A.** A subordination agreement reverses the order of claims in default between two creditors. If the seller can obtain such an agreement, it places the seller in a preferred position relative to the other claimant and thus increases the buyer's creditworthiness.

Below are typical essay questions which are likely to appear on the CCE examination:

**1. Q.** Explain why analysis of accounting ratios may not capture the true financial condition of a firm, even if the firm's statements are prepared using GAAP.

   **A.** The main reason why a firm's accounting statements may not capture its true financial condition concerns the difference between accounting conventions and market value. It is the market value of assets that best represents their earning power and liquidation value, but accounting values may diverge from these market values for several reasons. First, GAAP is a broad set of guidelines, and some accounting conventions produce accounting values which are closer to market values than do others. Second, all GAAP relies, to a great extent, on historic cost in computing asset value, and historic cost is frequently not representative of current market value. The classic example is land, which is held on the books at its purchase price, regardless of the relationship between that price and its value today. If accounting data do not fully capture market values, ratios based on these accounting data will be inaccurate in measuring true financial condition.

2. **Q.** Give and discuss the important characteristics of business credit that distinguish it from other types of credit.

**A.** Business credit, also known as trade credit, can be distinguished from other types of credit in a number of ways. Consumer credit is granted directly to end-users of products or services, and business credit is granted by one business to another.

3. **Q.** Discuss two important considerations in deciding whether credit functions should be centralized or decentralized.

**A.** Any two of the following are correct:
   1. The advantage of physical proximity to customers. A decentralized credit department, with field offices near customers, can monitor and visit customers at lower cost.
   2. Structure of the sales function. If the sales function is decentralized, contact and coordination with salespersons is facilitated if credit is also decentralized.
   3. Need for coordination, communication, and common training among credit personnel. Use of uniform policies and procedures is more difficult when the credit function is decentralized and communications among credit personnel are thus more cumbersome. Similarly, it is harder to schedule training and development activities when personnel must come from several locations.

**4. Q.** Explain the tradeoffs between using a simple system for automated approval of initial orders (for example, one based on agency ratings) versus a system where more initial credit investigation is performed.

**A.** The main advantage of a simple system is a reduction of the direct and indirect costs of credit investigation. This expense is reduced because: (1) out-of-pocket costs of credit investigation, such as the costs of agency reports, are avoided, and (2) the time of the credit manager is saved for other activities. Further, order entry is expedited, since such a system produces quick decisions. Set against these advantages are the costs of somewhat less accurate credit-granting decisions. Agency ratings are only rough guidelines; some customers will be granted credit based on these ratings who would be refused if more investigation was performed, and some customers will be refused credit who would be granted credit under other credit investigation systems.

**5. Q.** Explain the effects of a sale-and-leaseback arrangement by a customer on that customer's creditworthiness.

**A.** A sale-and-leaseback arrangement involves the sale of a major asset (such as a headquarters building) and the long-term leaseback of this asset by the firm. Entering into such a transaction has long- and short-term effects on creditworthiness. In the short term, cash (and thus liquidity) are increased. However, long term, the firm takes on increased payment obligations (via the lease payments) which result in cash outflows and thus decreased creditworthiness.

**6. Q.** Explain the differences in (1) income tax treatment and (2) liability for debts between a Subchapter S corporation and a sole proprietorship.

**A.** There are small differences in income tax treatment. For a sole proprietorship, all income is taxed as personal income to the proprietor. For the Subchapter S corporation, income which is distributed to the stockholders is taxed as personal income, and income which is not distributed is taxed personally based on the percentage of ownership. The differences in liability are much greater. Subject to state laws (such as homestead laws), the proprietor is liable for the debts of the business, while the liability of shareholders of Subchapter S corporations is limited to the amount invested.

**7. Q.** Explain the effects on (1) default risk and (2) recovery to creditors in liquidation if a debtor sells preferred stock and uses the funds to repurchase its own common stock.

**A.** Under most circumstances this change does not affect recovery in liquidation, since both common and preferred shareholders come after debtholders in the distribution of liquidation proceeds. There is some increase in default risk, however, because preferred stock generally requires a fixed stream of dividend payments. While failing to pay these dividends does not constitute default in the same way it would if the firm financed with debt, there generally are penalties for nonpayment of preferred dividends which management would prefer to avoid. Consequently, issuing preferred stock to replace common increases the default risk of the debtor by increasing cash outflows.

**8. Q.** In analyzing a firm's financial statements, you see a rather large liability labeled "deferred taxes." What insight might this item give you regarding the value of the firm's depreciable assets?

**A.** This liability usually results from differences between the depreciation schedules used for tax and reporting purposes. When the firm depreciates assets faster for tax purposes than for reporting purposes, taxes are deferred and this liability is created. While it is always in the firm's interest to delay paying taxes as long as is legally possible (because of the time value of money), a large entry of this sort may indicate that the firm has elected to depreciate assets very slowly for reporting purposes. Such a depreciation schedule may result in assets which appear at values larger than their current market value.

**9. Q.** Discuss why liquidity ratios are very important in the analysis of debtors when the creditor is granting short-term credit.

**A.** When the debt is due in a very short time (say, 60 days or less), as is typical with trade credit, the ability of the debtor to pay is to a great extent determined by the debtor's sources of short-term cash and the amount of cash needed to pay debts coming due. That is, this ability to pay will be determined by the amount of the debtor's current cash balance, the conversion of the debtor's existing short-term assets (typically, receivables and inventory) into cash, and the payments that the debtor must make on existing obligations. Liquidity ratios measure these factors.

**10. Q.** Explain how Sight Draft/Bill of Lading (SD/BL) terms are used in domestic collections.

**A.** These terms can be used when the customer must obtain a negotiable bill of lading in order to take possession of the goods. Under SD/BL terms, the seller sends both the bill of lading and a draft to the customer's bank. The customer must agree to pay the draft in order to obtain the bill of lading (and thus the goods). The major risks to the seller are: (1) paperwork errors in which the buyer obtains the merchandise without agreeing to pay the draft, and (2) transportation costs for returning the goods if, on receipt of the bill of lading and draft at the bank, the customer refuses to accept the draft.

**11. Q.** You are selling to a firm whose business is seasonal, with its peak selling season occurring at Christmas. Discuss the yearly patterns in this firm's cash, accounts receivable, inventory, and accounts payable if the firm is financially healthy.

**A.** In a business such as this, inventory is accumulated prior to the selling season, and should peak just before that season starts, declining as the season progresses. Sales from inventory will result in receivables, which follow a pattern opposite to that of inventory; receivables should be at their lowest level at the beginning of the selling season and the highest at the end. Cash should follow a pattern slightly lagging receivables, with a peak just after the selling season as receivables are collected. Payables will generally follow the pattern of inventories.

**12. Q.** In analyzing a customer's financial statements, the credit manager may elect to "adjust" the statements by increasing or reducing the value of some assets or liabilities or may change the maturity of these items (for example, by analyzing certain long-term debt as current debt instead). Explain why the credit manager might want to make these changes, even if the financial statement is prepared based on GAAP.

A. There are several reasons why the credit manager may want to make such adjustments, even if the debtor's accounting statements are based on GAAP. First, GAAP is based on historic costs and prices, and the credit manager may want to adjust statements to reflect current market values of assets, which may be greater or less than accounting values. For example, the credit manager might decrease the value of machinery and equipment (and adjust the firm's net worth to reflect these changes) if he or she feels that this equipment is worth less than accounting value. Second, GAAP assumes a "continuing firm"; that is, that the firm will continue to operate much as it currently operates. But it is the credit manager's job, in part, to anticipate changes from the current structure. Thus, for example, the credit manager might choose to treat a long-term loan from a shareholder as current debt under the assumption that such a debt would be paid off early if the debtor experiences financial difficulties.

13. Q. Explain the difference between cash discount and an anticipation discount.

A. The difference lies in how the dollar amount of the discount is calculated. For a cash discount, the dollar amount of the discount (say, 2% of the invoice value) is the same as long as the invoice is paid before a certain date (say, ten days after the date that the invoice is rendered). For an anticipation discount, the dollar amount of the discount is calculated based on a yearly discount rate (say, 5% per year) and the fraction of year before the due date that the invoice is paid. Thus, the dollar amount of the anticipation discount will vary with the time that payment is made.

15. Q. A debtor has come to you with a proposal for a voluntary settlement for less than the amount of the receivable, and states that, if the settlement is refused, the debtor will probably be forced to seek bankruptcy protection. Discuss the advantages and disadvantages of accepting the voluntary settlement relative to bankruptcy proceedings.

A. There are several advantages to the voluntary settlement. First, such a settlement typically involves payment over a reasonably short time (though longer-term arrangements are sometimes used), while bankruptcy proceedings are often stretched out over extended periods. Second, acceptance of the voluntary arrangement removes some of the uncertainty regarding the amount of the recovery; the voluntary settlement gives a promised payment schedule, while the amount that would be recovered by creditors if the firm was liquidated is uncertain. Finally, voluntary settlements avoid the out-of-pocket costs of legal proceedings, such as attorney costs, which occur in bankruptcy for both the debtor and creditor. However, the voluntary settlement also has disadvantages. First, the amount recovered may be less than the potential recovery in bankruptcy. The credit manager would need to perform estimates and calculations to assess this. Second, the debtor may default on the voluntary settlement, resulting in bankruptcy anyway. Finally, a voluntary settlement does not present protection from other creditors; unsatisfied creditors can still sue, to the detriment of creditors bound by voluntary agreements for deferred payment.

16. **Q.** Explain the advantages of a comprehensive written credit policy over an unwritten policy relying on oral communications.

**A.** While a credit policy based on oral traditions can be almost as formal as a written one, there are several advantages to putting credit policy in writing. First, the very process of producing the document requires that any differences among credit managers about policy be resolved. Second, a written policy continues beyond the individual credit managers currently employed. Third, written policy promotes consistency in decision-making among analysts. Finally, a written policy provides an advantageous basis for training of new credit personnel.

17. **Q.** Explain why DSO can give misleading implications regarding receivable turnover when sales volumes change over time.

**A.** DSO is usually computed by dividing the accounts receivable balance by average sales and multiplying this by the number of days in the year. The problem stems from the relationship between average sales and receivables balances when sales change over time (due, for example, to seasonality or growth). When average sales are compared to receivable balances from months when sales were different from this average, the result can be a DSO that fluctuates when no change in customers' payment patterns has occurred or a DSO does not indicate a change when, in fact, payment patterns have changed considerably.

**18. Q.** Explain the advantages and disadvantages of form letters as collection devices.

   **A.** The advantage of form letters is that they are inexpensive relative to other collection alternatives such as telephone calls or individually prepared letters. However, while modern printing technologies have made it more difficult to identify form letters as such, they still generally elicit fewer payments than other follow-up devices.

**19. Q.** You are a credit manager and one of your accounts is growing very rapidly. From conversations with management, you understand that the firm, which is currently a partnership, is considering incorporation. Explain the implications for credit management should the firm make this change.

   **A.** The principal disadvantage of this change of legal form is that the personal wealth of the general partners will be shielded from creditors. However, creditors should also see a positive feature in this procedure, considering the firm's rapid growth. Rapidly growing firms are starved for capital, and may overuse trade credit financing (including paying creditors slowly). Incorporation makes it much easier for the firm to finance via the sale of equity, which may relieve the burden on trade creditors.

**20. Q.** For typical discount terms of sale (such as 2%, 10, net 30), is the effective cost of lost discount higher or lower than the typical borrower's cost of capital? What are the implications of this comparison for the credit manager selling to accounts on such discount terms?

   **A.** For most terms of sale, the effective cost of lost discount is far beyond the typical borrower's cost of capital. For 2% 10 net 30, for example, the effective cost is greater than 36% per year. In fact, for most discount terms, the cost of lost discount is so high that even rapidly growing, capital-starved firms would not find skipping the discount to be an attractive financing mechanism. Firms who skip the discount are usually firms who are: (1) very unsophisticated financially, or (2) in such poor financial condition that they cannot obtain financing elsewhere.

## CASE STUDY. ACME INDUSTRIES

You are a credit manager; your employer is a manufacturer of metal products. Your firm has an annual sales volume of $50M. The firm was founded over 30 years ago and has been very successful. However, the recently hired Vice President of Finance (the prior VP had retired) has brought some new ideas to the firm. The new VP has been examining various financial policies, including credit policy, with the intent of increasing profits and reducing risks wherever possible. Acme Industries has been identified as an account where profits might be improved or risk reduced.

Acme Industries, a contractor-distributor, has been a customer for five years and has developed into your firm's largest account; yearly sales to Acme are approximately $2M. Your terms of sale are 2% 10 days, net 30 days, which are also the terms on which Acme buys most of its materials from other vendors. Acme pays your invoices in four or five months (losing the cash discount in the process); the balance owed varies between $600,000 and $800,000. (Audited financial statements for Acme for the fiscal year just ended are presented in Exhibit 11.1.) Acme obtains part of its short-term financing via a revolving line of credit, which is secured by the firm's inventory and receivables. The interest on this line is 1.5% above prime, and the balance currently owing is $700,000.

## CASE QUESTIONS. ACME INDUSTRIES

1. You have obtained the following industry average ratios for firms similar to Acme:

| | |
|---|---|
| Liquidity Ratios | |
| Current Ratio | 1.50 |
| Quick Ratio | 0.90 |
| Debt Ratios | |
| Total Debt/Total Assets | 0.60 |
| Total Debt/Equity | 1.50 |

Turnover Ratios

| | |
|---|---|
| Sales/Total Assets | 2.50 |
| Sales/Accts. Rec. | 8.00 |
| Avg. Collection Period (days) | 45.00 |
| CGS/Inventory | 6.00 |

Profitability Ratios

| | |
|---|---|
| Income after Tax/Sales | 2.00 |
| Income after Tax/Total Assets | 5.00 |
| Income after Tax/Equity | 12.50 |

Compare Acme's financial position to that of the average firm in this industry. Discuss differences in liquidity, debt, turnover, and profitability.

2. One way in which a credit manager may increase profitability and reduce risk is by counseling customers. Suggest ways by which Acme might, at relatively little cost, improve its financial position to the advantage of both itself and its trade creditors.

3. Suggest several credit strategies by which sales to Acme might be made more profitable or less risky.

## SAMPLE ANSWERS TO ACME INDUSTRIES CASE QUESTIONS

1. The required ratio analysis is:

| Ratio Analysis: | Acme | Industry |
|---|---|---|
| Liquidity Ratios | | |
| Current Ratio | 1.163 | 1.500 |
| Quick Ratio | 0.546 | 0.900 |
| Debt Ratios | | |
| Total Debt/Total Assets | 0.834 | 0.600 |
| Total Debt/Equity | 5.012 | 1.500 |
| Turnover Ratios | | |
| Sales/Total Assets | 3.022 | 2.500 |
| Sales/Accts. Rec. | 7.242 | 8.000 |
| Avg. Collection Period (days) | 48.960 | 45.000 |
| CGS/Inventory | 4.667 | 6.000 |

Profitability Ratios

| | | |
|---|---|---|
| Income after Tax/Sales | 0.70 | 2.00 |
| Income after Tax/Total Assets | 2.13 | 5.00 |
| Income after Tax/Equity | 12.79 | 12.50 |

Liquidity ratios show that the firm is less liquid than the average firm in the industry. Turnover ratios for accounts receivable and inventory show these major current assets to be near industry levels (though inventory balances are a bit high), so the atypically low liquidity is almost certainly due to relatively heavy short-term borrowings. This is evidenced by the debt ratios, which show that debt financing is much higher than average. This higher leverage, along with higher sales/assets, allows the firm to provide a similar return on equity to other firms in the industry, even though Acme makes less profit on each unit sold. Low liquidity and high debt make the firm an above-average credit risk.

2. Acme is burdened by high short-term debt owed to trade creditors and to the bank. One solution would be to obtain more long-term financing, secured by fixed assets, but the fixed assets' value is not sufficient to provide much help ($100,000 in financing at a maximum). Other possible solutions include factoring of accounts receivable or an inventory loan secured by the firm's inventory. There is significant available collateral, since these accounts total $3.8M and the banks' credit line exposure is only $700,000. When suggesting these alternatives, the credit manager should point out to Acme two advantages of replacing trade debt with financing of these sorts. First, the cost of such financing would be partly offset by the ability to take cash discounts. Second, paying promptly would increase Acme's bargaining power with suppliers with regard to price and shipping schedules.

3. Three possible alternatives for increasing the profitability or reducing the risk in selling to Acme are:

   a. The seller can institute a late charge program. While such programs are usually resisted, late charge revenue will increase the profitability of sales to Acme.

   b. The seller can reduce the balance owed by Acme by trading orders more aggressively. This may, of course, result in lost sales.

c. The seller may take a secondary security interest in Acme's account receivable and inventory. This will make the account less risky by raising the recovery in default, though it may adversely affect Acme's ability to obtain trade credit from other sellers.

## EXHIBIT 11.1 Acme Industries Financial Statements for Fiscal 1990

(all figures are in rounded thousands)

### Income Statement

| | |
|---|---|
| Sales | $12,500 |
| Cost of Goods Sold | 9,800 |
| Selling and Admin. Exp. | 2,500 |
| Interest Expense | 90 |
| Income Before Tax | $110 |
| Federal & State Inc. Tax | 22 |
| Income After Tax | $88 |
| Dividends | 30 |
| Additions to Retained Earnings | $58 |

### Balance Sheet

| | | | |
|---|---|---|---|
| Cash | $118 | Accounts Payable | $2,400 |
| Accts. Rec. less reserve | $1,700 | Bank Credit Line | 700 |
| Inventories | 2,100 | Current Portion of Long | |
| Prepaid Expenses | 40 | Term Debt | 50 |
| Total Current Assets | $3,958 | Dividends Payable | 8 |
| | | Accrued Bonuses | 55 |
| | | Accrued Expenses | 176 |
| Buildings | 22 | Due to Empl. Profit Shar. | |
| Vehicles | 200 | Fund | 9 |
| Furniture & Fixtures | 100 | Federal Inc. Tax Due | 6 |
| Machinery & Equipment | 90 | Total Current Liabil. | $3,404 |
| Leasehold Improvements | 20 | | |
| Gross Fixed Assets | $432 | Long Term Debt | 44 |
| Less: Accum. Deprec. | 279 | Common Stock | $200 |
| Net Fixed Assets | $153 | Retained Earnings | 488 |
| Surrender Value Life Ins. | 25 | Total Equity | $688 |
| Total Assets | $4,136 | Total Liab. & Equity | $4,136 |

# CHAPTER TWELVE

# QUESTIONS AND ANSWERS APPLICABLE TO ALL EXAMINATIONS

## INTRODUCTION

Contained herein are sample questions and answers of the variety that are likely to appear on all designation examinations and the Credit Administration Program (CAP) including the Advanced Credit Administration Program (ACAP).

It is important to keep in mind that the questions and answers selected relate to skills used on a day-to-day basis in the credit function. Do not feel that you must be totally correct on every question or problem. If, for example, you get about two thirds correct, you are well advised to consider your answers as minimally passing.

The pool of questions has been edited to assure correct grammar usage and has undergone a review to minimize any ambiguities. The minimum passing grade for each designation level is geared to satisfy professional standards. Test specifications are set by the NACM Accreditation Committee which has oversight responsibility for all of the professional designations. The specifications define content areas to be covered by examination questions, the emphasis of each content area, appropriateness of question type, what the total number of questions should be, time allowance for the examination, and whether failing candidates are to be provided with diagnostic information. The Accreditation Committee seeks input from both practitioners and content experts in the formulation of examination questions.

Please keep in mind that the more difficult the question reviewed, the higher the level, i.e., supervisory, management, and senior management or basic, intermediate, and advanced. Further, because the CAP and ACAP academic programs prepare individuals for the Career Roadmap progression leading from CBA to CBF to CCE, the questions encountered with CAP and ACAP courses are of the type likely to appear on designation tests as well.

## SAMPLE FORMAT OF EXAMINATION

1. **Q.** How do you go about planning to hire staff for the credit department?

   **A.** Prepare job descriptions and job specifications for the openings and then recruit individuals who closely match job requirements.

2. **Q.** Name the four areas the credit management functions are divided into.

   **A.** 1) Credit approval process, 2) order processing, 3) accounts receivable administration, and 4) collection & adjustment.

3. **Q.** Can a sales order be approved without a credit investigation? Explain.

   **A.** Yes. Requirements accounts, usually top companies, are rated on company capacity and do not require a separate investigation.

4. **Q.** What is the main difference between bank credit and business credit?

   **A.** With bank credit, no cash changes hands when a loan is made. Instead, a paper amount is established in the borrower's account. With business credit, credit is granted by a supplier selling goods for resale at a profit, terms are short, sales are unsecured on open account, and cash discounts may be offered for payment before the net due date.

**5. Q.** Name and describe three forms of credit, e.g., agriculture credit.

**A.** 1) Agriculture: highly seasonal, high risk, hence involvement of the federal government in financing farm ventures.
2) Investment: Placement of funds in productive assets to earn a profit.
3) Consumer: Credit used by banks and businesses to encourage consumer sales.

# CREDIT MANAGEMENT TYPICAL QUESTIONS & ANSWERS

## PART I

**1. Q.** What does A/R administration mean from a credit viewpoint?
   **A.** Control of open Accounts Receivable.

**2. Q.** Who is ultimately responsible for customer account status?
   **A.** The credit manager and his superior.

**3. Q.** For adequate reports to each control point, what is needed?
   **A.** A systematic follow-up system.

**4. Q.** Should controls and guidelines be established? Why?
   **A.** Yes, to ensure that all accounts are monitored.

**5. Q.** Who should set guidelines and parameters to be used by data processing people establishing computer systems for credit, collection, and A/R?
   **A.** The credit manager and his superior.

**6. Q.** What does interdependence of sales and credit boil down to?
   **A.** Credit needs sales and sales needs credit.

**7. Q.** What is said to be a key function of the corporate credit manager?
   **A.** To ensure that cash flow is maintained at optimum levels.

**8. Q.** The management of credit occurs at three principal levels. Name the three levels.
   **A.** Requirements accounts, average accounts, and marginal accounts.

**9. Q.** What are the five goals of dynamic credit management?
   **A.** 1. Increased sales and profits.
   2. Improved quality of work performed.

      3. Increased efficiency.

      4. Decreased cost per unit of work performed.

      5. Greater satisfaction attributable to results achieved.

**10. Q.** What is effective control based upon?

     **A.** Conscientious monitoring and follow-up of all accounts.

*If you have not turned in an interim case study evaluated by the instructor, you will be furnished with a mini-case from which to draw conclusions and arrive at a decision.*

# CREDIT MANAGEMENT TYPICAL QUESTIONS & ANSWERS

## PART II

**1. Q.** What purpose does a credit policy serve?

     **A.** Serves to guide all credit department personnel on a day-to-day basis.

**2. Q.** What is the best way to establish a credit policy?

     **A.** By involving top management, sales, and credit department personnel.

**3. Q.** What is a credit file?

     **A.** A file containing information on an account approved for credit.

**4. Q.** What is a chronological file?

     **A.** A numbered file which is suspended for follow-up on a future date.

**5. Q.** What is an open invoice?

     **A.** An invoice for sales which has not yet been paid.

**6. Q.** Why is a credit manual said to be useful?

     **A.** Provides a reference source for procedures on day-to-day activities.

**7. Q.** Name three types of float.

     **A.** Post-dated check, late payment of an invoice, and use of credit cards.

**8. Q.** Briefly describe each of the above types of float.

     **A.** A post-dated check is a check that contains a future date. Late payment of an invoice means paying later than allowed by the terms of the sale. The use of credit cards refers to charging the balance due to a credit card.

9. **Q.** Name four methods of gathering cash.

   **A.** Direct mail, lock box, factor, and cash before delivery (CBD).

10. Mini-case study furnished by the instructor.

The case study will vary from one instructor to another.

Refer to NIC's Credit Management Cases which are available from NIC.

# CREDIT MANAGEMENT TYPICAL QUESTIONS & ANSWERS

## PART III

1. **Q.** When questions arise concerning particular application of state laws, what is the best source to consult?

   **A.** NACM's *Credit Manual of Commercial Laws.*

2. **Q.** Why is the credit manager concerned with the legal composition of a business?

   **A.** To determine management composition and competence.

3. **Q.** Briefly describe a joint venture.

   **A.** Business venture between two or more parties on a one-time basis where profits, losses, and control are shared.

4. **Q.** Why enter into a joint venture?

   **A.** Profit or loss is shared between two or more parties.

5. **Q.** Why would a company want credit insurance?

   **A.** To reduce the level of bad debt.

6. **Q.** Is it necessary to obtain a financial statement on all accounts over $5000? Explain.

   **A.** Not necessarily, it depends on the reputation of the firm.

7. **Q.** What purpose do balance sheet ratios serve?

   **A.** To assess the company's financial condition and draw conclusions from a comparison with others in the same industry.

8. **Q.** What is a pro-forma statement? How is it useful?

   **A.** One that is prepared in advance of the official financial statement.

9. **Q.** Why are nonfinancial factors considered to be important in evaluating a new account?

    **A.** They provide insight on management and valuable antecedent information.

**10.** **Q.** Mini-case study furnished by instructor.
    **A.** See NIC's Credit Management Cases.

# CREDIT MANAGEMENT TYPICAL QUESTIONS & ANSWERS

## PART IV

*NOTE: Students are to use pocket calculators to make calculations.*

**1.** **Q.** Explain accrual accounting.
    **A.** The method of recognizing income when earned and expenses when incurred regardless of when cash is received or disbursed.

**2.** **Q.** You are given the following information for XYZ company.

| | Credit Sales | |
| --- | --- | --- |
| | Year 1 | Year 2 |
| January-August | $215,000 | $15,000 |
| September | 5,000 | 30,000 |
| October | 5,000 | 5,000 |
| November | 5,000 | 5,000 |
| December | 30,000 | 5,000 |

The company had to close down for the first half of year 2. That's why sales were only $15,000 from January to August. Credit terms are set 45 days, customers pay on time, sales are spread evenly during the month, and for simplicity, assume 30-day months. Given the above information, the A/R balances at the end of the last 3 months were:

| | Year 1 | Year 2 |
| --- | --- | --- |
| October | $ 7,500 | $20,000 |
| November | 7,500 | 7,500 |
| December | 32,500 | 7,500 |

    a. Compute the DSO for years 1 and 2 using the end of December receivables balance in the numerator and the average

daily sales for the last 360 days in the denominator.
   b. Compute the DSO for years 1 and 2 using the NASM procedure.
   c. Comment on the impact of the use of average and ratios.
   **A.** a, b, and c. The decision to whether to grant or deny credit depends on corporate policy, therefore no absolute answer is provided.
3. Case study furnished by the instructor.

# CREDIT MANAGEMENT TYPICAL QUESTIONS & ANSWERS

## PART V

*NOTE: Students are to use pocket calculators to make calculations.*

1. **Q.** It was Steve's second week as a credit analyst for XYZ Bank. His assignment was to perform an in-depth analysis of a local firm. The firm's net income for the past year was $25,000 and depreciation expense was $15,000. Steve told his boss that the firm's cash flow for the year was $40,000. If you were Steve's boss, how would you respond.
   **A.** I would ask Steve to show me how he arrived at his conclusion.
2. **Q.** Explain why and how certain assets and current liabilities change automatically with sales.
   **A.** Because there is a cause and effect relationship. With sales, e.g., there is an increase in receivables and a reduction in working capital.
3. **Q.** What is an accrued expense? How does it differ from other liabilities?
   **A.** This refers to acknowledged current expenses provided in a fiscal period but not yet paid. Other expenses may not be acknowledged until payment is received.
4. **Q.** Explain what the suitability principle is.
   **A.** The suitability principle, also known as the matching principle, states that expenses incurred to generate revenue should be recorded in the same period the revenue is recorded.
5. **Q.** Explain why the procedures used to compute net working capital and cash flow from operations and the net amount

spent on fixed assets give estimates and not exact amounts.

A. Because we do not know for sure how revenues and expenses affect net working capital until we analyze a firm's internal records.

6. Case study furnished by instructor.
   See NIC Credit Management Cases which are available from NIC.

7. Q. Name and describe 3 forms of credit, e.g., agricultural credit.
   A. 1. Bank Credit. Principal difference is that no cash changes hands when a bank loan is made. A paper amount is set up in borrower's account.
      2. Investment Credit. Primarily loans made to business for purchase of capital needs.
      3. Consumer Credit. Used by banks and businesses to encourage consumer purchases, e.g., charge accounts, installment, credit, loans, credit cards, etc.

8. Q. What are the main differences between bank credit and business credit?
   A. Essentially the type of resource in question, the amounts involved, the length of terms and the depth of the pre-approval analysis.

9. Q. Can a sales order be approved without a credit investigation?
   A. Yes, if it meets certain parameters covered by company policy, e.g., orders under $1000 or AAAI accounts.

10. Q. Name the 4 areas the credit management functions are divided into.
    A. 1. Setting objectives
       2. Planning
       3. Organizing
       4. Structure

11. Q. How do you go about planning to hire staff for the credit department?
    A. 1. Know requirements of job and criteria to measure results.
       2. Determine what the employee has to do (the job description), and the background that is needed (the job specification).
       3. Define the kind of person you want.

**12. Q.** What is effective control based upon?

    **A.** Standards, usually based on a statement of mission.

**13. Q.** What are 5 goals of dynamic credit management?

    **A.** 1. Increased sales and profits.

        2. Continuing improvement of the quality of work in the department.

        3. Increased productivity.

        4. Decreased cost per unit of work performed.

        5. Satisfaction as a professional.

**14. Q.** The management of credit occurs at 3 principal levels. Name the 3 levels.

    **A.** 1. General policy making and control.

        2. Day-to-day administration of operations.

        3. Counseling services.

**15. Q.** What is said to be a key function of the corporate credit manager?

    **A.** To integrate and coordinate the department's defined responsibilities with the treasury department and other parts of the company.

**16. Q.** What does interdependence of sales and credit boil down to?

    **A.** Establishing a viable credit-sales relationship. Emphasis is on credit' role in increasing sales.

**17. Q.** Who should set guidelines and parameters to be used by data processing people establishing computer systems for credit, collection, and A/R?

    **A.** The credit department manager.

**18. Q.** Should controls and guidelines be established? Why?

    **A.** Yes. To provide for timely evaluation of key functions and ensure prompt decisions to enable appropriate action to be taken.

**19. Q.** For adequate reports to each control point, what is needed?

    **A.** Quantitative and qualitative data should be available.

**20. Q.** Who is ultimately responsible for customer account status?

    **A.** The credit department.

**21. Q.** What does A/R administration mean from a credit viewpoint?

    **A.** The credit parameters established for customers, along with a historical summary of the transactions that have occurred.

**22. Q.** What is customer counseling?

    **A.** Suggestions from the credit manager to help the small business grow and help the seller nurture a more substantial customer.

**23. Q.** What is the key point to keep in mind regarding customer counseling?

    **A.** The advice must be sought by the customer.

**24. Q.** What is organization of the credit department all about?

    **A.** Determining the requirements of the specific business regarding size and type of credit department, e.g., centralized, decentralized, etc.

**25. Q.** What are some of the important considerations with regard to organization of the credit department?

    **A.** Customer service, credit and sales relationships, controlling credit exposure, delegation of authority, communication, training and development, and costs vs. benefits.

**26. Q.** Control and administration of credit is classified into three broad types of operations. What are they?

    **A.** 1. Controlled and administered at a principal office.

        2. Controlled at a principal office but administered from a decentralized location.

        3. Controlled and administered from decentralized locations with a staff office maintained at headquarters.

**27. Q.** Describe (1) a job description and (2) a job specification.

    **A.** 1. Statement of duties, responsibilities, and authorities of each position.

        2. Statement of the qualifications that one should have to fill a particular job, including educational requirements, experience requirements, and special characteristics and abilities.

**28. Q.** What is the primary objective of a training program?

    **A.** To provide employees with the opportunity to progress to whatever level of responsibility they can achieve.

**29. Q.** Does training simply mean mastery of skills?

    **A.** No! It means developing one's ability to think, to reflect, and to analyze. Then one will have the ability to arrive at good solutions.

**30. Q.** A good training program has numerous requirements; name at least five of them.

**A.** 1. Supervision by qualified people.
2. Adequate preparation time.
3. Optimal use of A/V augmentation.
4. Environment conducive to learning.
5. Outlines of job routines and procedures.
6. Testing and follow up.
7. Describing day-to-day operations.
8. Introduction to forms, files, etc.
9. Introduction to successive steps in order processing.
10. Follow-up on how well done.

**31. Q.** What are NIC and GSCFM?

**A.** NIC, National Institute of Credit, is the education arm of NACM that provides continuing education up to the graduate level and professional development programs. GSCFM, the Graduate School of Credit & Financial Management, provides education at the graduate level for those who want to develop leadership skills. This program is internationally known for excellence.

**32. Q.** What is a Credit File?

**A.** It is an accumulation of credit information derived from the department's own experience with a customer.

**33. Q.** What is a Chronological File?

**A.** A system utilizing 12 folders, one for each month, and 31 folders for days of the month. The files serve as a reference to keep up-to-date on a daily and monthly basis on accounts suspended.

**34. Q.** What is an Open Invoice File?

**A.** A file system consisting of folders for each customer, in which is placed a copy of the invoice or credit advice that was mailed to the customer.

**35. Q.** Name three types of float.

**A.** 1. Mail Float
2. Processing Float
3. Availability Float

**36. Q.** Briefly describe each of the above types of float.

**A.** 1. Days elapsed from when customer mails payment until

check is recorded.
2. Time lost due to sorting and recording information after check is recorded and until check is deposited.
3. Time elapsed from when check is deposited until funds are credited to depositor's account.

**37. Q.** What purpose does a credit policy serve?

**A.** It acts as a guide to determine how to handle given kinds of problems. It does not offer definitive solutions, but rather presents a range of solutions within which the credit manager is free to exercise judgment.

**38. Q.** What is the best way to establish a credit policy?

**A.** To give all who are directly affected a voice in policy development.

**39. Q.** Name four methods of gathering cash.

**A.** 1. Bank lockbox.
2. Courier package.
3. Preauthorized debit system.
4. Hand-carry method.

**40. Q.** Why is a credit manual said to be useful?

**A.** It serves as a reference book; larger companies need it as a standard guide and smaller companies use it to help train employees.

**41. Q.** What is the primary objective of an automated credit system?

**A.** Gathering information for credit decision making.

**42. Q.** Name one advantage of credit approval based on an agency rating.

**A.** Time saved for other, more pressing duties.

**43. Q.** What is the purpose of a credit line?

**A.** A guide for order approval, to minimize upward referral of orders, and call prompt attention to any charge in purchasing or paying habits of the customer.

**44. Q.** What is one characteristic of a marginal account?

**A.** Finances are inadequate. The firm is either not well capitalized for the volume transacted or they are not generating sufficient profits.

**45. Q.** When questions arise concerning particular application of state laws, what is the best source to consult?

    **A.** NACM's *Credit Manual of Commercial Laws.*

**46. Q.** Why is the credit manager concerned with the legal composition of a business?

    **A.** Because it is important to know about (1) the continuity of the business, (2) the capital-raising potential, and (3) the liability of the principals.

**47. Q.** Briefly describe a joint venture.

    **A.** A combination of two or more persons (including corporation) formed to perform a specific contract or business transaction.

**48. Q.** Why enter into a joint venture?

    **A.** Usually the contract or business transaction is too large in scope to be completed by one of the coadventurers alone.

**49. Q.** How does factoring work?

    **A.** A/R are purchased by the factoring company or bank, which assumes credit risk without recourse to the seller.

**50. Q.** Why use factoring?

    **A.** It provides the means for a business to convert receivables into cash before they are due without retaining liability for their payment.

**51. Q.** Why would a company want credit insurance?

    **A.** The policy provides protection against excessive bad debt losses, promotes safe sales expansion, provides collection assistance, strengthens borrowing and purchasing power, improves planning and budgeting accuracy, and provides loss prevention guidance on key risks.

**52. Q.** What is an intangible asset?

    **A.** One that is not available for payment of a debt, e.g., goodwill, trademarks, brands, etc.

**53. Q.** What is a negotiable promissory note?

    **A.** An "unconditional promise in writing made by one person to another, signed by the maker, agreeing to pay on demand or at a fixed or determinable future time, a sum certain in money to order or bearer."

**54. Q.** What is a guaranty of payment?

    **A.** When a guaranty of payment is obtained from a third party, the creditor may present the obligation for payment to the guarantor immediately after it becomes due if it is not paid by the original debtor.

**55. Q.** What is a security agreement?

 **A.** The security interest is a lien created by an agreement between the secured party and the debtor. Significant is the fact that all security devices are brought into one law and this provides the unified concept of a single lien.

**56. Q.** Goods are classified under the various categories in the UCC. Name them.

 **A.** Inventory, farm products, consumer goods, equipment, and fixtures.

**57. Q.** What is the CRF formula for DSO?

 **A.** $$\frac{\text{Average Trade Receivables Balance Last 3 Month Ends} \times 90}{\text{Credit Sales for Last 3 Months}}$$

[The source of answers to questions 58-63 is *Financial Analysis: Tools & Concepts*, Viscione, 1984; 9 and 12.]

**58. Q.** Explain the purpose of a creditors' committee.

 **A.** At the meeting of creditors, those eligible to vote may elect a creditors' committee of not fewer than three, and not more than 11. The elected committee may consult with the trustee regarding administration of the estate, make recommendations concerning performance of the trustee's duties, and submit to the court any question affecting administration of the estate.

**59. Q.** What is the principal duty of the trustee?

 **A.** Disbursement to creditors of payments under the plan.

**60. Q.** What is the purpose of the International Monetary Fund?

 **A.** To promote exchange stability and to provide resources to assist members in solving their payment problems.

**61. Q.** Why is an aging of accounts a good measure of collection performance?

 **A.** Because it provides a direct statement of the importance of past due accounts.

**62. Q.** What is an operating statement?

 **A.** The statement of retained earnings, i.e., sales, cost of goods sold, gross profit expenses, net operating income, other income and expenses, income taxes (federal), and net income.

**63. Q.** What is accrual accounting?

**A.** Method where revenue is recognized when earned and expenses recognized when incurred regardless of when cash is received.

**64. Q.** Indicate what the Trading Ratio measures and the calculation.

**A.** It measures the turnover of invested capital efficiency in addition to management ability. The calculation is:

$$\frac{\text{Net Sales}}{\text{Tangible Net worth}} = \text{Number of times turnover}$$

**65. Q.** What does net income plus depreciation show?

**A.** "Net income plus depreciation gives an estimated flow from operations. Moreover, if changes in deferred taxes are significant, then this computation will not even give a decent estimate of net working capital from operations."

**66. Q.** When do certain current assets and current liabilities automatically change?

**A.** "Certain current assets and current liabilities automatically change when sales change." Examples are accounts receivable, accounts payable, and accrued liabilities.

**67. Q.** What does an accrued expense represent?

**A.** "An accrued expense represents an expense that has not been paid for as of the balance sheet date. Unlike other kinds of liabilities, resources do not flow into the firm. Nevertheless, an accrued expense is properly viewed as a source in the sense that the firm would have to obtain another source of resources if this liability did not exist."

**68. Q.** What is referred to as the suitability principle?

**A.** The suitability principle states that "uses of funds should be financial with the right kind of sources. Temporary uses require temporary sources and permanent uses require permanent sources."

**69. Q.** What do you need to have access to in computing net working capital?

**A.** In computing net working capital, to figure out exact amounts, one needs access to a firm's internal accounting record. For instance, there may be an item included in other expenses that has not decreased net working capital and it is likely one would be unable to detect this from published financial statements.

**70. Q.** Does bankruptcy reorganization mean irreversible business failure?

**A.** No. Leveraged firms remain operationally viable and are important accounts before the filing, during the procedure, and following the reorganization.

# CREDIT MANAGEMENT TYPICAL QUESTIONS & ANSWERS

## PART VI

**1. Q.** What is meant by the interdependence of sales and credit?

**A.** Each party needs the other, i.e., credit needs sales and vice versa. One should help the other. They can do this by providing information that is more easily obtained by one department to the other department. It is also important that both are essential to the profitability of the company.

**2. Q.** There are three basic types of business entities: 1) Proprietorship, 2) Partnership, and 3) Corporation. Briefly describe the composition of each type of entity.

**A.** 1) Proprietorship. Pluses: Total control and profits do not have to be divided. Minuses: Illness or absence of the owner can impact negatively on profitability. Death of the owner can tie up monies due to creditors for a year or more until the estate is settled.

2) Partnership. This form of organization consists of two or more individuals who agree to share profits and losses. The agreement may be oral, written, or implied. And a partnership may result from actions and understandings, without the formal expression of intent to create a partnership. Any written agreement reflects the rights and obligations of each partner and is referred to as "articles of partnership." Partners are usually active in the management of the business. An exception would be with a limited partner who does not share in the management and whose liability is limited to the amount of his investment in the business. The personal assets of general partners may be attached when the assets of the partnership

are insufficient to satisfy a judgment. Consequently, there is shared business and personal liability.

3) Corporation. A corporate entity is formed to carry on a business or to provide a service. It differs from a partnership in that it is a legal entity separate and independent from its owners. Once a charter is issued, a new corporation takes over all contracts made on behalf of the corporation. A certificate of incorporation is drawn up by the stockholders. Once approved by the state the certificate of incorporation becomes the corporate charter. The principal advantage of this form of organization is protection against loss of one's personal estate to satisfy creditors.

**3. Q.** In this era of mergers and acquisitions, indicate in order of preference at least three ways to acquire another company.

 **A.** a. Leveraged buyout
  b. Exchange of stock
  c. Cash or short-term financing
  d. Long-term financing
  e. Equity-financing

**4. Q.** One of your slow pay accounts was acquired by a large nationally known corporation. Will your account improve from a credit standpoint? Explain.

 **A.** Yes. Because the surviving company assumes liability for debts of the companies party to the acquisition.

**5. Q.** Alco Co., a partnership between Steve Frank and Joseph Menco, manufactures log homes at their own facility. Most of the venture capital for the enterprise came from Menco who inherited extensive real estate holdings from his parents. As a credit grantor to Alco, what must you be aware of with regard to the partners?

 **A.** Determine whether Menco is a limited or general partner. If Menco is a limited partner and the business fails, his personal assets are not subject to any creditor's claims.

**6. Q.** Credit managers are no longer relying as heavily on the use of current ratio to measure risk potential. Why?

 **A.** Essentially because current assets are not distinguishable as to degrees of liquidity. Based on the premise that all current assets can be converted to cash with equal ease, a distorted picture unfolds. Inventory often becomes the questionable item and many analysts obtain a clearer picture. This ratio will fluctuate with movement of receivables and respond to their forces, e.g., sales, fixed-asset investment, and profit and loss.

**7. Q.** Entries have a plus or minus effect on the balance sheet. Indicate opposite each entry whether the effect was plus or minus.
   a. Net worth account credited      _____
   b. Liability account credited      _____
   c. Net worth account debited      _____
   d. Asset account credited      _____
   e. Asset account debited      _____

**A.** a. Increase
   b. Increase
   c. Decrease
   d. Decrease
   e. Increase

**8. Q.** Explain the purpose of each of the following:
   a. Trial Balance
   b. Accounting Journal
   c. General Ledger
   d. Subsidiary Ledger

**A.** a. A listing of account balances as of the closing date. Balances are adjusted by entries and are used for the balance sheet and income statement.
   b. A book of original entry in which all transactions are recorded. Included are: purchase journal, sales journal, and cash journal. These entries are posted to the General Ledger.
   c. The General Ledger contains a separate page for each account. Entries are made from the journals to ledger accounts. Account totals are ascertained and the excess debit or credit is compiled in the Trial Balance.
   d. The Subsidiary Ledger contains details of a General Ledger account, e.g., a Materials Ledger or a Manufacturing Expense Ledger.

**9. Q.** Indicate two examples of contingent liability.

**A.** a. Pending law suits.

b. Possible additional taxes for prior years. These are not liabilities in fact, but liabilities may result because of existing circumstances.

**10. Q.** Differentiate between liability reserve and surplus reserve.

**A.** Liability Reserve—set up as a current liability for an existing liability where the exact amount cannot be determined.

Surplus Reserve—setting aside a portion of earned surplus for future use. This reserve is available for payment of dividends. It represents an amount set aside for future expansion or other contingency.

**11. Q.** What are the determinants of whether to use FIFO and LIFO inventory accounting methods.

FIFO—in a period of rising prices, FIFO gives larger final inventory value because it is priced at the cost of the most recently acquired material. This method therefore gives higher final inventory value and lower cost of goods sold, consequently a larger net profit.

FIFO—gives lower final inventory value and higher cost of goods sold. LIFO therefore reflects a smaller end inventory and smaller current asset figures.

Either can be used to advantage depending on whether prices are declining or increasing.

**12. Q.** Ratio Analysis. Keep in mind that a ratio is simply a mathematical relationship between two quantities, of value to the analyst because it results in a measurement of the adequacy of one particular item on a financial statement relative to another. Credit managers commonly use up to 15 such ratios. Care, however, must be exercised in the use and interpretation of ratios. Ratios are useless unless compared with industry averages or norms which are available through business credit reporting agencies. Indicate how the following ratios are computed:

a. Current liabilities to net worth

b. Total liabilities to net worth

c. Inventory to working capital

d. Long term liabilities to working capital

e. Net profit to net worth
f. Net sales to fixed assets
Which of the above ratios measures three aspects of business debt structure?

**A.** All of the above ratios measure three aspects of business debt structure to some extent, for the following reasons:

a. Current liabilities to net worth: Divide all current liabilities by the tangible net worth of the company. This ratio measures solvency.

b. Total liabilities to net worth: Add long-term liabilities to current liabilities to obtain total debt, then divide by net worth.

c. Inventory to working capital: Subtract current liabilities from current assets and then divide the book value of inventory by working capital. This ratio measures liquidity.

d. Long-term liabilities to working capital: Divide long-term liabilities by the firm's working capital. This ratio measures solvency.

e. Net profit to net worth: Divide profit after taxes by tangible net worth to arrive at percent of return on invested capital. This ratio measures profitability.

f. Net sales to fixed assets: Divide net sales by book or depreciated value of fixed assets. The answer is expressed in time, not percent. This ratio measures efficiency.

Ratios are an important element in the understanding of financial management.

**13. Q.** Indicate the effects of each of the following transactions on the firm's current and quick ratios, assuming that each ratio is initially above 1.0. Each transaction may increase (+), decrease (−), or not affect (0) each of the ratios.

|  | Current Ratio | Quick Ratio |
|---|---|---|
| a. The firm sells stock, using the proceeds to increase cash. | _____ | _____ |
| b. The firm sells stock, using the proceeds to retire long-term debt. | _____ | _____ |

c. The firm increases inventory, financing
by borrowing short-term from its bank. ———— ————
d. The firm increases inventory, financing
this by reducing cash. ———— ————
e. The firm purchases fixed assets, financing
this by reducing cash. ———— ————
f. The firm pays off part of its short-term
debt due to its bank, financing this by
selling stock. ———— ————

| A. | Current Ratio | Quick Ratio |
|---|---|---|
| a. The firm sells stock, using the proceeds to increase cash. | + | + |
| b. The firm sells stock, using the proceeds to retire long-term debt. | 0 | 0 |
| c. The firm increases inventory, financing by borrowing short-term from its bank. | – | – |
| d. The firm increases inventory, financing this by reducing cash | 0 | – |
| e. The firm purchases fixed assets, financing this by reducing cash. | – | – |
| f. The firm pays off part of its short-term debt to its bank, financing this by selling stock. | + | + |

14. **Q.** A firm is incorporated as a Subchapter S corporation; such a corporation does not pay federal income taxes, and its shareholders pay taxes on income from the corporation at personal tax rates. If the firm defaults, are shareholders personally liable for its debts?

**A.** No. While a Subchapter S is taxed as a partnership, equity investors in Subchapter S corporations are limited in liability to the amount of their investment.

15. **Q.** A firm, which previously borrowed on a secured basis only from its bank, grants a secondary secured position on its assets to another trade creditor. Is the credit risk of the account

affected? If so, how?

**A.** The probability of the debtor's default is not affected in any major way by a transaction such as this. However, since one creditor is secured, the recoveries of the other creditors are reduced should the debtor default; credit risk is increased in this sense.

# CREDIT MANAGEMENT CASES

## CASE I. COMMERCIAL PRINTING INK CORPORATION

Review and analyze the case shown in Exhibit 12.1 on "Commercial Printing Ink Corporation."

Determine whether the $10,000 order from Commercial Printing Ink Corporation should be accepted. Explain your reasoning.

*NOTE: Students are to use pocket calculators to make calculations.*

# EXHIBIT 12.1
## COMMERCIAL PRINTING INK CORPORATION

Copyright© 1992 by National Association of Credit Management

You are the credit manager of American Container Corporation, Queens, New York, which is a moderate size manufacturer of cans, drums and other metal containers. You are faced with a decision on a $10,000 second order from Commercial Printing Ink Corporation of Wilton, Connecticut. The first order from this firm had been for $1,200 in cans and was placed more than six months ago. It was paid in 90 days with management of the customer firm claiming they payment was really as agreed, though American selling terms are net 30 days.

American Container Corporation operates on a modest profit margin and because of competitive pressures has been forced in numerous instances to accept marginal accounts.

The credit file on Commercial Printing contains a credit report, comparative financial statements, an interchange report, a bank letter and a letter from John Taylor, President of Commercial Printing.

### CENTRAL CREDIT REPORTS CORPORATION

April 15, 1990

Commercial Printing Ink Corporation
Wilton, Connecticut

John Taylor, President
Gregory Billing, Vice President
Ronald Tuttle, Secretary-Treasurer

**BACKGROUND:** Firm was incorporated in 1987 under Connecticut laws with a paid in capital of $25,000. Taylor has been in this line for many years. Prior to starting this business, principal was general manager of a much larger firm in this industry. Billings, primarily active in sales, was associated with Taylor in other firms in the past. Tuttle is plant manager.

**LOCATION:** Company owns, subject to mortgage, a 10,000 square foot, one story building and also owns three mills and other necessary production equipment, subject to undisclosed encumbrances.

**DISTRIBUTION:** Sells primarily to printers in the Metropolitan New York area.

**FINANCIAL:** Withheld

**PAYING RECORD:** Erratic

**RECOMMENDATION:** Absence of financial particulars precludes a recommendation.

## EXHIBIT 12.1 (cont'd)

### COMMERCIAL PRINTING INK CORPORATION

| | 12/31/91 | 12/31/90 |
|---|---|---|
| Cash | $ 2,800 | $ 1,200 |
| Accounts Receivable (Net) | 51,700 | 44,600 |
| Inventory | 15,200 | 13,700 |
| Current Assets | 69,700 | 59,500 |
| | | |
| Fixed Assets | 42,400 | 43,400 |
| Total Assets | 112,199 | 102,900 |
| | | |
| Accounts Payable | 58,300 | 47,800 |
| Long Term Debt-Current | 4,300 | 4,300 |
| Other Payables | 600 | 2,700 |
| Current Liabilities | 63,200 | 54,800 |
| | | |
| Long Term Debt | 14,900 | 18,400 |
| | | |
| Common Stock | 25,000 | 25,000 |
| Retained Earnings | 9,000 | 4,700 |
| Total Liabilities & Capital | 112,100 | 102,900 |
| | | |
| Sales | 407,000 | 324,000 |
| Gross Profit | 68,000 | 61,000 |
| Income Before Taxes | 13,500 | 9,800 |
| Net Income | 9,800 | 7,400 |

## EXHIBIT 12.1 (cont'd)

**EXHIBIT III**

NATIONAL ASSOCIATION OF CREDIT MANAGEMENT

### NATIONAL BUSINESS CREDIT REPORT

REPORT ON: ID # 00000000     DATE 03/15/90      REPORT FOR MEMBER #
Commercial Printing Ink Corporation
Wilton, CT

ON FILE SINCE

| BUSINESS CATEGORY | YR. OPEN | DATE REPTD | LAST ACTIVITY | HIGH REPTD | ACCOUNT BALANCE | ACCOUNT STATUS CURRENT | 1-30 | 31-60 | 61 & OVER | PAYMENT TERMS | CMNTS |
|---|---|---|---|---|---|---|---|---|---|---|---|
| Chem | 89 | 12/89 | 12/89 | 9400 | 7200 | – | – | 3000 | 4200 | ½-10-30 | |
| Chem | 88 | 2/90 | 2/90 | 8500 | 5000 | 2500 | – | 2500 | – | N30 | |
| Cont | 89 | 1/90 | 1/90 | 6000 | 6000 | – | 6000 | – | – | N30 | |
| Chem | 88 | 11/89 | 11/89 | 1000 | 500 | – | – | – | 500 | ½-10-30 | up to |
| Cont | 89 | 9/89 | 9/89 120+ | 8000 late --- | account | placed | for collection | | – | N30 | 120 due |
| Chem | 90 | 2/90 | 2/90 | 3600 | 3600 | 3600 | – | – | – | N30 | |
| Pap | 89 | 11/89 | 11/89 | 500 | – | – | – | – | – | N30 | |
| Chem | 89 | 2/90 | 2/90 | 1400 | 1400 | – | 1400 | – | – | ½-10-30 | |
| Chem | 89 | 1/90 | 1/90 | 2700 | 1400 | – | 1000 | 400 | – | N30 | |

## EXHIBIT 12.1 (cont'd)

### BANK LETTER

### THIRD COMMERCIAL BANK AND TRUST COMPANY

December 15, 1991

American Container Corporation
Attention: Credit Manager
Queens, New York

Re: Commercial Printing Ink Corp., Wilton, Connecticut

Dear Sir:

At your request we have checked with the subject's bank in Wilton and are told that a modest four figure balance is maintained on a routine basis. The account has not requested accommodation, so little is known of the company's operating ability.

Very truly yours,

T. Reynolds
Assistant Vice President

## EXHIBIT 12.1 (cont'd)

*Commercial Printing Ink Corporation*
*Wilton, Connecticut*

September 12, 1991

American Container Corporation
Attention: Credit Manager
Queens, New York

Dear Sir:

We are very much aware of the terms of sale printed on your invoice and do not have to be reminded that our account is running "slow." As we explained to your salesman Mr. Moore, when he solicited the order in question, we are a relatively new business and we expect to grow. Our customers do not pay us in thirty days and consequently we are unable to be concerned with printed terms and therefore we are not concerned.

Our obligation to you will be retired when our position permits. If this arrangement proves unsatisfactory, please advise and we will arrange to place our container business elsewhere.

Very truly yours,

John Taylor
President

## MODEL SOLUTION CASE I. Commercial Printing Ink Corporation

*Note to Student: Your answer to the questions posed in this case has been personally reviewed by the grader. His or her comments are made directly on your answer sheet. While the summary given below should by no means be construed as a complete answer, it does include the main points that you should have included in your response.*

A $10,000 order represents considerable profit potential if there is reasonable expectation of collection within terms. The attractiveness of the order diminishes with an increase in the period necessary to make collection unless a service is imposed to compensate for slowness.

The financial condition of this business leaves much to be desired despite a favorable sales and earnings trend. Schedule I shows that the company's principal sources of funds are accounts payable and retained earnings. The funds are applied primarily to finance the growth in accounts receivable (turnover of which has improved) and to reduce other payables and long-term debt.

An internal analysis shows that the financial condition of December 31, 1989 continues unbalanced. Indebtedness is almost double the net worth, fixed assets as well in excess of net worth, and net working capital is extremely thin. It is apparent that the company relies heavily on creditor's funds.

Information of a detailed nature is needed regarding the mortgage indebtedness. To whom is it owing? What is its retirement schedule (only $3,500 was retired during the year)? Perhaps an informal meeting with Mr. Taylor could be arranged where this and other aspects of the business could be discussed. Areas that may be considered are financing arrangements such as a second mortgage on the plant and equipment, a bank loan secured by personal collateral of Mr. Taylor, or a corporate note personally endorsed by Mr. Taylor or a third party with a good credit reputation.

Improved relations between the sales and credit departments of American are needed if American's salesman is being quoted accurately by the President of Commercial. Certainly a direct checking is warranted with the container supplier that placed this account for collection.

Schedule I

| | 12/31/88 | 12/31/89 | Use | Source |
|---|---|---|---|---|
| Cash | $1,200 | $2,800 | $1,600 | |
| Accounts Receivable | 44,600 | 51,700 | 7,100 | |
| Inventory | 13,700 | 15,200 | 1,500 | |
| Current Assets | 59,500 | 69,700 | | |
| Fixed Assets | 43,400 | 42,400 | | $1,000 |
| Total Assets | $102,900 | $112,100 | | |
| Accounts Payable | $47,800 | $58,300 | | $10,500 |
| Long-Term-Debt | | | | |
| (Current) | 4,300 | 4,300 | | |
| Other Payables | 2,700 | 600 | 2,100 | |
| Current Liabilities | $54,800 | $63,200 | | |
| Long-Term Debt | 18,400 | 14,900 | 3,500 | |
| Common Stock | 25,000 | 25,000 | | |
| Retained Earnings | 4,700 | 9,000 | | 4,300 |
| Total Liabilities and Capital | $102,900 | $112,100 | $15,800 | $15,800 |
| Net Working Capital | 4,700 | 6,500 | | |
| Days Sales Outstanding | 50.2 Days | 46.4 Days | | |
| Fixed Assets to Net Worth | 146% | 125% | | |
| Total Debt to Net Worth | 246% | 230% | | |

This order should be accepted only upon further investigation, firm establishment of a repayment schedule for the order, and careful consideration of the profit potential in dealing with this account.

## CASE II. XYZ CORPORATION

Review and analyze the case shown in Exhibit 12.2 on XYZ Corporation.

1. As a member of the creditors committee of XYZ Corporation, what are your recommendations?
2. Should the possibility of finding a buyer for the business be explored? Why?

## EXHIBIT 12.2

## XYZ CORPORATION

Copyright© 1992 by National Association of Credit Management

This company was formed in 1964 when it acquired the radio speaker production facilities of a large manufacturing concern in Indiana. Its management and control has been under the direction of one man since inception.

The general line of products included radio communication and electronic equipment such as radio and television loud-speakers, coils, transformers, headsets, earphones, and microphones. These were sold to the radio and TV industry, distributors, joggers and the U.S. Government. Production facilities were located in Indiana, Oregon and Kentucky.

Over a period of years the company operated with moderate success through the development and sale of new products along with their regular line of communication and electronic items. Among its new products was a tape recorder dictation machine which the company decided to manufacture in 1987 and sell through a separate concern that the principal of XYZ Corporation had formed to handle its distribution. Its invested capital was negligible.

THE XYZ Corporation had no difficulty in adapting facilities at one of the Indiana plants to produce this new line. For a period of time it was readily able to purchase materials and component parts on credit, to manufacture the dictation machines.

The sales affiliate sold the machines purchased from the XYZ Corporation to dealers located throughout the United States. (It was later learned that the principal at interest also owned tow of these dealerships.) In view of the keen competitive market existing in the office machine field, the sales company was obliged to extend longer than usual credit terms to its dealers. Many of the dealers did not have well established selling organizations. Further, since this was a new product, shipments in many cases were made on a trail basis.

Due to the limited financial position of the sales concern, it was only able to pay the XYZ Corporation for machines as proceeds were received from its dealers. The amount owing the XYZ Corporation grew to such an extent within a year that it strained its liquidity. As a consequence, XYZ Corporation was forced to ask some of its larger suppliers to take trade acceptances maturing monthly over a period of several months in settlement of overdue accounts.

Many large creditors agreed to this acceptance arrangement on the assurance from XYZ Corporation that it was only temporary; the company financial position would improve as soon as the sales affiliate succeeded in realizing the increased volume then in prospect.

At the time of the meeting, the committee learned that the debtor's order backlog totaled $750,000, of which $500,000 was Government business.

# EXHIBIT 12.2 (cont'd)

In October 1990, the committee reviewed the financial consultant's report which showed:

- Operations disorganized.

- Lack of key personnel and proper cost system.

- XYZ Corporation paying the rent for the principal's apartment, for which the company had paid $8,000 for furniture.

- Plant in Kentucky closed down; the consultant recommended discontinuance.

- Oregon plant profitable; consultant recommended continuance.

- Dictation machine business unprofitable; consultant recommended attempting to sell it as a going business.

The committee agreed to continue to cooperate with the principal if he would:

- Give the committee an irrevocable proxy of the company stock.

- Permit appointment of a new manager with authority to effect economies in operations.

- Assign affiliate stock and receivables to XYZ Corporation.

The principal agreed to consider the proposals.

By January 1991, the principal had failed in his efforts to attract new capital. The Committee proposed a voting trust agreement, but the principal refused to have his company managed by anyone else, particularly since the order backlog had rise to $1.3 million. Instead, he asked an independent adjustment firm to devise a settlement plan. The firm proposed 100 per cent settlement in no-interest debentures payable over five years on the following schedule:

## EXHIBIT 12.2 (cont'd)

| Payment | Date | Amount | Payment | Date | Amount |
|---------|--------|--------|---------|---------|----------|
| 1 | 8-20-91 | 5% | 6 | 2-20-94 | 10% |
| 2 | 2-20-92 | 5% | 7 | 8-20-94 | 12 1/2% |
| 3 | 8-20-92 | 7 1/2% | 8 | 2-20-95 | 12 1/2% |
| 4 | 2-20-93 | 7 1/2% | 9 | 8-20-95 | 15% |
| 5 | 8-20-93 | 10% | 10 | 2-20-96 | 15% |

As an option to this proposal, the XYZ Corporation offered an immediate cash settlement of 50 per cent on claims up to an aggregate of $2,000,000. The principal claimed that he had $100,000 with which to pay up on the 50 per cent basis.

By February 1991, most of the creditors had elected to take the 50 per cent settlement. However, the Government filed a tax lien of $89,733 and the customer was unable to pay both the tax lien and the 50 per cent settlements.

Attached are a balance sheet at June 30, 1990 and comparative operating statements for 12-month periods ending June 30, 1989 and 1990.

An unaudited balance sheet issued by the XYZ Corporation for December 31, 1990 showed:

| | |
|---|---|
| Current Assets | $1,001,000 |
| Current Liabilities | 933,000 |
| Surplus | 190,000 |

An operating statement for the 6-month period ending December 31, 1990 showed:

| | |
|---|---|
| Sales | $1,333,000 |
| Cost of Sales | 860,000 |
| Net Loss | (5,500) |

## EXHIBIT 12.2 (cont'd)

### XYZ CORPORATION

### BALANCE SHEET

### June 30, 1990

| ASSETS | | LIABILITIES | |
|---|---|---|---|
| Cash | $ 19,500 | (2) Bank Loan | $ 158,000 |
| (1)Accounts Receivable | 472,000 | Notes & T/A Payable | 271,000 |
| Inventories | 509,000 | Accounts Payable | 170,000 |
| Other Receivables | 1,500 | Accrued Salaries & | |
| Total Current | | Expenses | 60,000 |
| Assets | $1,002,000 | (3)Withholding Taxes & | |
| | | F.I.C.A. | 112,500 |
| | | Local Taxes | 20,500 |
| | | Federal Income Tax | 11,500 |
| | | Federal Excise Tax | 34,500 |
| | | Total Current | |
| | | Liabilities | $ 838,000 |
| Machinery & Fixtures | | | |
| (Net) | 180,500 | | |
| Deferred Charges | 15,500 | | |
| | | (4)Long Term Debt | 99,000 |
| | | Capital Stock | 46,000 |
| | | (5)Surplus | 215,000 |
| | | Total Liabilities & | |
| Total Assets | $1,198,000 | Capital | $1,198,000 |

Notes:
*(1)$283,000 due from affiliated company*
*(2)V-Loan - secured by assignment of receivables and inventory on Government contracts*
*(3)Payable $6,000 monthly per agreement*
*(4)$27,500 owed on 1989-90 renegotiation - being paid $250 per month + $25,000 owed*
*attorney for company + $46,500 owed officers of company.*
*(5)Includes $103,000 increase in valuation of assets - 1988*

### Profit & Loss Statement

| | June 30, 1989 | June 30, 1990 |
|---|---|---|
| Sales for Year | $ 2,915,000 | $ 3,053,000 |
| Less - Cost of Sales | 1,819,500 | 1,982,500 |
| Gross Profit | 1,095,500 | 1,070,500 |
| Less - Expenses | | |
| Sales & Administrative | 388,000 | 373,500 |
| Factory | 566,000 | 586,500 |
| Engineering | 112,000 | 146,000 |
| Financial | 13,000 | 24,000 |
| Total Expenses | 1,069,000 | 1,130,000 |
| Profit for 1989 | 26,500 | |
| Profit for 1990 | | 59,500 |

## MODEL SOLUTION CASE II—XYZ CORPORATION

*Note to Student: Your answer to the questions posed in this case has been personally reviewed by the grader. His or her comments are made directly on your answer sheet. While the summary given below should by no means be construed as a complete answer, it does include the main points that you should have included in your response.*

Actual liquidation of this business would not benefit creditors as a good part of the assets are questionable and tied up with liens.

The comparative profit and loss statements reflect a retrogressive trend. Despite an increase in sales, operations are now at a loss. However, a favorable factor is the $1.3-million order backlog. With creditor control, the company might be placed on a profitable basis permitting a long-term payout of obligations in full.

The immediate concern is to encourage the cooperation of the principal as an alternative to bankruptcy proceedings. This would include giving the committee an irrevocable proxy of the company's capital stock, permitting the appointment of a new manager with authority to inaugurate proper economies in operation, and assigning the affiliate's stock and receivables to the company.

As proposed by the financial consultant, possible transactions include the sale as a going business of the unprofitable dictation machine operation, discontinuance of the plant in Kentucky that is closed, and cessation of payment of the principal's personal expenses.

The possibility of finding a buyer for the business might be explored with the principal being encouraged to sell. Under new management and possible infusion of additional capital, the company would have a good chance to prosper.

It appears that in the case of a forced liquidation, creditors would receive little or nothing on their claims.

## FINANCIAL ANALYSIS TYPICAL QUESTIONS & ANSWERS

Indicated below are additional typical questions of the kind that may appear on any of the credentialing examinations addressing financial analysis and related problems:

1. A firm to which you sell has decided to finance its operations by factoring its receivables. The firm's factoring arrangement will re-

place unsecured bank credit borrowing. Discuss the effects of this change on the firm's creditworthiness.

2. A firm is financed in part by short-term bank borrowings which are renewed each quarter. Explain why the firm would be a lower credit risk if this financing were replaced by a long-term amortized loan.

3. You are examining the trend in a debtor's inventory turnover and find a substantial change in this ratio during the past year. On examining the footnotes to the firm's financial statements, you find that the firm changed inventory valuation methods for reporting purposes during this year. Interpret this situation relative to the firm's creditworthiness.

4. A debtor has two divisions of approximately equal size. These divisions are in unrelated business lines. Explain why such a firm has lower credit risk than a similar firm in only one business line.

5. A debtor changes auditing firms. Explain the implications for the debtor's creditworthiness.

## ANSWERS TO FINANCIAL ANALYSIS QUESTIONS

1. In general such a change will increase the firm's creditworthiness. The firm will be able to borrow more money via the factoring arrangement than it could via unsecured borrowing, should such funds be needed to cover a cash shortfall. Further, the firm will have additional financial flexibility, since it does not need to wait until customers pay in order to access funds.

2. While short-term borrowing is, on average, cheaper in that interest rates are generally lower than for long-term borrowing, the potential difficulty that the firm faces is refunding risk. Financial intermediaries seem prone to periodic "credit crunches" during which they withdraw credit to some borrowers. If this occurs, the debtor will not be able to renew the short-term financing. Long-term amortized loan financing would lessen this refunding risk.

3. A change in inventory valuation method will alter the firm's inventory turnover ratio even if the turnover of physical inventory remains the same since the change alters the accounting value of the inventory. The change in accounting value, in itself, has no effect on the firm's credit worthiness, as the same units of inventory are simply assigned a different accounting value. Nor is there any tax effect if

the change is for reporting purposes only. The problem is that the change in accounting method may take place at the same time as a change in physical turnover, and the accounting change may mask or exaggerate measurement of the change in physical turnover. Any reduction in physical turnover may indicate the accumulation of obsolete inventory, which would be detrimental to the debtor's creditworthiness.

4. All other things being equal, the two-division firm is less risky because of the portfolio effects of its two units on total cash flow. When one unit is doing badly, the other may be doing well, decreasing the possibility that the firm will experience cash flow difficulties. A single-business firm does not experience this advantageous portfolio effect.

5. A change in auditor may have negative implications for the debtor's creditworthiness. Firms sometimes change auditors due to a difference of opinion between the firm and its auditor over the application of GAAP to its accounting statements. When such differences of opinion occur, the firm usually prefers an accounting treatment that makes it seem more financially successful than the auditor believes is appropriate. Rather than obtaining an auditor's report containing a qualified opinion, the firm will change auditors.

## CASE STUDY I. ALTA INDUSTRIES CORPORATION

You are credit manager of Budd Convertors Corporation, a medium size converting operation which buys unbleached yarn, has them dyed and finished, and then sells the piece goods to dress manufacturers in the women's cutting-up trade, primarily in New York City.

The American textile manufacturing industry is heavily concentrated in New York City. It is highly seasonal and most manufacturers have two main seasons, spring and fall.

With styling critical, it is not unusual for a clothing manufacturer to reap large profits from a well-accepted line during one season, then to sustain substantial losses in the following season because its styles are poorly received.

Many clothing manufacturers are undercapitalized and, consequently, trade heavily on equity. Typically, also, at the end of each season, many firms discontinue operations, while many others are formed by principals who want to try their luck.

Clothing manufacturers usually purchase piece goods on both 60 and 70 day terms, and use contractors for the actual manufacture of dresses. Their regular selling terms to retailers are 8/10 EOM.

You have received an order from Alta Industries Corporation, New York, New York for $18,000 in piece goods, to be delivered immediately. Your credit file contains the information shown on the following pages.

Review this case and determine whether the Alta order should be shipped and document why.

Alta Management:   *Frank Mann, President*
                            *Vincent Argo, Vice President*
                            *Mark Masko, Secretary-Treasurer*

The President is 54 years old and is well experienced in this line. He was formerly employed by several dress houses as an executive until helping to establish this firm in 1980. He holds a 60% stock interest in the company.

Argo has been selling in this field for his entire commercial career of 20 years. He was a principal in Paris Fashion Corporation which compromised its indebtedness to creditors for 40% in 1967. He then worked as a salesman until he helped form this company. He holds a 20% stock interest.

Masko was employed as an accountant by a big eight accounting firm which has specialists in textile work. He has been in charge of finances here from the outset and handles all financial details.

## Method of Operation

The company is located in New York, New York where it was formed under New York laws in 1980. The firm manufactures ladies' wear, primarily in the low to medium price range. Alta employs 20 people including officers.

## Background Information

The organization started in a small way in 1980 and after several years in which earnings were slim or non-existent, a favorable trend then set in. Volume has expanded sharply in recent years and it is management's intent to triple the 1988 sales by 1995.

## Financial Statements

You have received two sets of financial statements from Budd: those representing the firm's last fiscal results (for the year ending May 31, 1990) and interim figures (for the ten months ending March 31, 1991). The interim figures are incomplete in that no inventory numbers are given. Instead "breakeven inventory" appears. Breakeven inventory is a balancing figure, and is the amount of inventory necessary for the firm to break even and for the total assets to equal total liabilities plus equity.

### Alta Industries Corporation
### BALANCE SHEET—May 31, 1990

| | | | |
|---|---|---|---|
| Cash | $ 28,500 | A/Payable | $ 52,200 |
| A/Rec. | 75,400 | Notes Payable | 20,300 |
| Inventory | 39,700 | Taxes Payable | 1,200 |
| CURRENT ASSETS | 143,600 | CURRENT LIABILITIES | 73,700 |
| | | | |
| Fixed Assets | 2,200 | Common Stock | 50,000 |
| Other Assets | 1,800 | Earned Surplus | 23,900 |
| TOTAL ASSETS | 147,600 | TOTAL LIAB. & NET WORTH | 147,600 |

### PROFIT & LOSS—YEAR ENDED MAY 31, 1988

| | |
|---|---|
| Net Sales | $960,400 |
| Cost of Goods Sold | 780,200 |
| Expenses | 166,200 |
| Taxes | 5,800 |
| Net Income | 8,200 |

## TRADE CLEARANCE—AUGUST, 1990

| High Credit | Owing | Past Due | Term | Payment |
|---|---|---|---|---|
| $18,000 | $18,000 | — | 2–10–60 | — |
| 12,400 | — | — | N 70 | PPT |
| 16,500 | — | — | 2–10–60 | DISCOUNT |
| 4,000 | 4,000 | — | N 70 | PPT |
| 800 | 800 | — | N 70 | PPT |
| 6,900 | 6,900 | 6,900 | 2–10–60 | DISPUTE |
| 21,200 | 21,200 | — | 2–10–60 | PPT-FEW |
| 7,400 | 7,400 | 7,400 | N 30 | 30 SLO |
| 8,000 | 8,000 | — | N 70 | PPT |

## Alta Industries Corporation
## TRIAL BALANCE—MARCH 31, 1990

| | | | | |
|---|---|---|---|---|
| Cash | $ 27,300 | Accounts Payable | | $ 84,300 |
| A/Receivable (Net) | 96,400 | Bank Payable | | 27,600 |
| | | Contractor Payables | | 8,400 |
| | | Taxes & Accrual | | 4,600 |
| Fixed Assets | 1,600 | Current Liabilities | | 124,900 |
| Other Assets | 1,700 | | | |
| | | Common Stock (3/31) | | 50,000 |
| | | Earned Surplus (3/31) | | 23,900 |
| Asset Exclusive of | | | | |
| Inventory | 127,000 | | | |
| Breakeven Inventory | 71,800 | | | |
| Total Assets | 198,800 | Total Lia. & Net Worth | | 198,800 |

### PROFIT & LOSS FOR 10 MONTHS ENDED 3/31/88

| | | |
|---|---:|---:|
| GROSS SALES | $980,000 | |
| Less Returns & Discounts | 60,000 | |
| Net Sales | | $920,000 |
| Beginning Inventory | 39,700 | |
| Purchase | 707,200 | |
| Labor | 172,600 | |
| Factory Overhead | 59,300 | |
| Other Expenses | 13,000 | |
| Total Expenses | | 991,800 |
| Inventory to Breakeven | | 71,800 |

## CASE I QUESTIONS. ALTA INDUSTRIES CORPORATION

1. Give your preliminary impressions of Budd Converters as a credit applicant. As part of this process, analyze management's ability to run the firm, payments to trade, and financial position as of May 31, 1990.

2. At this stage, your credit investigation of Budd Converters is incomplete. Give and explain the information you would require as part of the next stage of this investigation.

## CASE STUDY I. SOLUTION

1. Management's Ability. This is clearly one of the firm's strengths. Mr. Mann and Mr. Argo have substantial experience in the fabric and fashion industry. Further, in an industry where failure is frequent, they have been able to keep Budd afloat for ten years.

Payments to Trade. These payments are generally being made in accordance with terms. The only substantive slowness is being experienced by a firm whose terms of sale are thirty days, whereas normal terms to this industry are much longer.

Analysis of Financial Position. Here are some financial ratios for the firm as of May 31, 1990:

Liquidity Ratios
Current Ratio              1.95
Quick Ratio               1.41

Debt Ratios
Total Debt/Total Assets    0.50

Turnover Ratios
Sales/Total Assets         6.51
Sales/Accts. Rec.         12.74
CGS/Inventory             19.65

Profitability Ratios
Net Income/Sales          0.85%
Net Income/Total Assets   5.56%
Net Income/Equity        11.10%

These ratios show a fairly strong financial position. Liquidity is reasonably high without being excessive. Debt position (about a 50/50 debt/equity split) is typical for small firms. The asset base is somewhat small to support sales of these levels, but this is probably typical for firms in this industry. Receivables and inventory show rapid turnover, but this may be due to the date of the statement. For firms like this which have substantial seasonality in sales, financial statements are traditionally generated during the slack season when accounts receivable and inventory are lowest. Profitability is adequate.

2. Substantial additional information is needed to complete the financial analysis of Budd Converters. Of primary concern is the level of inventories as of March 31. In a fashion-oriented business such as this one, healthy firms should sell most inventory by the end of the selling season. If information on actual inventory levels is not available, financial statements as of March 31 for prior years should be obtained and inventory turnover ratios computed based on breakeven inventory figures. If this year's ratio does not compare favorably with those of prior years, the firm may be in trouble.

Another set of information which would aid in the financial analysis of Budd would be financial statements as of prior year-ends and industry average figures for financial ratios. The former would aid in analyzing trends in the firm's financial structure, while the latter would aid in assessing the firm's credit risk relative to other firms in the converting industry.

Finally, information should be obtained on the composition of the firm's debt to banks. Is this debt secured? How?

## CASE STUDY II. APEX CORPORATION

Apex Corporation was started in 1925 as an iron ore mining and processing firm. It subsequently acquired interests in nonferrous metals and has grown substantially. At present, it has annual sales volume approaching $60 million. About 50% of this volume is derived from production and processing of its own materials; the remainder is commission work for other firms.

Among the metals handled for its own account is titanium. Long used as a brightener in paints and paper, titanium is also used as a raw material for parts in the construction of supersonic aircraft and missiles. In the early 1950's, titanium was in short supply, and a sellers' market existed. However, in recent years, supply has increased considerably and profit margins have eroded.

Steven Bender, credit manager of Apex Corporation, has received an order for $12,000 of titanium from Miller Paper Corporation which, if approved, would bring the total exposure to $30,000. Though Apex's terms of sale are net 30 days, Miller has indicated that payment for this order will be made in 90 days.

Mr. Bender decided that the situation should be discussed with his firm's Treasurer and arranged for an appointment with her. The Treasurer, Linda Sheppard, asked Mr. Bender for background information on the account. Mr. Bender indicated that Miller had been a customer for 12 years. Volume had started small and had increased over time. Prior to this extended terms request, Miller had always paid promptly. Mr. Bender knew that Miller obtained some working capital financing from its bank, but no financial statement was in the credit file. Nor had Miller made financials available to credit reporting agencies.

Ms. Sheppard asked Mr. Bender how similar requests from other customers had been handled in the past. Bender advised that each request for any out of the ordinary credit extension was examined individually and decided on its merits. Ms. Sheppard then inquired as to when financial statement information was a prerequisite for shipping to a customer. Mr. Bender said that statements were requested, but he did not insist on receiving these if bank and trade information were favorable.

The discussion between Ms. Sheppard and Mr. Bender then touched on other areas of credit policy. It became clear that many credit decisions were made in an ad hoc fashion, and that there was a general lack of consistency in reaching decisions.

Both the Treasurer and the Credit Manager realized that Apex Corporation needed a written credit policy on which sound decisions could be based. Ms. Sheppard instructed Mr. Bender to prepare a written policy for the corporation.

## CASE II QUESTIONS. APEX CORPORATION

1. Prepare a statement of credit policy goals for Apex Corporation, stating in general the objectives of any credit department.

2. A complete credit policy should include specific procedures for handling various credit policy decisions, such as credit investigation, credit granting, terms of sale, and collection. The situation with respect to Miller Paper involves credit investigation and terms of sale decisions. Write sample policy statements for Apex in each of these areas which would address the questions raised by the Miller situation.

## CASE STUDY II. SOLUTION

1. Policy has been defined as a general course of action in recurring situations designed to achieve established objectives. Credit policy must spell out specific guides for day-to-day activity but should also allow for considerable latitude for judgment on the part of the credit executive.

Practices are implied in a good policy but fall under the scope of procedures. A sample credit policy statement might read as follows:

> The Credit Department shall function under the direction of the Corporate Treasurer, and its activities shall be coordinated with overall company policy and the activities of the Billing and Sales Departments.

The Credit Department is to help build a broad and durable customer relationship for (the) company. In the discharge of this duty, the Credit Department shall maintain an interdependent cooperative attitude toward the Sales Department and strive to promote sales.

Adhering to the bounds of sound credit practices, the Credit Department shall strive to find an acceptable credit basis upon which to deal with each customer whom the Sales Department wishes to have purchase our goods or services. The decision on what constitutes an acceptable credit basis shall rest with the Credit Department. The Credit Department understands that no customer shall be denied the right to purchase our products until every prudent means of dealing with the customer has been exhausted.

2. The credit investigation question raised by Miller Paper is: at what level of exposure should the customer be required to provide a financial statement for analysis? This question is part of the larger policy issue: what practices shall the firm use in performing credit investigation? An appropriate credit policy with respect to credit investigation might be:

Credit Investigation. Credit investigation is undertaken with the intent of reducing the uncertainty in making credit-granting decisions. The more credit investigation is undertaken, the more accurate will be the resulting credit decisions, but the more expense will be expended in credit investigation. Thus, in deciding how much credit investigation to perform, the credit manager must weigh the costs of credit investigation (including his or her own analysis time) against the accuracy required for the decision. The general principal of credit investigation is: the credit manager should investigate until the cost of the next stage of investigation is not economical, given the characteristics of the customer on which the credit-granting decision is being made. This will mean that higher levels of credit investigation are undertaken when: (1) exposures are larger and (2) the creditworthiness of the customer is more uncertain. More extensive credit investigation is warranted in such cases since greater accuracy in credit granting is required to control bad debt expense and receivable carrying costs.

Relative to these principles, it is not at all clear that Mr. Bender made the wrong decision in not requiring a financial statement from Miller. Miller had a long history of prompt payments which is an important indication of a strong financial condition, and obtaining and analyzing financial statements is an expensive and time-consuming process.

The terms of sale policy question raised by Miller is trickier because of its legal implications. Apex may have violated the antitrust statutes in the past by granting extended terms to some customers while not offering the same terms to other customers. Policy in this area needs to address the "meeting competition in good faith" provisions of the antitrust statutes:

> Terms of Sale. Terms of sale for each product are set jointly by the marketing and credit departments. Because of antitrust considerations, extensions of these terms of sale may not be granted unless it can be confirmed that competitors are offering these extended terms for the same product. When it can be confirmed that such terms are being offered by competitors, the credit and marketing departments will jointly determine whether Apex will match these terms.

## PRACTICE PROBLEM

Return on Investment (ROI) measures profitability.

The DuPont method is among the more widely used approaches in calculating return on investment. It links efficiency in controlling assets with efficiency in producing a profit.

The formula is as shown below:

ROI—Earnings as a percent of sales times asset turnover, e.g.:

$$\text{Earnings as a percent of sales} = \frac{\text{Net profit}}{\text{Net sales}}$$

$$\text{Asset turnover} = \frac{\text{Net sales}}{\text{Total assets}}$$

Exhibits 12.3 and 12.4 on National Metals Company are provided for practice purposes. Exhibit 12.5, the chart entitled "Dupont Systems Applied to National Metals" shows answers and how they were reached.

## EXHIBIT 12.3
## NATIONAL METALS COMPANY INCOME STATEMENT
### Year Ending December 31
### (Thousands of Dollars, Except for Per-Share Data)

|  | 1990 | 1989 |
|---|---|---|
| Gross Sales | $3014 | $2860 |
| Bad Debt Expense | 14 | 10 |
| Net Sales | $3000 | $2850 |
| Cost and Expenses |  |  |
| Labor and materials | $2544 | $2850 |
| Depreciation | 100 | 90 |
| Selling expenses | 22 | 20 |
| Administrative expenses | 40 | 35 |
| Lease payments on buildings | 28 | 28 |
| Total operating costs | $2734 | $2586 |
| Net Operating Income (EBIT) | $ 266 | $ 264 |
| Less Interest Expense: |  |  |
| Interest on notes payable | $    8 | $    2 |
| Interest on first mortgage bonds | 58 | 45 |
| Total Interest | 66 | $   47 |
| Pretax Earnings | $ 200 | $ 217 |
| Federal & State taxes (40%) | 80 | 87 |
| Net Income | $ 120 | $ 130 |
| Preferred Dividends | $    8 | $    8 |
| Available for Common Stockholders | 112 | 122 |
| Dividends to Common Stockholders | 92 | 82 |
| Amount Added to Retained Earnings | 20 | 40 |
| Earnings Per Share (50,000 shares) | 2.24 | 2.44 |
| Dividends Per Share | 1.84 | 1.64 |

## EXHIBIT 12.4
## NATIONAL METALS COMPANY
### December 31 Balance Sheets
### (Thousands of Dollars)

|  | 1990 | 1989 |
|---|---|---|
| Cash | $ 50 | $ 55 |
| Marketable securities | 0 | 25 |
| Accounts receivable | 350 | 315 |
| Inventories | 300 | 215 |
| Total Current Assets | $ 700 | $ 610 |
| Gross plant and equipment | $1800 | $1470 |
| Less accrued depreciation | 500 | 400 |
| Total Assets | $2000 | $1680 |
|  |  |  |
| Accounts payable | $ 60 | $ 30 |
| Notes payable | 100 | 60 |
| Accrued wages | 10 | 10 |
| Accrued taxes | 130 | 120 |
| Total current liabilities | $ 300 | $ 220 |
| Long term debt | $ 800 | $ 580 |
| Stockholder's equity |  |  |
| Preferred stock | 20 | 20 |
| Common stock | 50 | 50 |
| Paid-in capital | 80 | 80 |
| Retained earnings | 750 | 730 |
| Total stockholders' equity | $ 900 | $ 880 |
|  |  |  |
| Total liabilities and equity | $2000 | $1680 |

## EXHIBIT 12.5 Dupont Systems Applied to National Metals

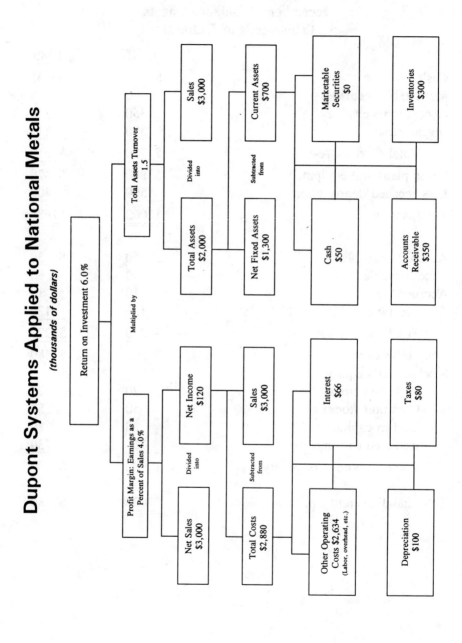

Dupont Systems Applied to National Metals

*(thousands of dollars)*

Return on Investment 6.0%

Total Assets Turnover 1.5

Multiplied by

Profit Margin: Earnings as a Percent of Sales 4.0%

Sales $3,000

Divided into

Total Assets $2,000

Current Assets $700

Subtracted from

Net Fixed Assets $1,300

Marketable Securities $0

Cash $50

Inventories $300

Accounts Receivable $350

Net Income $120

Divided into

Net Sales $3,000

Sales $3,000

Subtracted from

Total Costs $2,880

Interest $66

Other Operating Costs $2,634 (Labor, overhead, etc.)

Taxes $80

Depreciation $100

## HUMAN RELATIONS-BEHAVIORAL TYPICAL QUESTIONS & ANSWERS

Indicated below are typical questions of the kind likely to appear on any of the credentialing examinations addressing human behavior. Each question is followed by a model answer.

1. Q. Indicate at least five ways to improve one's ability to listen and explain.

   A. a. Don't talk or interrupt. Concentrate on what is being said instead of what you will say next. We learn more if we listen carefully.

   b. Be empathetic. Convey to the person speaking the impression that you are attentive and understanding. It helps to appear interested and looking toward the speaker. To look away, at the ceiling or reading your notes, is distracting to even very experienced speakers. Care should therefore be exercised to avoid doing these things.

   c. Demonstrate patience. Do not jump to premature conclusions—give the speaker time to make a point. Do not yawn or interrupt . . . such conduct is discourteous and impedes the exchange of information.

   d. Criticism. Unless your criticism is constructive, i.e., you have a solution to offer, avoid being argumentative lest you make the speaker defensive which would not benefit either party.

   e. Freely ask questions. Asking questions indicates interest and connotes that you are open-minded and have been listening. People who ask questions invariably learn more quickly because the correct interpretation is immediately imparted. The alternative is to take notes and look up, however, this creates additional work and is obviously time consuming.

2. Q. Is there any value to non-verbal communication? Explain.

   A. Yes. That portion of the message we do not wish to communicate verbally is left to non-verbal communication. For example, you know that one of your colleagues did something that you perceive to be unethical. Rather than to cause him to lose face, you generalize on the issue while looking at him, saying nothing to indicate that he is the offender. You and he are aware of the transgression.

3. Q. How can the grapevine be useful in an organization?

 A. Although it should not be used in place of formal channels of communication, this additional source is a way of gathering information to and from employees and it can provide insight into their beliefs and attitudes.

4. Q. Are excellent companies perceived as such because there is good communication of their goals to employees?

 A. Usually. When employees understand the organization's goals at all levels, they will better understand and appreciate why certain actions are taken. This leads to commitment to these actions and precludes the circulation of rumors.

5. Q. Why does upward communication within an organization often break down?

 A. Often, while the message to the manager from his people is quite clear, he or she either does not hear it or fails to see it in proper perspective. For example, in the collection department, three people suddenly resign. The question raised is "Did you (the manager) see it coming?"

6. Q. Why is feedback important?

 A. Unless we know what we have said is received, communication is incomplete. Feedback from the receivers of our information lets us know if understanding has occurred or whether there is any confusion.

7. Q. Give an example of teamwork.

 A. Teamwork in a credit department: The department consists of five credit analysts and a manager. Each member of the department is authorized to approve credit and collect from those accounts granted credit. Each analyst has responsibility for achieving one-fifth of the department's goal objective, e.g., the monthly A/R is $500,000 divided by 5. One analyst is nearing end with $85,000 which reflects a $15,000 shortfall. The manager discusses this with the group and they decide on a strategy to help the below-goal analyst achieve target. By month-end although the struggling analyst attains another $10,000, the overall goal is met because another analyst pulled in $105,000. This is teamwork in action.

8. Q. Indicate and explain three factors that are common to informal work groups.

A. Group norms, cohesiveness, and leadership. The group norm, whether verbalized or not among members, refers to what constitutes acceptable behavior within that group. Cohesiveness refers to the extent of attraction each individual has for the group. Cohesiveness is affected by group size, previous accomplishments, attitudes, and behaviors. Groups tend to choose their leader in terms of an individual they view as being most able to help them achieve their objectives. The leader is expected to have good communication skills who can provide direction and disseminate information for the group.

9. Q. Does team building have anything to do with awareness of the work group?

A. Yes. The group must be aware of anything that could prevent it them from functioning more effectively. Awareness prods the group to take initiatives to eliminate conditions that have a negative effect on functioning.

10. Q. Why do informal groups exist in organizations?

A. Because of mutual interests, a desire to realize social needs, friendships, work conditions, management, technology, and the manager's style.

11. Q. Management theorists refer to a creative process. Explain what is meant by the creative process.

A. The process consists of four steps, i.e., preparation, incubation, illumination, and verification. Preparation entails the conscious examining of an issue, problem, or topic. This requires thinking and study. Eventually one steps back away from the matter being examined and at this time, there is no thought about the issue, problem, or topic—this is known as the incubation stage. Ostensibly, unconscious mental processes related to the matter go on during incubation. Illumination manifests itself when suddenly the solution appears— what some refer to as the "Ah Ha" reaction. Verification involves the testing and refinement of the solution.

12. Q. Is brainstorming helpful to the creative individual? Why?

A. Yes. In brainstorming, where the problem is presented to a group, many ideas are generated and there is consequently likelihood of constructive criticism and possible solutions.

13. Q. What is meant by the statement that some employees are "following the beat of a different drum"?

A. This usually refers to those who deviate from the norms of the organization. If employees do not see their goals as being in harmony with organizational goals, then deviation may occur.

14. Q. What causes job frustration?

A. This occurs when a drive or motive is blocked before the goal is achieved. The cause usually emanates from a top management decision.

15. Q. What is goal conflict?

A. This is an occurrence that results when one attempts a goal that has both positive and negative features or when several competing goals exist.

16. Q. What is the cause of burnout? Describe the symptoms.

A. The cause is negative stress, i.e., attempting to do too much usually without adequate resources in terms of people and money. You are at odds with your role, society, and self. Observable symptoms are usually feelings of emotional exhaustion, looking at others in a harsh light, e.g., a "people be damned" attitude, and a self assessment that is critical and negative. Although you are still productive and effective in your role, you do not perceive yourself in that light anymore.

17. Q. In using a Management by Objective (MBO) approach to setting goals, is it simply a matter of handing each employee instructions on the departmental goals?

A. No. To be effective, MBO properly applied must make employees a part of the decision-making process. By giving each employee an opportunity to provide input, each individual identifies with the goal objectives. This results in a balance where company goals are in harmony with individual goals. The important thing to remember is that when an employee identifies with the process, he or she will make sure that goals are achieved even if extraordinary measures have to be used. This may require putting in extra time and/or doing more than usual in terms of day-to-day routine.

18. Q. What determines the most appropriate structure for a credit department, e.g., line organization, line and staff organization, matrix organization, or committee organization?
    A. The key is to adopt the structure that helps in achieving good performance. Carried further, studies have concluded that the kind of structure is dependent not only on organizational objectives but also on the technology and rate of change in the micro environment.
19. Q. Differentiate between intrinsic and extrinsic rewards for employees.
    A. That which is intrinsic is internal to the individual and emanates from involvement with certain tasks and duties. Extrinsic rewards are more tangible and are controlled and distributed by the company.
20. Q. The media frequently refers to "Human Oz Accounting." What does this mean?
    A. This refers to a process of assigning a dollar estimate to the value of a firm's human assets. This value is obviously not one that is shown on a balance sheet.
21. Q. What is employee development?
    A. The process which focuses on behavior and attitudes of individuals for the purpose of increasing productivity and goal attainment. The aim is to have more effective employees.
22. Q. Name some common methods of employee development.
    A. In-house training sessions, performance review, coaching, and other forms of on-the-job training.
23. Q. What are the sequential steps to follow in training employees?
    A. Tell the trainee, show the trainee, have the trainee do the task, check up on how well it is done.
24. Q. What is the advantage of having satisfied employees?
    A. People who enjoy their work and like their supervisors and company are usually more productive. They are also more committed to goal achievements.
25. Q. Are employees essentially motivated by money?
    A. Not unless it serves to satisfy an unsatisfied need. Money alone will not satisfy needs for self esteem or recognition. For many, once their basic needs are satisfied, money is less of a motiva-

tion. Abraham Maslow explained that man is not primarily an economic animal. He is first a spiritual human being. His greatest urges are those of the spirit. His feelings are stronger than his thoughts; his reactions come quicker from the heart than from the world. We are only logical to the extent that our feelings let us be.

26. Q. Is there any creditability to the attitude that employees are productive only to the extent that they are closely monitored and supervised?

   A. No. This is a rigid, extreme view held by some managers. Employees prefer to have an opportunity to schedule their own work and want the responsibility to accomplish a job by themselves. Studies have shown that productivity suffers when people cannot see their work completed from start to finish.

27. Q. Who is the management researcher who created Theory X and Theory Y?

   A. The creator of Theory X and Theory Y is Douglas McGregor.

28. Q. Who created the concept of a hierarchy of needs?

   A. Abraham Maslow created the concept.

29. Q. Name the different levels that comprise Maslow's Need Hierarchy.

   A. The need levels are: Physiological, Safety, Social, Esteem or Ego, and Self Actualization.

30. Q. What purpose does reference to Maslow's Hierarchy of Needs serve?

   A. The Hierarchy of Needs provides a framework designed to facilitate understanding of human needs and wants. According to Maslow, people start with the lower order of needs and move up the hierarchy one step at a time as present level needs become satisfied. More detail on Maslow and other theorists may be obtained from textbooks on management.


## SCENARIO TO ANALYZE

A scenario is not as detailed as a case, however, it follows a similar format for study and analysis.

## *They Give 110% to the Job*

Operating a credit department requires meeting deadlines, adhering to schedules and achieving results. Steve Kay as credit manager is responsible for accounts receivable of $150 million and a department of four people. He complains about not having the luxury of enough time to concern himself with personalities. He therefore hires only "hard workers" who follow instructions and give 110% to the job. Two of his credit analysts are new. They replaced experienced people who were with him for six months. The new analysts are coming along but are slower and make mistakes that could be avoided if they were more careful. In the two years he has been credit manager, he has not found employees who work as hard and as effectively as he feels he did while climbing the ladder.

He often thinks of how much better it would be if people were more motivated. To achieve goals he has to spend extra time going over the work of his analysts and is constantly under stress to meet a deadline. What is the problem and how can it be resolved?

## Scenario Model Solution

Steve must learn to understand that results depend upon his ability to motivate the analysts. To do so, he must be able to please them emotionally . . . skill in this area can be developed.

Over and above the effort an analyst normally gives to the job, he or she has a reserve amount of ability and energy to give if he or she feels like it . . . if he or she is motivated to do so.

There is no way to force an analyst to give Steve his reserve ability and energy, but he will willingly give it to him if he takes the time to motivate him . . . when Steve creates in him the will to work. No company can buy an employee's enthusiasm, loyalty, the devotion of hearts, minds, and souls. Steve must learn that helping others to uncover and utilize their full range of talents is an integral part of his responsibility as credit manager.

Frederick Herzberg advanced a theory of motivation which related to job satisfaction. The motivational factors of achievement, recognition, advancement, the work itself, the possibility of personal growth and responsibility are said to be job centered. The maintenance factors include company policy and administration, technical supervision, interpersonal relations with supervisors, interpersonal relations with peers, interpersonal relations with subordinates, salary, job security, personal life, work conditions and status. These factors are said to be peripheral to the job and related to the external work environment (Herzberg, 1966).

Another researcher, Abraham Maslow constructed a hierarchy of needs comprised of five levels, i.e., physiological, safety, social, esteem and self actualization (Maslow, 1954).

Later, Victor Vroom expanded on the work of Maslow and Herzberg and developed an "Expectancy Theory of Motivation." According to Vroom, his theory views motivation as a process governing choices. Therefore, a person who has a given goal must perform some behavior to achieve the goal. The theory is said to explain how the goals of individuals influence their effort and how the behavior that people select has to do with their assessment of whether it will lead to the goal objective (Vroom, 1964).

Behavioral aspects include the meaning of motivation, and in addition, the following theories: *Motivation-Maintenance*, *Preference-Expectancy*, and *Reinforcement*. Questions are likely to address the areas of managing conflict, leadership, encouraging effort, developing abilities, pay satisfaction, job descriptions, quality control, and business ethics.

Readers unfamiliar with the various concepts related to the Hierarchy-of-Needs theory, the Motivation/Hygiene Theory, and Theories X or Y should refer to current university material on this subject. Guidance is available to individuals registered with the National Institute of Credit. Simply contact NIC stating your need and oral or written information will be provided.

# APPENDIX A

# GET CONTROL OF YOUR CAREER

*On the following pages, the Career Roadmap is summarized to provide you an overview of the certification process.*

## GET CONTROL OF YOUR CAREER

The Career Roadmap is the approved vehicle to guide career practitioners toward earning a designation for each skill level from supervisory to senior management responsibility.

Point values are assigned to each of the following major categories and facilitate career progression:

- work experience and special interest;
- participation, local and national;
- college and continuing education; and
- special consideration activities.

Applications for designations must include a Career Roadmap, NIC registration form with fee, an indication that official college transcripts are being sent, and a resume of experience. Roadmap points needed for each designation level are:

- Credit Business Associate (CBA)                                                 50
- Credit Business Fellow (CBF)                                                      100
- Certified Credit Executive (CCE)                                                 125

Once registered with NIC and having a Career Roadmap certified with 50 points, an applicant is ready to be evaluated by NIC for the

CBA designation and if the requirements of Plan A or Plan B are met can proceed to take the examination. Registration is processed through the local NACM affiliate to NIC.

## CREDIT BUSINESS ASSOCIATE (CBA)

### Plan A

Satisfactory completion (grade average must be "C" or better) of the following courses:

> Introductory Accounting
> Intermediate Accounting
> Macro Economics
> Micro Economics
> Credit and Collection Principles
> Financial Analysis
> Business Communication

To substantiate the above, have the university send an official transcript to your local NACM office.

### Plan B

An alternate plan requires meeting the following criteria:

A. Three years' experience in business credit administration and completion of the Credit Administration Program (CAP). This requires an official transcript, minimum grade of "B" and a current resume.

B. CAP courses required are:

> Credit and Collection Principles
> Financial Analysis
> Credit Management Cases

With 50 Career Roadmap points and meeting requirements of Plan A or Plan B, applicants are admitted to the CBA examination. The examination is administered at the local NACM affiliate office.

Upon successful completion of the examination, a notification is sent and followed by an engraved CBA certificate forwarded to the applicant's NACM affiliate for presentation at its next meeting.

## CREDIT BUSINESS FELLOW (CBF)

The next benchmark level requires 100 Career Roadmap points and meeting the course or experience requirements under Plan A or Plan B of the CBF designation.

### Plan A

Have official college transcripts sent to the local NACM affiliate office showing satisfactory completion (grade average of "C" or better) of the following nine courses:

Business Law I
Business Law II
Speaking
Marketing
*Credit Management Cases
Psychology
Management
2 elective business courses (from approved list)

* Candidates who used this course under Plan B of the CBA may not use it again here.

Under Plans A or B, candidates must have earned the CBA designation.

### Plan B

An alternative which requires meeting the following criteria:

A. Transcripts showing completion of a Master's Degree in Business or completion of a Bachelor's Degree in Business and a resume detailing a minimum of three years' teaching experience at the college level.
B. A resume detailing a minimum of five years of experience in credit management (up to two required courses may be substituted for experience, e.g., two courses for first and second year). Experience should be at the management or supervisory levels.

Once the Career Roadmap point requirements under Plan A or Plan B are verified by NIC, applicants are admitted to the CBF examination.

Examinations are scheduled for the Spring and Fall of each year and are taken at local NACM affiliate offices nationwide.

Upon successful completion of the three-part examination, a notification is sent and followed by an engraved certificate forwarded to the applicant's NACM affiliate for presentation at its next meeting.

Candidates may now prepare for the CCE designation.

## CERTIFIED CREDIT EXECUTIVE (CCE)

### Plan A

A. Applicant submits an updated Career Roadmap showing 125 earned points. This roadmap is certified by the NACM affiliate and routed to NIC.

B. Upon receipt at NIC, the examination date is scheduled through the local NACM affiliate.

C. Upon successful completion of the examination, a notification is sent and followed by an engraved certificate forwarded to the applicant's NACM affiliate for presentation at its next meeting.

### Plan B

This alternative is designed for candidates already at the executive level in their careers.

*A. Complete an NIC Registration, application, and Personal Data Form and submit to the local NACM affiliate for processing to NIC. The registration and application forms are processed by NIC and the Personal Data Form is point-scored by the Accreditation Committee.

B. The weighted score determines whether an applicant is admitted to the examination.

C. If the applicant is not admitted to the examination, a new application may be submitted after six months.

D. If the applicant is admitted and passes the examination, notification is sent, followed by an engraved certificate forwarded to the applicant's NACM affiliate for presentation at the next meeting.

**E.** Candidates are certified for three years and must therefore recertify every three years thereafter until they reach age 60. A CCE Recertification Report is available for this purpose and may be obtained from NIC.

* Applicants who wish to complete a Career Roadmap showing 125 or more points certified by the local NACM affiliate may be admitted to the examination. *(This alternative was approved by the Accreditation Committee on June 5, 1990).*

# APPENDIX B

# Professional Designation Update

The following pages are designed to be used by coordinators and instructors who wish to impart to a group the sequential steps leading from one designation to another.

Each page may be enlarged and used as an overhead transparency to facilitate imparting the information.

Because changes may be made from time to time, check with the National Institute of Credit (NIC) before making a presentation using this material.

# PROFESSIONAL DESIGNATION

# UPDATE

The National Institute of Credit, NIC, is the national agency empowered to administer the issuance of professional designations for:

☞ Corporate Credit Management Personnel

☞ Bankers, Controllers, Treasurers and Financial Analysts

☞ City, County, State and Federal Finance Employees

There are three nationally recognized designations, one for each level:

**CBA** - Credit Business Associate: Supervisory Level

**CBF** - Credit Business Fellow: Management Level

**CCE** - Certified Credit Executive: Upper Management Level

## Getting Started

## How?
Use of the Career Roadmap.

## Why?
Because the benefits include:

1. An objective point scoring system to guide applicants.

   ☞ Points earned through education, participation and work experience count toward admission requirements for each designation.

2. A clear progression is mapped out.

3. Admission to qualifying exams is facilitated.

## How do designations make a difference?

In many ways, which include:

1. Increasing the likelihood of recognition in terms of salary, promotion and higher esteem.

2. Helping companies to identify and retain top performers.

3. Making recruiting easier once it is known that each career level has certified people available.

4. Strengthens the profession and moves practitioners closer to parity with CPA's, CCM's and other designation holders in business fields.

# CBA - Credit Business Associate

1. The applicant completes a registration form which is available from NIC or the NACM Affiliated Association.

## Plan A

2. *The applicant includes with the registration form transcripts or grade reports showing satisfactory completion (grade average must be C or better) of the following courses:

>  2 Accounting Courses
>
>  2 Economics Courses
>
>  1 Financial Analysis Course
>
>  1 Credit & Collections Principles Course
>
>  1 Business Communications Course

## Plan B

3. Three years of experience in business credit administration and completion of the required Credit Administration Program (CAP). This requires an official transcript, minimum grade of B and a certified resume.

*A portfolio containing documentation of formal and informal learning experiences may be submitted to NIC for evaluation to determine if equivalency may be granted in lieu of certain formal courses. The applicant should contact NIC for instructions.*

*Transcripts may be sent directly to NIC from the university.*

4. The applicant completes a "Career Roadmap" which is available from NIC or the NACM Affiliated Association.

☞      The Career Roadmap awards points for education, career activity participation and work experience.

☞      50 Points, certified by the applicant's NACM Affiliated Association are needed to qualify applicants to the exam.

☞      Applicants, upon earning 50 points and meeting course requirements, receive a credit supervisory candidate letter and are admitted to the exam.

5. The CBA exam is sent to the applicant's NACM Affiliate. Applicants are given up to 3 hours to complete it.

6. The completed exam is then returned by the Affiliate to NIC Headquarters for grading.

7. Within 6 weeks, notification is sent to both the applicant and Affiliate as to whether or not a passing grade was achieved.

☞      If the exam is passed, the applicant is notified by mail and receives a Request for Certificate form.

☞      On failed exams, the applicant is notified to arrange for a re-take.

8. An engraved CBA certificate is sent to the applicant's NACM Affiliate for presentation at their next meeting.

# CBF - Credit Business Fellow

1. Applicants contact NACM Affiliate when ready to apply for the CBF designation. (The applicant must have already earned the CBA.)

2. A "Career Roadmap", updated with proof of an additional 50 points for a total of 100 points, is certified by the NACM Affiliate.

**PLAN A:**

☞ Transcripts or grade reports showing satisfactory completion (grade average must be C or better) of the following 9 courses:

>2 Business Law Courses
>
>1 Public Speaking Course
>
>1 Marketing Course
>
>1 Cases in Credit Management Course
>
>1 Psychology Course
>
>1 Management Course
>
>2 Elective Business Courses

3. Applicants then receive a credit management candidate letter and are admitted to the next CBF exam.

# CBF - Credit Business Fellow
---CONTINUED---

## PLAN B:

4. Substitution of the following for the course work requirements:

☞    *    Transcripts showing completion of a Master's Degree in Business

☞      Transcripts showing completion of a Bachelor's Degree in Business and a resume showing at least three years of teaching experience

☞      A resume showing at least five years of experience in Credit Administration (up to 2 required courses may be substituted for experience, e.g., 2 courses for first and second year)

5. Applicant receives a credit management candidate letter and admission to the next CBF exam.

*A portfolio containing documentation of formal and informal learning experiences may be submitted to NIC for evaluation to determine if equivalency may be granted in lieu of certain formal courses. Contact NIC for instructions.*

6. Within 6 weeks, notification is sent to the applicant and Affiliate as to whether or not a passing grade was achieved.

☞      If the exam is passed, applicant is notified by mail and receives a Request for Certificate form.

☞      On failed exams, applicant is notified of which part(s) to retake.

7. An engraved CBF certificate is sent to applicant's NACM Affiliate for presentation at their next meeting.

## CCE - Certified Credit Executive
### "Career Roadmap" Routing

1. Applicants notify the NACM Affiliate when ready to apply for the CCE designation.

2. Applicants submit an updated "Career Roadmap" showing an earned additional 25 points (a total of 125 points), certified by the NACM Affiliated Association.

3. Upon receipt of the certified Career Roadmap from the NACM Affiliate, an application for admission to the CCE exam is sent by NIC.

4. Once NIC receives the application, applicant is classified as a Certified Credit Executive Candidate and asked to arrange to take the exam at the Affiliate.

5. After an exam is completed, it is promptly returned to NIC Headquarters for grading.

6. Within six weeks, notification is sent to the candidate and Affiliate indicating whether or not a passing grade has been achieved.

☞   If the exam is passed, a certificate is engraved and sent to the Affiliate for presentation at their next meeting. CCE recipients are also recognized in Business Credit Magazine and at the Annual Credit Congress.

☞   On failed exams, the candidate is advised of areas needing review and asked to retake the exam.

*NOTE: Certification is for three years...candidates must complete 6 points over the next three years, i.e., 3 education and 3 participation points to qualify for recertification.*

## For CCE Candidates
## Already at the Executive Level
Application is Subject to Affiliate
and NIC verification and approval

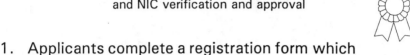

1.  Applicants complete a registration form which is available from NIC or the Affiliated Association.

2.  Applicants then complete an application and Personal Data Form and send it to the NACM Affiliated Association.
    *See exception below

3.  Upon receipt of these forms, NIC forwards them to the NACM Accreditation Committee for point scoring.

☞      If the applicant achieves an average point score at or above the minimum, a notification letter is sent advising of approval to take the exam.

☞      If the applicant falls below the minimum average point score, he or she is asked to reapply at a later date.

4.  Qualified exam candidates must notify their NACM Affiliate, who notifies NIC to forward the exam for a scheduled date.

*Applicants who wish to complete a Career Roadmap showing 125 or more points certified by the local NACM affiliate may be admitted to the examination. (This alternative was approved by the Accreditation Committee on June 5, 1990).*

# APPENDIX C

# SAMPLE CERTIFICATES

Sample copies of the certificates which are awarded to successful candidates of the CAP, ACAP, CBA, CBF, and CCE designations have been reproduced on the following pages for your reference.

# SAMPLE CERTIFICATE

The National Institute of Credit

Be it known that

**Boris Yeltsin**

has satisfactorily completed the prescribed study requirements of the
National Association of Credit Management's

**Credit Administration Program**

Administered by the Credit Research Foundation
and is therefore presented this
Certificate of Achievement

In witness thereof, given this 12th day of April 19 92

President,
National Association of Credit Management

President,
Credit Research Foundation

Vice President, Education
Credit Research Foundation

The National Institute of Credit

Be it known that

Vladimir Posner

has satisfactorily completed the prescribed study requirements of the
National Association of Credit Management's

Advanced Credit Administration Program

Administered by the Credit Research Foundation
and is therefore presented this
Certificate of Achievement

In witness thereof, given this  22nd  day of    April      19 92

President,
National Association of Credit Management

President,
Credit Research Foundation

Vice President, Education
Credit Research Foundation

# The National Institute of Credit

## This Certifies that

### Phillip Donahue

has completed the prescribed course of study and has met all other requirements for the Associate Award and is hereby entitled to the designation as a

## Credit Business Associate

with all the honors and rights pertaining thereto.

IN WITNESS WHEREOF, for and on behalf of the NATIONAL INSTITUTE OF CREDIT, duly incorporated under the Laws of the State of New York, we have hereto set our hands and seal

this        first        day of        April        19 92

President
National Association of Credit Management

Vice President
Director of Education

The National Institute of Credit

This Certifies that

**Albert C. Bracuti**

has completed the prescribed course of study and has met all other requirements for the Fellow Award and is hereby entitled to the designation as a

Credit Business Fellow

with all the honors and rights pertaining thereto.

IN WITNESS WHEREOF, for and on behalf of the NATIONAL INSTITUTE OF CREDIT, duly incorporated under the Laws of the State of New York, we have hereto set our hands and seal

this          second          day of          April          19 92

President
National Association of Credit Management

Vice President and Director
National Institute of Credit

# National Association of Credit Management

CCE / CERTIFIED CREDIT EXECUTIVE

THROUGH ITS ACCREDITATION BOARD
CONFERS ON

## Donald R. Mosher

THE DESIGNATION OF

### CERTIFIED CREDIT EXECUTIVE

IN RECOGNITION OF EXPERIENCE AS A CREDIT EXECUTIVE,
ADHERENCE TO PROFESSIONAL STANDARDS, ADVOCACY OF SUPERIOR
BUSINESS CREDIT MANAGEMENT, AND FOR SUCCESSFULLY
MEETING PRESCRIBED REQUIREMENTS.

IN WITNESS THEREOF, GIVEN THIS  12th  DAY OF  April  19 92

CHAIRMAN OF THE BOARD

PRESIDENT

VICE PRESIDENT OF EDUCATION

CHAIRMAN ACCREDITATION BOARD

1100

# CANONS OF BUSINESS CREDIT ETHICS

A copy of the *Canons of Business Credit Ethics* has been reproduced for your reference. The canons may be purchased as a plaque to hang on a wall.

# CANONS OF BUSINESS CREDIT ETHICS

**I** Justice, equity and confidence constitute the foundation of credit administration.

**II** Agreements and contracts reflect integrity and should never be breached by either party.

**III** The interchange of credit information must be based upon confidence, cooperation, reciprocity and confidentiality.

**IV** It is deemed unethical to be a party to unwarranted assignments or transfers of an insolvent debtor's assets nor should creditors participate in secret arrangements.

**V** Creditors should cooperate for the benefit of all in adjustment or liquidation of insolvent estates or companies.

**VI** Creditors must render all possible assistance to honest debtors who become insolvent.

**VII** Dishonest debtors must be exposed and referred to the authorities.

**VIII** Cooperation, fairness and honesty must dominate in all insolvent debtor proceedings.

**IX** Costly administrative procedures in the rehabilitation or liquidation of an insolvent debtor shall be avoided at all times.

**X** Members pledge themselves to uphold the integrity, dignity and honor of the credit professional in all of their business dealings.

# NATIONAL ASSOCIATION OF CREDIT MANAGEMENT

# CASE STUDY METHOD OF INSTRUCTION

The case study method of instruction may be new to some individuals. We have therefore provided suggestions to facilitate the understanding of case studies and thereby maximize results in their use.

# The Case Method Of Instruction

Whatever method of instruction is best suited to the material being presented will be used in classes. The "case method" is the approach most commonly used.

Under this method, the participant is presented with a case, a description of an actual business transaction. Placing himself in the position of the executive responsible for acting in this situation, he must evaluate the facts, arrive at a decision, and formulate a plan of action. Through the analysis of cases, he practices making decisions in new situations and translating these decisions into action.

Learning by the case method is not based on accumulation and memorizing facts. There is no one right answer to a case. One solution may differ from another; both may differ from the instructor's. Seldom is there full agreement. Any solution may be considered satisfactory if it is based on facts and sound reasoning.

The case method is new to many participants. The following suggestions for working through a case may be helpful:

1. **Read the Case Carefully.** Remember that this is a real situation; as in your own experience, the account of the situation may include irrelevant facts, or opinions and rumors masquerading as facts.

2. **Define the Problem.** Often this is the most difficult part. Be sure that you understand what the problem is and that you are aware of its implications.

3. **Find the Facts.** It is often helpful to outline them in writing. If it appears that opinions, rumors, or feelings should be considered, set them down with the objective facts, but recognize them for exactly what they are. Recheck to be sure that you have all the facts.

4. **Evaluate the Facts.** Weed out those that are of no importance. Determine the relative importance of those which remain. It may be helpful to indicate which are most important, which less important, by a system of checks, asterisks, or other marks.

5. **Develop Alternative Solutions Based On Facts.** Do not look for a quick solution; seldom is there only one. It may be helpful to write down all the possible solutions.

6. **Make the Decision.** Decide which of the possible solutions you would select. Support the decision with facts from the case. Be sure you know why you select this solution. Recognize your own prejudices, feelings, and experience, and if your decision is based on these in addition to the facts, say so.

7. **Formulate a Plan of Action.** In light of the facts, decide how to put your decision into effect. Be sure to consider such questions as these: When should the decision go into effect? In what order will various steps be taken? What problems may arise from adopting this decision? How can they be prevented or solved? What will determine whether the decision is considered satisfactory? If it proves unsatisfactory, what alternatives will be open?

# GLOSSARY AND TERMINOLOGY

## INTRODUCTION

Every profession—law, accounting, economics, psychology, and medicine, and many others—has a body of terminology that is used rather perfunctorily by its practitioners. Within the credit and financial establishment, there are such terms which are esoteric to the uninitiated and yet important to day-to-day communication, and it is important to have a working knowledge of those terms that relate to the practice of credit administration.

It is in this context that we encourage the reader to become familiar with the glossary of legal terms that follows, as well as the everyday credit terminology. In addition, various competency-based tests, whether finals or comprehensive exams, often include the terms in a true/false question or open-ended question format.

Because the list is not intended to be all inclusive, your attention is directed to other texts such as *Credit Executives Handbook* by George Christie and Al Bracuti, and *The Dictionary of Business and Credit Terms* by Ben Berman. Both publications may be ordered through the NACM Publications Department, 8815 Centre Park Drive, Suite 200, Columbia, Maryland 21045-2117.

## REVIEW SUGGESTIONS

Check your knowledge of the words contained in this listing by practice. As you become familiar with each word move on to the next until you know all of the listed meanings. Grouping the words into smaller segments may be helpful. Some prefer to use index cards, with a separate card for each word.

Those using this review are from various levels of experience with different learning styles. Consequently there is no one best way to review the material. Try different methods until you find the one best suited to your way of learning.

## GLOSSARY OF LEGAL TERMS

The following terms are reprinted from the *Credit Manual of Commercial Laws,* a reference book covering all federal and state laws dealing with commercial transactions which is updated annually. The book is published by NACM, 8815 Centre Park Drive, Suite 200, Columbia, Maryland 21045-2117 and is available from the NACM Publications Department.

*Acceptance (with respect to negotiable instruments).*   The drawee's engagement to honor the draft as presented.

*Accord and Satisfaction.*   An agreement by which a claim is satisfied and discharged.

*Accommodation indorser.*   One who places an indorsement of commercial paper without compensation, in effect, as a guaranty of payment.

*Acknowledgment.*   The statement of a competent officer, usually a notary public, that the person who has executed an instrument, has appeared before the officer and has sworn to the facts of its execution.

*Action.*   A suit at law or in equity.

*Actionable.*   Affording grounds for a legal action.

*Administrator.*   One appointed to manage and distribute the estate of a deceased person who has not left a will, or where for some reason an executor has not been appointed or qualified under the will.

*Affidavit.*   A statement sworn to or affirmed before an official who is authorized to administer oaths, usually a notary public.

*After-acquired property.*   Property a debtor acquired after the execution of a mortgage or other form of indebtedness and which secures such indebtedness.

*Agent.*   A person who acts for another person who is referred to as the principal.

*Amicus curiae.* Friend of the court. A term frequently used to designate one not a party to the proceeding but who has filed a brief with respect to the issue or principal of law to be decided.

*Arbitration.* The determination of a dispute by a disinterested third person, or persons, selected by the disputants.

*Arrangement.* Setting in order. A term used with respect to certain types of compositions with creditors such as an arrangement under Chapter 11 or 13 of the Bankruptcy Act.

*Assignment.* The transfer of property rights by one person known as the assignor to another person known as the assignee.

*Assumpsit.* A form of action for the recovery of damages for the nonperformance of a contract.

*Attachment.* Taking property into custody of the court, either to secure a judgment or as a method of acquiring jurisdiction.

*Attestation.* The act of witnessing the execution of an instrument.

*Attorney-in-fact.* A person who is authorized by power of attorney to act for another.

*Bailment.* The delivery of property by one known as the bailor to another known as the bailee to be held in custody for certain purposes.

*Bequest.* A gift of personal property by will.

*Bill of exchange.* A written order, which may be negotiable or non-negotiable, directing one party to pay a certain sum of money to him or to a third party.

*Bill of lading.* Receipt and contract issued by a common carrier for the shipment of goods.

*Bill of sale.* A written instrument by which one transfers his rights or interest in chattels and goods to another.

*Blank indorsement.* Indorsement that consists only of the signature of the indorser and does not state in whose favor it is made.

*Blue sky laws.* State legislation that regulates the issuance and sale of corporate securities.

*Bona fide.* In good faith.

*Bona fide purchaser.* One who buys property without knowledge or notice of the interest in it of a third party.

*Bulk transfer.* The transfer of inventory or trade fixtures of a portion thereof not in the regular course of business.

*Caveat emptor.*    Let the buyer beware. In the absence of a warranty, a buyer purchases goods at his own risk, unless the seller is guilty of fraud.

*Certiorari.*    A writ of a higher court issued to a lower court directing the lower court to transmit its proceedings for review.

*Chattel.*    Any type of personal property as distinguished from real property.

*Chattel mortgage.*    Indebtedness secured by chattels, title and possession of which may be in the debtor but which may pass to the creditor upon the debtor's default.

*Chose.*    A thing; personal property.

*Chose in action.*    Property not in possession but a right of action for such possession. A claim or right to recover a debt or damages.

*Collateral security.*    A separate obligation that is given to secure the performance of the primary obligation in a contract.

*Common carrier.*    One whose business it is to transport passengers or freight for the public.

*Consideration.*    The required element in all contracts by which a legal right or promise is exchanged for the act or promise of another person.

*Consignment.*    The shipment of goods or chattels by means of a common carrier from one person known as the consignor to another known as the consignee; also, the transfer of property to another for sale by him or her.

*Conveyance.*    The transfer of an interest in realty; a deed. May sometimes include leases and mortgages.

*Copyright.*    The exclusive right granted by the federal government to publish and reproduce copies of writings and drawings.

*Counterclaim.*    A claim asserted by the defendant against whom suit is instituted.

*Covenant.*    A promise by one person made to another.

*Devise.*    The gift of real property in a will. Also (as a verb): to give real property by will.

*Dishonor.*    The non-payment of a negotiable instrument on its due date.

*Draft.*    A bill of exchange.

*Drawee.*    The person on whom a bill of exchange is drawn.

*Drawer.* The person who draws a bill of exchange.

*Easement.* The right of one person to use the land, or a portion of the land, of another for a specific purpose without obtaining possession thereof.

*Eminent domain.* The power of a sovereign government to take private property for public purposes.

*Equity of redemption.* The right of a mortgagor to redeem his or her property after the mortgage is past due.

*Escrow.* The delivery of a deed or of personal property to a third party for delivery to the recipient thereof upon the happening of certain conditions.

*Estoppel.* The rule of law that precludes a person from denying certain facts because of previous inconsistent conduct or statements.

*Factor.* One who has received goods or merchandise for sale on behalf of another.

*Fee simple.* Absolute ownership of real property.

*Fixture.* A chattel that has been affixed to real estate and may or may not be severable therefrom without injury to the property.

*Foreclosure.* The legal act by which the owner of a mortgage cuts off the rights or interest of the mortgagor in the mortgaged property.

*Franchise.* A license, privilege, or right granted by a sovereign.

*Garnishment.* The legal process by which property due a defendant and in the hands of a third party is attached.

*Guarantee.* To assume the liability for such debts of another in the event of his or her default.

*Guaranty.* A contract by which one undertakes to be liable for the debt of another person in the event of his default.

*Inchoate.* Not yet completed or finished. Used in reference to rights that have not become absolute, such as a wife's inchoate right or dower during the lifetime of her husband.

*Indemnity.* Compensation paid for damage or loss sustained or anticipated.

*Indorsement.* The signature of a person transferring a negotiable instrument.

*Infant.* A person who dies without a will. Also (as an adjective): Having died without having made a will. Not having been disposed of by will.

*Joint liability.*   Liability imposed upon two or more persons.

*Joint tenancy.*   The ownership of property by two or more persons with the survivor taking the interest of the deceased.

*L. S. (Locus Sigilli)* An abbreviation following the signature to take the place of a seal.

*Laches.*   An unreasonable delay. Notwithstanding the provisions of statutes of limitations, a court of equity may deny relief because of laches on the part of the litigant.

*Lien.*   The right to satisfy a debt out of certain property owned by the debtor.

*Liquidated damages.*   The amount agreed upon between the parties asto the loss or damage sustained in the event of a breach of contract.

*Lis pendens.*   A pending suit. An instrument filed or recorded in a court or registry office that affords public notice of the pendency of an action, such as a proceeding to foreclose a mortgage.

*Minor.*   A person who has not reached legal maturity. An infant.

*Mortgage.*   A conditional conveyance of property to a creditor as security for a debt.

*Negligence.*   The failure by a reasonable person to use the sufficient care, diligence, and skill which he or she is required to use for the protection of others from injury or damage.

*Nisi prius.*   A term used to denote courts or terms of court held for the trial of civil actions with a jury.

*Nominal damages.*   The award of a nominal sum where no serious loss or damage has been sustained.

*Notary public.*   A public officer empowered to administer oaths and take acknowledgments.

*Per capita.*   By the head. In the law of descent and distribution, this term is used to indicate the right of descendants to take shares equally as members of a class who have the same relationship with one another.

*Per curiam.*   By the court. A term generally used to denote the opinion or decision of the court as a whole rather than that of a single judge.

*Per stirpes.*   By trunk or root. In the law of descent and distribution, this term is used to indicate the right of descendants to take share by representation of a deceased parent.

*Perjury.*   A false statement made under oath.

*Personal property.* All rights and interest owned in goods or chattels or against another person as distinguished from ownership of real estate.

*Pledge.* Bailment of personal property to secure a debt.

*Preference.* Paying or securing to one or more creditors, by an insolvent debtor, of all or a part of their claim to the exclusion of other creditors. Also a right acquired by a creditor by statute or legal proceedings to have his or her claim satisfied out of the debtor's assets before other creditors.

*Prima facie.* Evidence sufficient in law to establish a fact unless rebutted.

*Probate.* The act or process of proving a will or other instrument.

*Ratification.* The approval of the acts of another taken on one's behalf.

*Real property.* Land and everything that is permanently affixed to it.

*Receiver.* A person appointed by the court to take custody of property in litigation or insolvency.

*Reclamation.* A term used in bankruptcy to denote a right or proceeding on the part of a person having title to property to recover the same when it is in possession of the bankrupt, debtor, receiver, or trustee.

*Replevin.* An action to recover the possession of personal property taken or withheld from the owner unlawfully.

*Res adjudicata (or res judicata).* A matter that has been decided. This is a legal doctrine to the effect that once an issue has been finally decided between the parties by a court of competent jurisdiction, it cannot thereafter be litigated by those parties in a new proceeding before the same or any other court.

*Rescission.* The annulment of a contract as a result of which both parties are returned to their former positions.

*Satisfaction.* Written evidence of the payment of the debt.

*Seal.* Originally wax impression, but today consists of any written figure or form.

*Set-off.* A claim that one person has against another who has a claim against him.

*Statute of frauds.* A term applied to various statutes requiring agreements to be in writing.

*Statute of limitation.*   A law that limits the length of time within which a lawsuit must be commenced or the right to sue is lost.

*Subrogation.*   The substitution of one person in place of a creditor whose rights he or she acquires.

*Summons.*   A writ or notice requiring a person to appear before a court to answer a complaint.

*Surety.*   A person who agrees to be liable for the debt of contractual obligations of another.

*Tenancy by the entirety.*   The joint ownership of property by a husband and wife.

*Tenancy in common.*   The common and undivided ownership of property.

*Testator.*   A person who makes a will.

*Tort.*   A private or civil wrong exclusive of a breach of contract.

*Tortious.*   Wrongful; having the quality or nature of a tort.

*Turnover proceeding.*   A summary proceeding authorized under the provisions of the Bankruptcy Act requiring a bankrupt to turn over property to a receiver or trustee for administration. It may also be used in connection with property belonging to the bankrupt held by a third person.

*Ultra vires.*   The unauthorized acts of a corporation in violation of its certificate or charter of incorporation.

*Underwriter.*   A person who insures another.

*Usury.*   The charge of illegal interest.

*Venue.*   In law this term is used to indicate the county, district, or other place where a case is or will be tried. In many cases the law specifies the venue with particularity, such as the county of residence of one of the parties. The venue may be changed for the convenience of witnesses or other reasons.

*Waiver.*   The relinquishment or refusal to accept some right or benefit. A waiver may result from an express agreement, by the act of a party, or by failure to take appropriate action when required.

*Warranty.*   The representation that an article has certain properties, the breach of which subjects one to financial liability.

*Writ.*   A term derived from the common law referring to a precept issued in the name of the sovereign or state directing the person named therein to comply with the directions contained therein. Under the common law, all actions were instituted by the issuance of a specific form of writ and no cause could be instituted unless a recognized form of writ was executed thereof.

# EVERYDAY CREDIT TERMINOLOGY

There are certain terms that are consistently used during the course of discharging credit department responsibilities.

The following checklist of the most important terms was taken from *Everyday Credit Checking: A Practical Guide* by Sol Barzman, published by Thomas Y. Crowell Company in association with the NACM. [The book is now out of print and no longer available.]

*Accounts receivable.* Monies owed to you by your customers. To your customer, the credit department of your company is sometimes the accounts receivable department, i.e., the department responsible for receiving monies due. Conversely, to you, your customer's department responsible for paying is accounts payable.

*Anticipation.* Like the cash discount, a reward for prompt payment, although in this case, ahead of due time. In other words, you are permitting your customer to anticipate the date his or her invoice is to be paid. Anticipation is based upon the annual interest rate paid for commercial loans and is allowed only for each day ahead of the due date that payment is made.

*As of the 25th.* Another phrase frequently used. It is now the custom in some industries to consider that the shipping and billing month end on the 24th; if your customer requests that his invoice be dated as of the 25th, he or she is in effect asking for 30 days extra to pay the bill.

*Assets.* A company's resources, what it owns. Will be in the form of cash, both on hand and in the bank, inventory (merchandise), accounts receivable, equipment, fixtures, real estate, etc. Assets can be either current or fixed: current assets are those readily convertible and available at once to pay debts—cash, merchandise on hand to be sold, securities and insurance, and accounts receivable (money owed to your customer by people who purchased from him or her on credit); fixed assets are those invested in property, equipment, and fixtures.

*Automatic cancellations.*   Some accounts prefer complete shipments only and ask that you automatically cancel any balances due. Also, an order may show an outside shipping date; anything to be shipped after that date is considered automatically cancelled and will be returned to the supplier at his or her expense.

*Back orders.*   When orders are not shipped complete, the balance still to be shipped is a back order.

*Bill of lading.*   A contract for carriage and a shipping document, normally in several parts (determined by your own needs) and normally numbered. The bill of lading must indicate the full name and address of the consignee (the one to whom the shipment has been consigned), the number of cartons in the shipment, their total weight, and the type of merchandise being shipped. For proper control, an invoice number of order number should be included.

*Chargeback or debit memo.*   The document or notice used by your customer to advise you that he or she will deduct, or is deducting, from his or her payment for shortages, allowances, anticipation, freight charges, returns, etc.

*CIA, CBD, or COD.*   Cash in Advance, Cash before Delivery, or Cash on Delivery. Used when you refuse to sell to a customer on your normal terms.

*Common carrier.*   Any individual or organization who offers himself or herself to the public for hire to carry or transport freight. Usually refers to interstate truckers but also include railroads, airlines, freight forwarders, and express companies.

*Consolidating and consolidators.*   Consolidating is holding shipments for a customer until you have accumulated or consolidated one large shipment for him or her; this is then forwarded on one bill of lading (separate shipments require separate bills of lading, one for each shipment, and result in higher freight costs). Or your customer may request shipment to a consolidator who holds smaller shipments until he or she has accumulated, from other suppliers as well as from you, one large shipment for your customer.

*Credit checking.*   Examining, analyzing, approving and/or disapproving an order. In everyday credit parlance, to check on account normally means to approve an order from that account.

*Credit interchange.* Credit information exchanged with your colleagues in your own industry or in a group of industries.The interchange may be assembled by a credit agency, by a club or council of credit managers organized within an individual industry, or by a larger organization representing many industries, as for example, the National Association of Credit Management, which has branches in major cities all over the country.

*Credit ratings.* The classification of accounts by rating on numbered or letter scales, normally beginning with I or A. Dun & Bradstreet, for example, uses a combination of letter and number; other agencies may use letters only, while some agencies do not have specific ratings but offer "Recommended" for whatever the line of credit will be or "Not Recommended".

*Discount.* The allowable percentage your customer is permitted to deduct from your invoice total (if freight charges are included, your customer must deduct those charges before computing his or her discount—discount is figured against merchandise costs only). There are two kinds of discount: trade and cash.

*EOM.* A term frequently employed in the payment of bills denoting 'End of the month". If payment is to be made in the month following shipment, terms of sale will read, for example, Net 10 EOM, so that a shipment made in December will be paid for January 10, the tenth day after the end of the calendar month.

*Financial statement.* Often inadvertently called a balance sheet. Lists both the resources and liabilities of a business or individual. A financial statement shows the assets of the firm, its liabilities, and its net worth; it is normally dated at the end of the calendar year, December 31st. However, fiscal year end variances are numerous.

*FOB.* Free on Board. The most commonly used term for the shipment of goods. And the most frequently misunderstood. It does not mean freight on board, as so many people believe. Simply put, it means the point at which responsibility for the freight charges begin and title passes. If the terms read FOB Shipping Point, or FOB Factory or FOB Mill, the customer pays all shipping costs, and title to the goods passes to him or her at that point.

*High credit.* The highest aggregate amount of credit you've allowed a customer at a given time. It does not mean, as is often supposed, the largest individual order, but includes everything your customer owes you at one particular time. It can be less than his or her assigned line of credit, or it can be more.

*Insolvency.*    Inability to pay debts as they mature, or having more liabilities than assets. A solvent customer is one who can pay his or her bills although he or she may run slow.

*Invoices.*    The bills itemizing merchandise shipped, unit cost, and total cost. Invoices should be numbered in sequence. They are sometimes included with the shipment, but are more often mailed, either to the designated consignee or to a paying office.

*Ledger.*    A record of debits, credits, and all money transactions; there are subsidiary ledgers that go into greater detail for specialized analysis, but most credit managers are concerned only with the general ledger, which is the book of final entry. Whether your general ledger is kept by hand or by data processing, the basic format will be the same, with an individual ledger card or sheet for each customer. Additional cards are added as sales with that customer warrant. When you are asked by one of your colleagues for your ledger experience with a certain account, check the ledger card itself or an extract.

*Liabilities.*    What a company owes. Its debts will be in the form of obligations for merchandise purchased (trade debts), taxes, loans, etc. Liabilities are either current or long term; current liabilities are normally the trade obligations, taxes, accrued salaries, interest on loans, mortgages, etc. anything that is payable after a year.

*Line of credit.*    The amount of money you are willing to have an account owe you at a given time. Includes unpaid invoices, merchandise in transit, unfilled approved orders in the house, and new orders. Also, line of credit refers to the total suggested by credit agencies, which may be either higher or lower than yours.

*Manifest.*    Originally, a listing of the goods being shipped; this term is now more often used to list the stores being shipped, especially when you ship to a large chain and you are requested to make shipment to one central point for a number of stores on one bill of lading.

*Marginal accounts.*    Businesses with poor credit ratings and/or questionable prospects. Some credit managers have no problems at all with marginal accounts, since they simply refuse to ship any of them.

But most credit managers do ship some marginal accounts, and they have learned to watch these customers carefully.

*Net.*   The full amount your customer must pay. There will be instances where he or she will request and receive certain allowances, such as a percentage of the invoice total for a new store opening, or a set amount for advertising. In spite of such allowances, the terms will still read NET.

*Net worth.*   The owner's share in the assets of the business. Calculated by subtracting the total of all liabilities, both current and long term, from the total of all assets, both current and fixed. What is left is the net worth of the business.

*Open terms.*   Selling on credit, as opposed to selling for cash. When you offer a customer open terms, you have opened a line of credit for him or her.

*Past due.*   Any invoice that remains unpaid after the date it was scheduled for payment, or past the due date. Most credit managers use a series of reminders as their past due collection letters, with each reminder becoming progressively firmer. Or, statements are sometimes used as past due reminders.

*Personal Opinion or P.O.*   A credit analyst's own assessment of an account. The agency for which the credit analyst is working may not recommend a particular account, but in the opinion of the analyst, the account is worthy of shipment and he or she will suggest a line of credit.

*Pro forma.*   A Latin phrase meaning as a matter of form. In commercial terminology it has come to stand for a document prepared as a convenience, or as a matter of form, in place of or in advance of the official document. For example, you may be requested to send a pro forma invoice, which is no more than a preliminary dummy copy prepared before shipment is made. A customer's pro forma financial statement is a projection of what he or she expects his or her financial picture to be at a future date.

*Pro no.*   A number assigned to the delivery receipt, which has been prepared by the freight carrier making delivery to the point designated by your customer, or prepared by one carrier transferring your goods to another. Originally called pro forma number, common usage has shortened it to its present form, pro no.

*Proof of delivery.*   A signed receipt showing date of delivery to consignee, and signature of consignee or his or her agent.If you have been requested to ship to a consolidator, you generally will not be required to prove delivery beyond that point.

*Requirements accounts.*   Businesses that are eligible for any amount of credit they may require. Not all requirements accounts are alike in capitalization or net worth; some may be infinitely wealthier than others and require much higher lines of credit.

*ROG.*   Receipt of Goods. Used to calculate the due date of your invoice. If your customer specifies ROG, he wants his payment terms to begin from the date he receives his merchandise, not from the date you shipped it. ROG terms can often give a customer as much as 30 additional days, depending upon the length of time your goods will be in transit.

*Schedule.*   Sometimes called an aging schedule or "trial balance." It is a listing, either alphabetically by account name or numerically by account number, of total sales, current sales, monies owing, chargebacks, and credits. Computerized schedules are remarkably easy to read and will even include credit ratings and manner of payment; for the credit manager, they can be a useful and important tool—an advantage of a data processing system.

*Shipping memo or packing slip.*   A detailed listing of the merchandise shipped; if you use style or product numbers or names, colors, or sizes, these should appear on the memo. It also includes department number, order number, packing marks, etc., but should not include prices. Like the invoices, the packing slips should have their own numerical sequence for easy reference and control. Some suppliers use a combination invoice and shipping memo on the same form.

*Statements.*   Forms sent to your customers listing all open items on their ledger cards. These include unpaid invoices, unused credits, and any chargebacks that you have not allowed. Some customers insist upon statements before they will send you a check; others do not want statements at all.

*30x or extra dating.*   Thirty days extra for your customer to pay his invoice (a variation of "as of the 25th'). Or 60 days extra, and beyond, if you agree to give him that much additional time. The granting of extra dating is the supplier's prerogative alone, although many buyers now make it an integral part of their demands.

*Working capital.* Not to be confused with net worth. Calculated by subtracting the total of current liabilities only from the total of current assets only. What is left is the working capital of the business.

# ACRONYMS

Every credit professional should be familiar with the following acronyms:

1. CRF: Credit Research Foundation. CRF is the education affiliate of the NACM, organized in 1949. It is a member-supported research and education organization dedicated to developing and enhancing the skills, talents, knowledge, and leadership qualities of credit and financial executives.
2. FCIB: Finance Credit International Business. FCIB-NACM is the international arm of NACM and serves exporters and foreign trade chapters, providing credit reports on 400,000 overseas buyers. They publish weekly bulletins on world market conditions, conduct roundtable conferences and offer specific industry credit group services.
3. NACM: National Association of Credit Management. NACM is one of the oldest and largest professional associations in the world. Organized in 1896, NACM remains a grass roots organization. Power emanates from the individual up through the local organization to the national association, and services conceived nationally are administered locally.
4. NIC: National Institute of Credit. NIC, founded in 1918, is the accrediting and academic awards agency for the credit profession. The NIC charters chapters through local NACM affiliates nationwide.

# BIBLIOGRAPHY

Anderson, Ronald A. and Kumpf, Walter. *Business Law*. Cincinnati, Ohio, Southwestern Publishing, 1976.

Barzman, Sol. *The Complete Guide for Credit and CollectionLetters*. New York, National Association of Credit Management, 1983. [Book is now out of print.]

Brady, E. Michael and Margotta, Maurice H., Jr., 'Toward Certification of the Credit Executive," *Credit & Financial Management*, April 1985, pp. 9-13.

Brennan, Jay, ed. *The Time Life Family Legal Guide*. Time, Inc., New York, 1971.

Christie, George; Bracuti, Al. *Credit Executives Handbook*. New York, Credit Research Foundation, 1986.

Fisk, McKee and Snapp, James C. *Applied Business Law*. Cincinnati, Ohio, Southwestern Publishing, 1966.

Herzberg, Frederick. *Work and the Nature of Man*. Cleveland, World Publishing, 1966.

Maslow, Abraham. *Motivation and Personality*. New York, Harper & Row, 1954.

Mott, Sheryl S. *Ratio Analysis Workbook*. New York, National Association of Credit Management, 1984.

Naisbitt, John. *Megatrends*. New York, Warner Books, Inc., 1984.

Naisbitt, John and Aburdene, Patricia. *Reinventing the Corporation*. New York, Warner Books, Inc., 1985.

Nelson, Lester. *Credit Manual of Commercial Laws*. Columbia, Maryland, National Association of Credit Management, 1992.

Rue, Leslie W. and Byard, Lloyd L. *Management Theory and Application.* Homewood, Illinois, Richard D. Irwin, Inc., 1983.

Viscione, Jerry A. *Financial Analysis: Tools & Concepts.* New York, National Association of Credit Management, 1984.

Vroom, Victor. *Work and Motivation.* New York, John Wiley & Sons, 1964.

# REVIEW LITERATURE

## OUTSIDE REVIEW LITERATURE

*Modern Working Capital Management,* by Frederick C. Scherr, NJ, Prentice Hall, 1989.

*Thriving in Chaos,* by Tom Peters, New York, Knopf, 1987

## ADDITIONAL REVIEW LITERATURE

If, after going over this review book, you feel that you need additional information or insights into a particular subject area, your attention is directed to the texts below. Each of the books listed is available through the NACM Publications Department, 8815 Centre Park Drive, Suite 200. Columbia, Maryland 21045-2117. Please note that the books listed are subject to availability (certain items may fall out of print or be dropped from the NACM selection library). Also, the NACM Publications Department is continually updating its library—current brochures describing the books offered are available from the NACM Publications Department.

Item # Title

1      *Credit Manual of Commercial Laws,* NACM. Annual every January.

12     *Uniform Commercial Code and Related Procedures Manual,* Registre. Annual every January.

83    *Handbook of International Credit Management,* by Brian Clarke. Gower Publishing.

85    *The Check is NOT in the Mail,* by Leonard Sklar. Baroque Publishing.

86    *Analysis of Financial Statements,* by Leopold Bernstein. Business One Irwin.

87    *Handbook of Credit & Accounts Receivable Management,* by Rosie Bukics and Walter Loven. Probus Publishing.

88    *The Art of Business Credit Investigation,* by Peggy Mound. Advanced Verification Service.

92    *The Desktop Encyclopedia of Corporate Finance & Accounting,* by Charles Woelfel. Probus Publishing.

93    *The Complete Executives Encyclopedia of Accounting, Finance, Investing, Banking & Economics,* by Albert Link and Charles Woelfel. Probus Publishing.

94    *Turning Debts into Dollars,* by Dan Wolner.

96    *The Leadership Challenge,* by James Kouzes and Barry Posner, Jossey Bass, Inc.

97    *Compensation of Credit Executives.* Credit Research Foundation.

98    *Analysis for Financial Management,* by Robert Higgins, Business One Irwin.

99    *How to Interpret Financial Statements for Better Business Decisions,* by Barry Miller and Donald Miller. AMACOM.

100   *Principles of Business Collections.* NACM. (Due for release August 1992.)

101   *International Financial Management,* by Rose Marie Bukics. Probus Publishing.

# INDEX